The Court of St James's

The Court of St James's

The Monarch at Work from Victoria to Elizabeth II

Christopher Hibbert

QUILL

New York   1983

Library of Congress Catalog Card Number: 82-62185

ISBN: 0-688-03627-9
    0-688-01602-2 (pbk)

Printed in the United States of America

First Quill Edition

1 2 3 4 5 6 7 8 9 10

Contents

Illustrations

Author's Note and Acknowledgements

Most of the material in the earlier chapters of this book will be familiar to those who have read the standard biographies of the monarchs and their consorts whom I have discussed. I am especially indebted to books by Elizabeth Longford, Cecil Woodham-Smith, Daphne Bennett, Roger Fulford, Georgina Battiscombe, Philip Magnus, Harold Nicolson, John Gore, James Pope-Hennessy, Frances Donaldson, John W. Wheeler Bennett, Robert Lacey, Philip Ziegler, Philip Howard, Dorothy Laird and Basil Boothroyd. I have also drawn with gratitude upon the diaries, letters and memoirs of Sir Henry Channon, Sir Cecil Beaton, Lady Diana Cooper, Sir Harold Nicolson, Richard Crossman, Sir Henry Ponsonby, Lord Sysonby, Mr Harold Macmillan, Lady Hardinge, Victor Cazalet, Lord Chandos, Lord Avon, Lord Kilmuir, Sir Edward Marsh, Lord Home, Sir Harold Wilson, J. C. C. Davidson, Sir Robert Bruce Lockhart, Lord Lee, Lord Butler, Group Captain Peter Townsend, Lady Cromer, Lady Cynthia Colville, Hugh Dalton, Charles Hobhouse, Tom Driberg, Princess Marie Louise, Lady Airlie and Ramsay Macdonald.

I acknowledge the gracious permission of Her Majesty the Queen to publish passages of which she owns the copyright.

The second part of the book could not have been written without the generous help of Her Majesty's Household. I am particularly grateful to Mr W. F. P. Heseltine, the Queen's Deputy Private Secretary; Lieutenant-Colonel J. F. D. Johnston, Assistant Comptroller, Lord Chamberlain's Office; Mr Michael Shea, the Queen's Press Secretary; Lord Rupert Nevill, Private Secretary to the Duke of Edinburgh; and the offices of Her Majesty's Keeper of the Privy Purse, and of the Crown Equerry. Mrs Michael Wall, the Queen's Assistant Press Secretary, has patiently answered numerous questions and arranged for these chapters to be read by the various officers and members of the Royal Household without whose assistance their authenticity could not have been ensured. None of the departments of the Household is, of course, responsible for any of the opinions which I have expressed or comments which I have made.

I want also to thank Sir Robin Mackworth-Young, the Queen's

Librarian; Miss Frances Dimond, Assistant Registrar at Windsor; Mr Colin Peterson, the Prime Minister's Appointments Secretary; Mr Michael Ruffer, Assistant Secretary, the Duchy of Cornwall Office; Mr R. L. Sharp, Ceremonial Officer of the Civil Service Department; the Rev. Canon J. S. D. Mansel, Sub-Dean of the Chapel Royal, St James's Palace, Deputy Clerk of the Closet and Sub-Almoner; Mr M. J. Gravestock of the Crown Estate Commissioners' Office; Mr E. M. Blood of the Ministry of Defence; Mr J. P. Brooke-Little, Richmond Herald of Arms; Mr E. R. Wheeler, Clerk of the Council and Keeper of Records, the Duchy of Lancaster Office; Mrs M. E. Dunton of the Queen's Awards Office; Mr D. L. Joiner, Press Officer of the British Railways Board; Mr J. P. Stables of the Secretary's Office, the Post Office; Mr Stephen L. Roberts, Librarian, the United States Embassy; Brigadier R. J. Lewendon, Assistant Secretary (Historical) of the Royal Artillery Institution; Miss Meg Wilson of the Central Office of Information; and Mrs P. Forde of the Department of the Environment.

Finally I am most grateful for their help in a variety of ways to Mrs John Rae, Mrs Francis Pollen, Mrs John Street, Mrs Joan St George Saunders and to my wife for having compiled the index.

C.H.

The author and publishers are most grateful to the following for kind permission to reproduce the photographs: National Portrait Gallery, 1; Mary Evans Picture Library, 2, 3, 4, 9; Reproduced by Gracious Permission of Her Majesty The Queen, 5, 7, 8, 10, 12, 13, 14, 15, 16, 17, 18, 20, 21, 22, 23, 26, 30; Rowena Ross, 6 (photo: John E. Wells); Bassano and Vandyk, 11; National Library of Wales, 19; Radio Times Hulton Picture Library, 24, 25, 27, 28, 33, 36, 39, 41; Sketch of the Duke and Duchess of Windsor, 1938, by Etienne Drian © by A.D.A.G.P. Paris, 1979, 29; Weidenfeld Archives, 31; Topix, 32; Imperial War Museum, 34, 35; Popperfoto, 37; Fox Photos, 38, 42; Camera Press, 40 (photo by Baron), 53 (photo: Arthur Edwards), 55 (photo: Colin Davey), 56 (© The Times); The Press Association, 43, 44, 46, 51, 58 (photo: Ron Bell), 59; © ITC Incorporated Television Co. Ltd, 45, 47 (photo: Joan Williams); Serge Lemoine, 48, 49, 52, 54, 57; Central Press Photos Ltd, 50. The photographs on the front cover are reproduced by kind permission of the following: from left to right: Bassano and Vandyk; Bassano and Vandyk; Camera Press (photo: Peter Grugeon); Camera Press (study by Bassano); Camera Press (photo: Bassano); Camera Press (study by Karsh of Ottawa).

Prologue

At half past seven on the morning of 6 February 1952 a valet carrying a cup of tea entered King George vi's bedroom at Sandringham. His master did not wake, so he left him to finish his sleep. Twenty minutes later, hearing no sound, he went in again with a fresh cup of tea. He touched the King's shoulder and found that he was dead.

The King's successor, his elder daughter Princess Elizabeth, was in East Africa with her husband, the Duke of Edinburgh, on the first stage of a journey which, it had been intended, should take them on to Australia and New Zealand. She had spent part of the previous night in a tree house built into the branches of a huge fig tree overlooking a water hole beside which she had seen elephants and rhinoceros drinking, baboons playing and a fight between two waterbuck. That morning she had gone fishing after breakfast, and had landed a better catch than her husband. She was apparently in a cheerful and contented mood when the news was broken to her that her father had died.

She had loved him deeply. She had known how ill he was, as had all who had seen him on the news-reels the week before, looking tired and pale as he stood at the airport, waving her goodbye, the high wind ruffling his grey hair. So, while not expecting it so soon, she had been prepared for his death. Mourning clothes had been packed in her trunks as, indeed, they always were.

Although she 'broke down and wept for some minutes', she could not give way to her grief for long. There were telegrams of apology to be sent to the Australian and New Zealand Governments, arrangements to be made for the journey home, presents and signed photographs to be distributed, documents to sign. She was asked by what name she would be known as Queen: neither her father nor her uncle had chosen as their regal titles the names by which they had been known in the family. 'Oh, my own name,' she said decisively, 'what else?' Soon afterwards, then, Queen Elizabeth ii was in the air over Nanyuki airfield flying towards Entebbe where the aircraft which had brought her from England was to take her home again. She got up 'once or twice during the journey', the

1

Duke of Edinburgh's valet noticed, 'and when she returned to her seat she looked as if she might have been crying'.

In London that morning the Cabinet had sat for a few moments in silence at 10 Downing Street. Afterwards the Lord Chancellor as head of the judiciary, and the Speaker of the House of Commons, who had been specially asked to attend the Cabinet meeting, were both consulted as to the proper procedure to follow. The last time that a monarch had been proclaimed *in absentia* was in 1714 on the death of the childless Queen Anne. Her distant German relative, George Louis, Elector of Hanover, was proclaimed her successor in implementation of the Act of Settlement of 1701 by which, in order to deny the throne to the native dynasty of the Roman Catholic Stuarts, the crown had been required to pass to King James I's grand-daughter, the Electress Sophia, and her heirs, being Protestants. It was decided that the precedent of 1714 would be followed and that, in spite of the Queen's absence, the traditional Accession Council would be held at five o'clock that evening at St James's Palace.

The original palace was built by King Henry VIII on the site of a hospital, dedicated to St James the Less, Bishop of Jerusalem, for young women suffering from leprosy. The hospital, situated in what was then a desolate and lonely spot half a mile west of Charing Cross, was bought by the King in 1532. The leprous patients were sent elsewhere; 'a goodly manor' of red brick with blue diapering took the hospital's place; and south of it a large park was annexed and enclosed by a long brick wall. For over three hundred years St James's Palace remained one of the principal residences of the kings and queens of England. Here King Henry VIII's daughter, Mary, died; here Mary's half-sister, Queen Elizabeth I, held her glittering court; here their cousin, James I, and his friends watched the splendidly lavish productions of Ben Jonson's masques; and here James's son, King Charles I, spent the last cold night before his execution. After Cromwell's interregnum King Charles II returned gratefully to the palace upon his family's restoration to the throne and added thirty-six acres to the park where he could often be seen feeding the ducks on the lake and playing bowls and pall-mall with his mistresses. His brother, James II, also lived here; so did his nephew William III in whose reign the huge nearby Whitehall Palace was burned to the ground and St James's therefore became the main royal residence in London. William III's sister-in-law, Queen Anne, spent much of her time at St James's, within whose walls nearly all her numerous still-born or short-lived children were born. Anne's successor, King George I, lived at St James's, too, for several years; so did his son, George II, in whose days the gambling after the Twelfth Night Ball became notorious. George III was married here in the Chapel Royal. Here, also, most of his children were born, including his eldest son who was so drunk when *he* was married in the chapel that he nearly fell over during the ceremony and did fall over into the fireplace of the bridal chamber where, according to his disgusted bride, he spent what remained of the night. A few years later, in 1809, a large part of the palace was destroyed by fire. But under the supervision of the Prince Regent, it was sufficiently restored by 1814 for magnificent entertainments to be held here in celebration of Napoleon's defeat and in honour of those distinguished visitors to London who had helped to bring it about, the Emperor of Russia, the King of Prussia and Marshal Blücher. Blücher was provided with apartments overlooking Ambassador's Court where he could be seen through the window smoking contentedly, bowing to the passers-by and accepting with infinite complacency the compliments of ladies who came in to congratulate him and 'kiss his moustachios'.

By this time the Regent himself had moved to Carlton House, his fine new palace overlooking St James's Park, a little way beyond Marlborough House, the large mansion opposite Friary Court, which had been built by Sir Christopher Wren for the first Duke of Marlborough. But the Regent's brothers continued to occupy apartments at St James's Palace where one of them, the mysterious Duke of Cumberland, was attacked and nearly murdered by his valet. In 1825, after the Regent had become King George IV, two of his brothers were provided with new houses within the palace precincts: Lancaster House, also known as York House and Stafford House, which was designed for the Duke of York by Benjamin Wyatt; and Clarence House, the first London home of the present Queen, which was rebuilt for the Duke of Clarence, later King William IV, by John Nash.

After his accession King George IV decided that Carlton House, splendid as it was, was not a suitable residence for a king of England. He therefore had it demolished and erected a larger and even more imposing palace on the site of the modest London home of his parents, Buckingham House. Thus, Buckingham Palace, first occupied by the King's niece, Queen Victoria, became the main royal residence in London. Thereafter the State Apartments at St James's Palace were no longer lived in; and, although foreign ambassadors continue to be accredited in traditional style to the Court of St James's, they are received at Buckingham Palace. Certain functions take place at St James's, however, as they have done for generations. The accession of a new sovereign is still proclaimed here and Privy Councillors still assemble here for the Accession Council.

In the days of Queen Elizabeth I the Privy Council, consisting of about twenty of the most important and powerful men in the country, usually Ministers of State or officials of the Royal Household, was in effect the executive instrument of the sovereign. Its meetings, held in secret wherever the Queen happened to be at the time, were normally attended by less than half the total number of Councillors and quite often its business was transacted by only three or four of them. The Queen herself did not attend, leaving it to some such trusted adviser as William Cecil, Lord Burghley, her Secretary of State, to ensure that her wishes were made known. When power was transferred to a Cabinet responsible to Parliament, the authority of the Privy Council declined. But the fiction of its authority is still preserved, just as the fiction of the monarch's supreme authority is still preserved by every Act of Parliament beginning with the words: 'Be it enacted by the Queen's most Excellent Majesty, by and with the advice and consent of the Lords Spiritual and Temporal, and Commons, in this present Parliament assembled.' It is also maintained by the Queen sitting on her throne in the House of Lords, at the State Opening of Parliament each year, and summoning the Commons to hear her read the so-called Queen's Speech which is, in reality, the Prime Minister's programme of intended legislation.

The theoretical authority of the Privy Council is sustained by all members of the Cabinet having to be sworn in as Councillors if they are not already of their number – taking a secret oath in addition to the oath of allegiance – and by the power granted it by certain statutes to declare important decisions made by 'the Queen's Most Excellent Majesty in Council', such as declarations of war and the dissolving and summoning of Parliament. Appointments to the Privy Council are made for life and there are, therefore, far more Councillors than there were in the days of Queen Elizabeth I, as resignations are rare. In 1978 there were three hundred and fifty. As well as present and former members of the Cabinet, they included the Duke of Edinburgh, Earl Mountbatten, the Duke of Beaufort, the Archbishops of Canterbury and York and the Bishop of London, the Lord Chamberlain, statesmen of the Commonwealth, distinguished lawyers and leading members of the Liberal Party. The office of Lord President of the Council is a political appointment often held by the Leader of the House of Commons, though in May 1979 Mr Michael Foot was succeeded by Lord Soames. It is for him to decide who shall attend the meetings of the Council, a quorum being three, though there are usually four in attendance. All Privy Councillors, however, are entitled to attend the Accession Council; and most of them took advantage of this privilege in 1952.

4

The Accession Council traditionally consisted not only of Privy Councillors but also of 'the Lords Spiritual and Temporal ... and other Principal Gentlemen of Quality, with the Lord Mayor, Aldermen and Citizens of London'. At Queen Elizabeth II's accession, however, it was decided to add to these some distinguished delegates from other countries in the Commonwealth of which she was now head; and so, at the appointed time, several High Commissioners, representing the various countries of the Commonwealth, joined the large crowd of peers, Ministers, ex-Ministers and Privy Councillors who could be seen entering St James's Palace through Ambassador's Court and going up to the picture gallery. The Lord Mayor and Aldermen were in their robes of office; the rest in morning suits. When they were all assembled the Lord President read the declaration, proclaiming Elizabeth II Queen, by the grace of God, of the United Kingdom of Great Britain and Northern Ireland and of her other Realms and Territories. Then all present signed the great parchment Rolls of Allegiance which were laid out on the long table in front of them.

Two days later, on the morning of 8 February, the Privy Councillors re-assembled at St James's Palace in the Entrée Room. A few of them, including the Earl Marshal, the Duke of Norfolk, and the High Steward of Westminster, were in full dress, as were the officers of the Household Cavalry and the Brigade of Guards. But the rest were in morning suits as they had been on Wednesday; and the Minister of Housing, Harold Macmillan, said that in contrast these 'dark coats and striped trousers presented a rather scruffy appearance'. Promptly as the clock outside struck ten o'clock, the Lord President began the proceedings by nominating a small number of those present to wait upon Her Majesty. A few minutes later the Lord Chamberlain, the Earl of Clarendon, limped into the Entrée Room from the Throne Room next door to announce that the Queen was ready. The Councillors nominated by the Lord President, including the Duke of Gloucester, the Archbishop of York (the Archbishop of Canterbury was ill), the Prime Minister, the Leader of the Opposition and the Lord Chancellor, then went into the Throne Room from which the Queen shortly emerged alone, dressed in black with a black felt hat, making everyone else in the room, so the Secretary of State for the Colonies thought, suddenly appear 'immeasurably old and gnarled and grey'. She walked to the table, picked up the Declaration which had been mounted on a board, glanced at the Lord President who gave her a slight nod and then read the words written out for her. They ended with these:

My heart is too full for me to say more to you to-day than that I shall always work as my father did throughout his reign, to uphold the constitutional

5

government and to advance the happiness and prosperity of my peoples ... I pray that God will help me to discharge worthily this heavy task that has been laid upon me so early in my life.

It was, Lord Chandos thought, 'one of the most touching speeches' which he had ever heard; and he, 'like many others could hardly control [his] emotions'. Macmillan was also deeply moved. 'The firm yet charming voice in which she pronounced her allocution and went through the various ceremonial forms of the ritual', he wrote, 'produced a profound impression on us all.'

Others besides Macmillan remembered her calm, controlled voice. But as she went back to Clarence House the strain proved too much for her: she broke down and cried.

She soon recovered her composure, though. Like her great-great grandmother, who had been proclaimed Queen Victoria at St James's Palace one hundred and fifteen years before, she was determined to be a good and conscientious monarch, worthy of the crown that her family had worn for so long. She admired Queen Victoria most – she still admires her most – of all her predecessors. Those familiar with Queen Victoria's attitude towards her responsibilities and prerogatives, however, had good cause to hope that this admiration would not lead to too strict an emulation. For Queen Victoria's example was never one that could unreservedly be recommended to punctilious practitioners of constitutional monarchy.

Part 1
Exemplars

1 Queen Victoria and her Ministers

When Queen Victoria, the daughter of the Duchess of Kent and grand-daughter of King George III, came to the throne in 1837 she was just eighteen years old. A very small girl with large blue eyes and light brown hair, she delighted the Privy Councillors who assembled for the first Council of her reign by her combination of self-confidence and becoming diffidence. She entered the room in a black dress, 'of course quite *alone*', as she wrote herself, determined from the outset to display her independence from her mother and 'those others' who had so closely watched over her childhood. She was greeted by her two uncles, the Dukes of Cumberland and Sussex, brothers of her father and of the late King William IV, and was led to the throne where she read her declaration in an attractive voice, a little high and thin, but beautifully 'clear and untroubled', as John Wilson Croker, one of the Councillors, described it. 'Her eye was bright and calm, neither bold nor downcast, but firm and soft. There was a blush on her cheek – certainly she did look as interesting and handsome as any young lady I ever saw!'

After the swearing-in, she accepted the obeisances of her uncles and the Councillors, blushing prettily again as they kissed her soft hand, yet behaving throughout with quiet grace and simple dignity. 'There was never anything like the first impression she produced,' Charles Greville, Clerk-in-Ordinary to the Privy Council, thought, 'or the chorus of praise and admiration which is raised about her manner and behaviour ... It was very extraordinary, and something far beyond what was looked for.' Calm, modest and appealing, she acted 'with every sort of good taste and feeling', though occasionally appearing a little bewildered and looking enquiringly at the Prime Minister, Lord Melbourne.

The impression of vulnerability she gave was, however, rather misleading. She was certainly shy, apprehensive of seeming stupid and therefore disinclined to venture opinions on matters in which she felt out of her depth, being conscious when she did so, as she confessed herself, of sometimes 'saying stupid things in conversation'. But although her intellect was far from subtle and her knowledge very scanty, she had strong prejudices and, once her mind was made up, her Ministers soon learned that it was extremely difficult to alter it. For her judgements were never tentative; her confidence in her opinions was absolute. A thing was right, or it was wrong; a person was good or bad. Like most people who are themselves uncompromisingly truthful and direct, she had no understanding of those who are not. Nervous yet insensitive, usually shrewd but sometimes obtuse, she was to prove to be a queen as difficult, tiresome and demanding as she was conscientious, capable and effective.

Not long after her accession, her obstinacy, her tendency to the most excessive aversions, and that childish outlook on the world which her enclosed and lonely upbringing had done nothing to enlighten, resulted in two serious quarrels at Court that dissipated her early and almost universal popularity. The first arose from her dislike of Lady Flora Hastings, her mother's Lady-in-Waiting and, as she supposed, the mistress of the Duchess's Irish confidential secretary, Sir John Conroy.

At Kensington Palace, where much of her childhood had been spent, Conroy had been a dreaded and hated figure. Unscrupulous, scheming and overbearing with a kind of coarse, self-satisfied charm, he exercised a powerful influence over her susceptible mother. Victoria's governess, the strict and vigilant Baroness Lehzen, whom her little charge both loved and feared, also hated Conroy. And rightly suspecting that he hoped to profit from his closeness to the Duchess, the Baroness protected the child jealously from his company and taught her never to trust him. Victoria never did trust him. And when at the beginning of 1839 Lady Flora's stomach began to swell, she soon came to the conclusion that Lady Flora was pregnant and that the father of the unborn child was, as she wrote in her journal, that 'Monster & 'demon Incarnate' whose name she forbore to mention. Soon the supposed pregnancy was the talk of the Court; and it was decided that something would have to be done. It might have been supposed that the proper course would have been for Queen Victoria to speak to her mother about it. But at that time she was not on good terms with the Duchess, having immediately upon her accession severed the stiflingly close ties that had previously bound them together by decreeing that her mother should no longer share her bedroom, and insisting that she saw all her Ministers, as she had approached the Privy Council, 'quite ALONE'. So Lady Tavistock, an experienced Lady of the Bedchamber was, on Baroness Lehzen's advice, deputed to approach the Prime Minister.

Melbourne did not care for the Hastings family. They did not, he maintained, have 'an ounce of sense between them'; and he affected to find Lady Flora – who was, in fact, a gifted and attractive if rather withdrawn young woman – both plain and disagreeable, the ugliest woman he had ever seen. He had discussed her with the Queen and had given the impression that he shared Her Majesty's suspicions. When

Lady Tavistock broached the embarrassing subject with him, however, he was non-committal, advising her to say nothing but to keep a watch on developments. All the same he thought it advisable to send for Sir James Clark, the Duchess of Kent's doctor and the Queen's Physician-in-Ordinary.

Sir James, an abrasive though kind-hearted man with a pronounced Scottish accent, a large mouth and nose and a great deal of untidy, grey hair, had spent the early part of his medical career as a ship's surgeon; and before entering the service of the Duchess of Kent – to whom he had been recommended by her brother, King Leopold of the Belgians – he seems to have had little experience of gynaecological complaints. He had already been consulted by Lady Flora, for whose sickness and pain he had prescribed pills of rhubarb and ipecacuanha in conjunction with an embrocation composed of opium, sulphur and soap, though he now told the Prime Minister that he believed his patient might be pregnant rather than ill. He agreed, however, that for the moment it would be better to wait and see.

On further consideration, Sir James suggested that, having been unable to make a proper diagnosis through the material of Lady Flora's underclothes and dress, he should examine her 'with her stays removed'. This she refused to allow. She also declined to submit to examination by any other doctor. But next day she changed her mind. With her maid by the bedside and Lady Portman, the senior Lady-of-the-Bedchamber, by the window holding her face in her hands, she was examined by Sir James and by a specialist, Sir Charles Clarke. They found that she was a virgin. Yet even so, they entertained some doubts and told Lord Melbourne that they could not be positive as to her not being pregnant. Melbourne conveyed their uncertainty to the Queen who reported to her mother: 'Sir C. Clarke had said that though she is a virgin, still that it might be possible and one could not tell if such things could not happen. That there was an enlargement in the womb like a child.'

By this time the Hastings family, infuriated by the Court's behaviour towards Lady Flora, were demanding that the persons responsible for the insinuations about her should be named and exposed. Angry letters flew between the conflicting parties and found their way into the newspapers. The old Duke of Wellington, appalled that this 'slur on the palace' was bringing the monarchy into disrepute, was called in as arbitrator, a commission which he normally relished but which on this occasion he was unable to perform with much satisfaction to either party. The Queen, who had received the ill and trembling Lady Flora to express her sorrow for what had happened, now began to believe she did not deserve such sympathy. When she heard that Lady Flora had refused to shake hands with Lady Tavistock, with whom the Duchess of Kent declined to sit at the whist-table, she asked Lord Melbourne for his advice. Should she retaliate? Yes, Melbourne told her. 'Be more distant.' The Queen took the advice, cut Lady Flora and referred to her as that 'nasty woman', 'that wretched Ly. Flo'.

The Queen, in her turn, was now openly referred to as 'a heartless child'. In Tory circles it was suggested that she was party to a disgraceful conspiracy by the Whig ladies of the Court to ruin both Lady Flora and the Duchess of Kent. The Queen looked pale and distraught, refusing to read the newspapers, bursting into tears at the thought that the scandal might bring down the Whig government of her beloved friend, Lord Melbourne.

There was worse yet to come. At Ascot that year she was hissed as she drove down the race-course; and as she came out on to the balcony women's voices could be heard shouting at her, 'Mrs Melbourne!' She was also hissed at the opera, while Lady Flora was applauded. In the summer it became clear that Lady Flora was gravely ill. By the end of June, indeed, it was obvious that she might not have long to live; and the Queen, who went to visit her, found her 'literally a skeleton, but the body *very* much swollen like a person who is with child'. There was 'a searching look in her eyes, rather like a person who [was] dying'. Eight days after the Queen's visit Lady Flora did die; and at the post-mortem, which was carried out at her own request, it was found that the cause of her death was due to a growth on her liver.

For the Court the repercussions of Lady Flora's death were highly damaging. The newspapers, particularly the *Morning Post*, were outspoken in their condemnation, accurately reflecting the mood of public opinion. A well-publicized duel was fought between a Whig Member of Parliament and a Tory Member in protest against some stinging remarks made about the Queen by the Tory Member. Old Lady Hastings returned to the Queen a present of £50 which Her Majesty had given to Lady Flora's maid. At a dinner in Nottingham only one voice responded when Major-General Sir Charles Napier proposed the loyal toast, and that was his own. A force of police had to be despatched to protect the Queen's carriage which Melbourne thought ought to be sent to the funeral.

Although the Queen was clearly and deeply upset by the whole unfortunate affair, it was not grief for Lady Flora so much as anxiety for her own position that moved her; for she was not yet a compassionate person. Her immediate reaction when she heard the women shouting 'Mrs Melbourne' at Ascot was that she would like to have them flogged. Now she protested to Lord Melbourne that she felt '*no* remorse'. '*I* did nothing to kill her,' she said. But as Charles Greville observed, there was 'no doubt that an effect very prejudicial to [Her] M[ajesty] has been produced, and the public, the women particularly, have taken up the Cause of Lady Flora with ... vehemence'.

That year the Queen's reputation was also severely damaged by what later became known as the Bedchamber Plot, an affair during which the Queen behaved in a manner that a modern constitutional monarch would find unthinkable. At the beginning of May, in floods of tears, she had received the news that Lord Melbourne's government, facing defeat in the House of Commons, would have to resign. '*All* ALL my happiness gone!' she lamented in the pages of her journal, distressed and horrified. 'That happy peaceful life destroyed, that dearest kind Lord Melbourne no more my Minister!' 'I sobbed and cried much,' she continued after Melbourne had been to see her. 'I really thought my heart would break: he was standing near the window; I took that kind dear hand of his in both mine and looked at him and sobbed out, "You will not forsake me"; I held his hand for a little while, unable to leave go; and he gave me such a look of kindness, pity, and affection, and could hardly utter for tears, "Oh! no," in such a touching voice. We then sat down as usual and I strove to calm myself.'

She had recently told him that she thought the royal family ought always to be Whig: the Tories were amongst the things that she most hated in all the world. She would *have* to face the inevitability of parting with him, though, Lord Melbourne told her. At least it was the constitutional right of the sovereign to appoint her successor; and the right of the Prime Minister to offer his advice as to the most suitable successor should Her Majesty require it. The Queen did require it. Well, then, she should send for the Duke of Wellington who had been appointed Prime Minister by George IV in 1828 and had provisionally held the office after Melbourne's previous resignation in 1834. If Wellington declined, she was to send for Sir Robert Peel but on condition – a condition which she had, in fact, no right to make – that the Duke was in the Cabinet.

Wellington realized that the Queen would not at all relish the thought of either himself or Peel after she had become so fond of the charming Lord Melbourne. 'I have no small talk,' he said, 'and Peel has no manners.' Besides, he himself was old and deaf and completely out of touch with the House of Commons. So, when the Queen saw him in the Yellow Closet at Buckingham Palace, he told her that Peel was her man.

The Queen's heart sank at the thought of having to send for Peel, whose awkwardness and gauche mannerisms had so irritated her uncle, George IV. He was so unbending, so lacking in spontaneity and warmth. Nor was it only Peel she dreaded. She might be asked to accept all sorts of Tory Ministers who would be equally objectionable. Now, as always, the prospect of having to grow accustomed to strange, new faces appalled her.

'But what am I to do if he proposes appointments that are disagreeable to me?' she asked Wellington.

'Fight upon the details as much as you please,' he advised her. 'But make no conditions as to principles, and, depend upon it, there will be every disposition to consult your wishes and feelings in every respect.'

The Queen seemed to accept this; but then she added a condition to her reluctant acceptance of Peel which made Wellington realize how sketchy had been her political education. 'You must promise me', she said, 'to be Secretary of State for Foreign Affairs.' The Duke explained that he could not promise this; it was constitutionally impossible. All appointments to the Cabinet would have to be in the hands of the new Prime Minister. In that case, the Queen said at last, would the Duke please tell Peel to come to see her. Again Wellington had to demur: she was in duty bound to write to him herself. When the Duke left she burst into tears.

Her interview with Peel, who arrived in full dress in accordance with etiquette, was far more painful than that with the Duke. He was nervous and awkward as she had expected, 'cold, unfeeling and disagreeable'. Concealing her own embarrassment beneath a cool, even haughty, reserve, she accepted with an ill grace the Ministers he proposed, expressing her particular dislike of the future Lord Chancellor, Lord Lyndhurst – a man of highly dubious morals who had taken her mother's side in the recent squabbles – and of Lord Aberdeen, who was to be Secretary for War and who had expressed the opinion that the Queen was a baby in Melbourne's hands. But she put her foot firmly down when Peel went on to talk of changes in her Household which would, he said, be necessary to show her confidence in the new government.

Melbourne had told her what to say if these changes were mentioned. 'Your Majesty had better express your hope,' he had written to her in a memorandum, 'that none of Your Majesty's Household, except those who are engaged in Politics, may be removed.' And later, when advising her not to show too obvious a dislike of any Ministers that Peel might propose, he had added reassuringly, 'They'll not touch your Ladies.' To this the Queen had replied sharply that they had better not do so: she would never allow it.

To Peel she now said she must retain *all* her Ladies.

'All?' Peel asked.

'*All.*'

'The Mistress of the Robes and the Ladies of the Bedchamber?'

'*All!*'

After this interview the Queen again broke down, pacing up and down the room, the tears pouring down her cheeks. She was still in a highly emotional state when the Duke of Wellington, at Peel's request, went to see her again to try to persuade her to change her mind.

'Well, I am very sorry to find there is a difficulty,' the Duke said to her.

'Oh, *he* began it and not me,' she replied pertly, acting in a manner which the Duke afterwards described as of 'a *naïveté* so very girlish'. 'It is offensive to me to suppose that I talk to any of my Ladies upon public affairs.'

'I know you do not ... But the public does not know this.'

She would not give way, however, insisting that it was no good Peel saying that he would not deprive her of her lesser Ladies, that it was only the most prominent Ladies who must be changed. *These* were the Ladies, she protested, who were of more consequence to her than the others. In any case, queens had never in the past been required to part with their Ladies on a change of government. It was explained to her that her case was quite different: she was a reigning queen not a king's consort. Her case was *not* different, she maintained, obstinately standing her ground. Sir Robert must be very weak, she added tartly, if '*even* the *Ladies* must be of his opinion'.

'I was calm but very decided and I think you would have been pleased to see my composure and great firmness,' she wrote to Melbourne. 'The Queen of England will not submit to such trickery. Keep yourself in readiness for you may soon be wanted.'

So the Queen had her way: Melbourne resumed office; Peel and Wellington remained in opposition. 'One has often heard of the country going to the dogs,' one Tory remarked, 'but never before of a country going to the bitches.' The Duke spoke in the House of Lords of 'anomalous influences' at the Palace; while Greville lamented that it was 'a high trial of our institutions when the caprice of a girl of nineteen can overturn a great Ministerial combination'. 'The simple truth,' continued Greville, 'is that the Queen could not endure the thought of parting with Melbourne, who is everything to her. Her feelings, which are *sexual* though she does not know it, and are probably not very well defined to herself, are of a strength sufficient to tear down all prudential considerations.'

While the Tories condemned her obstinacy and the Whigs praised her constancy, the Queen herself, as mercurial as she was resilient, turned her back on this first great political crisis of her reign, which she had brought to such a dangerously triumphant conclusion, and abandoned herself to the pleasure of entertaining the Grand Duke Alexander of Russia, 'a dear delightful young man' with whom, as she confessed in her diary after dancing with him happily until a quarter past three in the morning, she was 'a little in love'.

Towards the end of her life the Queen admitted that her conduct towards Peel did not merit so gay a celebration. 'Yes! It was a mistake ... I was very hot about it,' she conceded, 'and so were my Ladies, as I had been so brought up under Lord Melbourne; but I was *very* young ... and never should have acted so again.'*

Peel felt sure that she would not have made the mistake at all had she then had the guidance of the man whom she was to meet later that year, Prince Albert of Saxe-Coburg and Gotha, that 'darling, dearest husband', 'so great, so good, so faultless', who was to transform her life. At first she declined to let the Prince take any part in political business, limiting his role as partner to what she herself ingenuously called a little 'help with the blotting paper', and bossily organizing his official life to such an extent that she chose all the officers of his Household, including his confidential secretary.

The Prince protested about this; but the Queen refused to give way. 'As to your wish about your gentlemen, my dear Albert, I must tell you quite honestly that it will not do,' she told him. 'You may entirely rely upon me that the people who will be round you will be absolutely pleasant people of high standing and good character ... Lord Melbourne has already mentioned several to me who would be very suitable.'

In Prince Albert's opinion this was precisely why they were not suitable. The crown, he believed, should not display partiality to any political party, as King William IV had done towards the Tories and as Queen Victoria did towards the Whigs.

I am very sorry [he replied to the Queen's rebuff] that you have not been able to grant my first request, the one about the Gentlemen of my Household, for I know it was not an unfair one ... As to your proposition concerning Mr Anson [Melbourne's Private Secretary who had been recommended as the Prince's], I confess to have my doubts ... I give you to consider, dearest, if my taking the Secretary of the Prime Minister would not from the beginning make me a partisan in the eyes of many? ... Think of my position, dear Victoria; I am leaving my home with all its old associations ... and going to a country in which everything is new and strange to me – men, language, customs, modes of life, position ... Is it not even to be conceded to me that the two or three

---

* There was, in fact no question of her acting so again. Only her Mistress of the Robes was to be changed in future; and by the time the next queen regnant, Queen Elizabeth II, had to accept a change of government no alterations at all were required. The Countess of Euston, who became the Duchess of Grafton on her father-in-law's death in 1970, was appointed Mistress of the Robes during a Labour administration in 1967, retained her office when the Conservatives came to power, and remains in office today.

persons who are to have the charge of my private affairs should be persons who already command my confidence?

No, it was not to be conceded. 'I am distressed to be obliged to tell you', the Queen answered, settling the matter, 'what I fear you do not like, but it is necessary, my dearest, most excellent Albert.'

But, although obliged to give way on this occasion, the Prince was not to be the subordinate partner for long. And after he had secured the departure of the officious and jealous Baroness Lehzen, who still stalked about the corridors of the palace, keys clanking importantly upon her hip, continuing to consider herself the Queen's principal adviser, the Prince himself gradually assumed that benign yet over-whelming influence over her which was to last until his death. Step by wary step he began to guide her and to train her as a queen, teaching her to bear with less resentment the actions and opinions of those she took to be her enemies, persuading her to take an interest in matters that she had previously felt need not concern her. Soon she was com-pletely dependent upon him. 'She is certainly an odd woman,' Charles Greville noted in his diary. 'Her devotion and submission seem to know no bounds ... It is obvious that, while she has the title, he is really discharging the functions of the Sovereign.'

He composed all her letters to the Prime Minister for her to copy out; he frequently took her place when the Government had need to consult the Crown. People began to refer to her as Queen Albertine. 'It is you who have entirely formed me,' she said to him. And to their eldest daughter she wrote: 'Papa is my father, my protector, my guide and adviser in all and everything, my mother – as well as my husband.'

Ministers were judged by their attitude towards him and by his feelings towards them. When Melbourne, on his retirement, advised her to put herself under the Prince's guidance since he understood 'everything so well' and had 'a clever able head', she wrote down the old man's words in her diary, delighted with him for having uttered them. She even began to change her attitude to Peel when it became clear how sincerely her new Prime Minister appreciated the Prince's qualities and sympathized with the Queen's wishes to grant him a more important constitutional position. Sir Robert, who did all he could to please the Queen over her Household appointments, was such an enlightened man, she eventually concluded. 'His opinion [was] invaluable'; and his enforced resignation in 1845 reduced her to floods of tears.

The Queen's attitude towards her next Prime Minister, Lord John Russell, was also conditioned by Prince Albert's, who distrusted him. The Prince considered Lord John hesitant and unreliable, tem-peramentally unsuited for the premiership, and he always felt uneasy in his almost dwarf-like presence. To the Queen, therefore, Russell was 'a dreadful' little man, incapable of making up his own mind: when it came to the appointments to her Household he must needs go scurrying to his colleagues for consultations instead of keeping it *'entre nous'* as dear Sir Robert had done.

Lord Derby, Russell's successor, was, however, quite a different case altogether. He was attentive and dutiful, clear in his expositions, a *real* Prime Minister. He paid careful attention when the Prince spoke to him about the dangers of appointing to the most coveted Court appointments the kind of people whom Lord Derby had in mind, the 'Dandies and Roués of London and the Turf'. No one whose moral character was not above reproach, the Prince insisted, should be granted a place about the Queen's Court. Lord Derby, pliable and accommodating, was sensible about this. He, at least, the Queen concluded, was one Conservative who could be trusted to do the right thing.

Looming powerfully in opposition to Lord Derby, however, was a man who could certainly not be trusted to do the right thing, Lord Palmerston. The Queen and the Prince were quite as much at one about him as about Melbourne, Peel and Derby. Before her marriage the Queen had got on quite well with Palmerston, a handsome, dashing man who enjoyed the pleasure of life to the full, the company of pretty women in particular. She found him 'clever', 'amusing' and 'agreeable'. To be sure he had rather shocked her when at the age of fifty-five he married Lord Melbourne's widowed sister, Lady Cowper, who was a grandmother of fifty-two; for the Queen always believed that widows ought to remain faithful to the memories of their departed husbands. And after that, as she told Lord Melbourne, who laughed at her naïvety, she found that she did not care for Lord Palmerston as much as she had done in the past. But she still enjoyed his company when he set out to please her. He was 'always so gay and amusing'; and she acknowledged that he was 'such a clever able man'. After her own marriage, however, she began to entertain serious doubts about his reliability. She became increasingly aware that he acted without consulting her; and she agreed that one should not be expected to countenance a man at Court who had once entered the bedroom of one of her Ladies, either in the hope of seducing her or of spending the night there with another Lady whose bedroom it had formerly been.

By 1848 Palmerston's high-handed foreign policy; his carefree contradictions of the Queen's and Prince Albert's notions; his sympathy with the aspirations of liberal Europe which went against their desire to see England dissociate herself from not only despotic but also from revolutionary governments; his habit of not forwarding the drafts of controversial despatches to the Palace until the final versions themselves had been sent off; and the intolerably insolent yet infinitely cheery manner in which he ignored any alterations that might be proposed to him on those occasions when changes were still possible, all seemed very good reasons to the Queen and Prince for getting rid of him as Foreign Secretary. The Queen, as heedless of her constitutional duty as Palmerston was negligent of his, consequently informed the Prime Minister that the time would soon come perhaps when she would be unable 'to put up with Lord Palmerston any longer, which might be very disagreeable and awkward'. As it happened, Palmerston's independent assurances to the French Ambassador of Britain's support for the *coup d'état* of Napoleon III brought about his downfall at the hands of the Prime Minister; and the Queen was saved on this occasion from an act which, in the unlikely event of its being committed, would have threatened the stability of the Crown.

The incompetent mismanagement of the Crimean War in 1854–5, however, rendered the return of Palmerston inevitable. He was seventy-one by then, rather deaf and extremely short-sighted; but he was the only man the nation would trust. Benjamin Disraeli, who had been Chancellor of the Exchequer in Derby's Cabinet and was now – as he was for most of his political life – in opposition, put the case for Palmerston with amusing over-emphasis in a letter to Lady Londonderry: he 'seems now the inevitable man, and tho' he is really an imposter, utterly exhausted, at the best only ginger beer and not champagne, an old painted Pantaloon, very deaf, very blind, and with false teeth, which would fall out of his mouth when speaking, if he did not hesitate and halt so in his talk – he is a name which the country resolves to associate with energy, wisdom and eloquence'.

The Queen and Prince Albert did all they could to avoid the apparently inevitable appointment. The Queen sent first for the Conservative leader, Lord Derby; but Derby said, 'it *must* be Palmerston; the whole country wants him'. She then sent for Lord Lansdowne, an elderly Whig grandee, who had been Lord President of the Council at the time of her accession; but Lansdowne protested that he was too old and decrepit to serve her. After Lansdowne she even tried Lord John Russell who said he would try to form a Government but failed to do so. At last, with deep reluctance she sent for Palmerston, lamenting 'what a trial' his premiership would prove to be.

To her pleasurable surprise she found Palmerston, as Prime Minister rather than Foreign Secretary, quite agreeable. And when the war was over she paid him this unexpected tribute in her journal: 'Albert and I agreed that of all the Prime Ministers we have had, Lord Palmerston is the one who gives the least trouble, and is most amenable to reason and most ready to adopt suggestions. The great danger was foreign affairs,

but now ... these are conducted by an able, sensible & impartial man,'
Lord Clarendon.

After the defeat of Palmerston's government in 1858, though, and
following the brief second administration of Lord Derby, when the
Queen and Prince Albert were faced with the prospect of Palmerston's
return to office they were dismayed, for they knew that he and Lord
John Russell – those two 'old Italian Masters' as the Prince caustically
referred to them – would endeavour to pursue a foreign policy to which
they were both rigidly opposed. They did all they could to deny
Palmerston the premiership, vainly endeavouring to bring into being a
government headed by the more tractable Lord Granville.

Two years later Prince Albert was dead. His beneficial influence over
the desolate Queen could not be denied. He had done much to form her
mind, to draw out her natural gifts, to persuade her to value the services
of gifted men, to extend the narrow range of her interests and to guide
her towards the creation of a new English monarchical tradition which
placed the throne above party. But, while more aware of them than his
wife, he never himself fully comprehended the limits imposed upon a
constitutional monarch. His former tutor, Baron Stockmar, that sardonic, moody, obsessively moral doctor whose voluminous memoranda
were placed with such regularity upon the Prince's desk, did not direct
and control him to the extent that many people supposed. Yet Stockmar's influence over the Prince was nevertheless considerable. He
stayed for months on end at Court where, permitted to ignore the rules
of etiquette imposed upon all others, he could be seen walking about in
the morning in his dressing-gown and slippers, in the evening going in
to dine without decorations and wearing ordinary trousers instead of
the regulation knee-breeches. And whether at court or at home in
Germany, Stockmar liked to consider himself an indispensable adviser.
Admittedly the advice he gave was generally shrewd, but it was sometimes dangerous. He held and forcibly expressed the opinion, for
instance, that the Prime Minister was merely the 'temporary head of
the Cabinet'; it was the monarch who was the 'permanent Premier'.
This doctrine, which strongly appealed to the Queen, was one that
Prince Albert could not bring her to reject.

There were, indeed, occasions when Prince Albert, who often overstepped the bounds of constitutional propriety by speaking in the
Queen's name, seemed to have subscribed to the doctrine himself. On
the fall of the Conservative Government in 1852, Derby, the defeated
Prime Minister, thought that Lansdowne should be sent for. Lord John
Russell thought that his own claims ought to be considered more
deserving. In fact, the Queen, rejecting them both, after consultations
with her husband, sent for Lord Aberdeen, that elderly, kindly, amen-

able gentleman whom the Prince considered 'safe'. On his arrival the Prince went so far as to hand Aberdeen a list of names which he considered suitable for inclusion in the Cabinet.

When the widowed Queen eventually emerged from the lugubrious seclusion into which she had retreated in her overwhelming and excessive grief, she was discovered by her new Ministers to be an even more formidable personality than they had expected. She did not hesitate to rebuke them sternly when they offended her. On hearing that General Gordon had been killed by the Mahdi's soldiers at Khartoum she wrote the Prime Minister (Gladstone) a letter which made him so indignant he considered resigning: 'These news from Khartoum are frightful, and to think that all this might have been prevented and many precious lives saved by earlier action is too frightful.' Nor did she hesitate to correspond direct with her generals without consulting the War Ministry; and when the War Minister objected she reacted furiously: 'The Queen always *has* telegraphed direct to her generals, and *always will* do so ... She thinks [the protesting Minister's] letter *very officious* and *impertinent in tone*. The Queen *has* the *right* to telegraph ... *to any* one, and won't stand dictation. She *won't* be a machine.' The Queen did not even refrain from writing to the heads of other states on important political matters without the knowledge and against the wishes of the Foreign Office. She did so in 1877 when the Foreign Secretary was, in her opinion, not being forceful enough with Russia. Bypassing him, she wrote direct to the Tsar. She knew she had no constitutional right to do so; but, as she told her daughter, it was 'a miserable thing to be a constitutional Queen and to be unable to do what [was] right!'

She threatened to abdicate if the Government allowed Russia to occupy Egypt; and, summoning to her presence the Colonial Secretary, Lord Carnarvon, who supported the Foreign Secretary's pacific policy, she 'pitched into him' with what she herself admitted to be 'vehemence and indignation'. 'He remained shrinking but still craven hearted! – wishing to say to the world that we cld. not act!!!' she continued: 'Oh! that Englishmen were now what they were!! but we shall yet assert our rights – our position – & "Britains never will be slaves" will yet be our Motto. I own I never spoke with such vehemence.'

Soon afterwards Carnarvon felt obliged to resign. So did the Foreign Secretary.

The Queen also acted most improperly by corresponding with her former Prime Ministers after they had left office and without the knowledge of their successors. Her youth and inexperience might well have been thought enough to excuse her in insisting that Melbourne should continue to write to her and to advise her after he had been replaced in office by Peel. But over forty years later she was still continuing the practice by maintaining a political correspondence with her former Conservative Prime Minister, Lord Salisbury, after his Government had been replaced by the Liberals. She was even capable not only of endeavouring to concert policies with the Opposition – as she did by writing *'confidentially'* and 'entirely on [her] own responsibility' to the Opposition leader, Lord Derby, over the issue of electoral reform in 1866 – but also of actively supporting and encouraging the Opposition, as she did twenty years later when her Government were endeavouring to bring in a Home Rule Bill for Ireland to which she objected.

Of all her Ministers none found the Queen more troublesome than Gladstone. This was partly his own fault. Unlike Disraeli, whom the Queen at first distrusted and then grew to adore, Gladstone, as his great rival put it himself, treated the Queen 'like a public department'. Disraeli treated her like a woman. 'The present Man will do well,' the Queen assured her eldest daughter when Disraeli became Prime Minister, 'and will be particularly loyal and anxious to please me in every way. He is vy. peculiar, but vy. clever and sensible and vy. conciliatory ... full of poetry, romance and chivalry. When he knelt down to kiss my hand wh. he took in both his – he said: "In loving loyalty and faith."'

This was the secret of Disraeli's success with her. Behind the calculating knowledge that the Queen's support could be of great value to him and the outrageous flattery which led him to assure her, for instance, that nothing in his life had ever been so interesting as his 'confidential correspondence' with one 'so exalted and so inspiring', there lay a genuine attachment to the throne.

Having sent her the collected edition of his novels and received in return a copy of the Queen's *Leaves from the Journal of Our Life in the Highlands*, he may well have said to her: 'We authors, Ma'am.' He certainly said to Matthew Arnold, 'You have heard me called a flatterer and it is true. Everyone likes flattery; and, when you come to royalty, you should lay it on with a trowel.' But he never underestimated the Queen's astuteness and he was genuinely fond of her. In treating her with elaborate courtesy he was behaving towards her as he did to all women he liked; in writing her his long, amusing, informative letters he was indulging a whim to please her rather than performing a necessary and arduous duty.

Gladstone was also deeply attached to the throne but he was quite incapable of expressing his attachment with Disraeli's seductive charm. Yet, whereas the Queen had not at first cared for the sound of Mr Disraeli, whose youthful escapades had been most reprehensible, she had initially liked Mr Gladstone. 'He is very agreeable,' she wrote in her journal, 'so quiet and intellectual with such a knowledge of all subjects, & is such a *good* man.' This was, however, almost the last compliment she was ever to pay him. She grew to dislike him intensely. What the Queen particularly objected to, what aroused her furious jealousy – since she felt that Gladstone was usurping her own prerogative – was the claim, which he made in his electioneering addresses, of speaking beyond all classes and factions to '*the nation* itself'. She would 'sooner *abdicate*', she eventually decided, 'than send for or have any *communication*' with that '*half-mad*' firebrand who wd. soon ruin everything & be a Dictator'.

Yet in 1880 the success of Gladstone's party at the polls made a Liberal Government inevitable; and it was he, perforce, who must lead it. The Queen looked desperately to others to save her from him. She considered Lord Granville; she thought of Lord Hartington; but in the end she had to succumb to Gladstone. She did so with the utmost ill grace; and was relieved beyond measure when his Government was defeated five years later.

But Lord Salisbury's Government, which succeeded it, lasted but a few months; and in her efforts to avoid a further series of unwelcome meetings with Gladstone, the Queen once again overstepped the limits of her prerogative. At first she refused to accept Salisbury's resignation; then, having done so, she made repeated efforts to find some means of preventing her 'dear great country' from falling into 'the reckless hands of Mr Gladstone'. Warned that the Liberals were severely critical of the delay, she sharply retorted: 'The Queen does not the least care but rather wishes it shd. be known that she has the greatest possible disinclination to take this half crazy & really in many ways ridiculous old man.' In the end, of course, she had to take him. But she told him firmly, when at last she summoned him to her presence, that the country's foreign policy must on no account be altered and she would not accept Granville as Foreign Secretary, a post which she and Salisbury had between them decided ought to go, as it did go, to a more congenial man, Lord Rosebery.

Defeated on the Home Rule issue a few months later, Gladstone was forced to resign. Accepting his resignation with unconcealed satisfaction, the Queen welcomed Lord Salisbury back and took her leave of a pale and haggard Gladstone in the reasonable expectation that, as he was now seventy-six and in failing health, she would never have to deal with him again.

In 1892, however, Salisbury's Government fell; and the Queen was faced once again with the necessity of entrusting the country to 'the shaky hand of an old, wild incomprehensible man of eighty-two and a half ... the really wicked' Mr Gladstone. It seemed to her 'a defect in our much famed Constitution to have to part with an admirable Govt. like Ld. Salisbury's ... merely on account of the number of votes'.

Having announced in the Court Circular, to the understandable annoyance of the Liberals, her 'regret' at Salisbury's resignation, she braced herself to receive his successor whom she found 'greatly altered and changed ... his face shrunk, deadly pale, a feeble expression about the mouth, & the voice altered'. She let him know at once that she would not allow him the Cabinet of his choice: Henry Labouchere, the radical Member for Northampton and proprietor of *Truth*, a weekly journal highly critical of the royal family, was certainly not to be given office. He was a man of most reprehensible character who, having fallen in love with a circus girl in Mexico, had joined her troupe and had afterwards lived in a camp of Chippewa Indians. A nephew of Lord Taunton, from whom he had inherited an immense fortune, Labouchere was, moreover, a notorious gambler as well as an agnostic and was reported to have lived with his wife, an actress, before they were married. A Cabinet post for such a man, the Queen repeated, was unthinkable.

Although the witty and cynical Labouchere was inclined to mock Gladstone in private – it was he who said of the Grand Old Man that there was no objection to his always having the ace of trumps up his sleeve, but only to his pretence that God had put it there – he always treated Gladstone with great respect in public. Besides, Labouchere was a powerful force in the House of Commons and his great talents certainly well fitted him for office. But the Queen was adamant. She would not have Mr Labouchere in any position in which there was a possibility of her meeting him personally. Labouchere protested that the Queen was acting unconstitutionally in objecting to him and would have made the matter public had not Gladstone, with characteristic loyalty to the throne, himself accepted the responsibility for his exclusion, not mentioning the Queen's veto. But the Queen insisted that it did not matter in the least what Labouchere said: by refusing to accept the appointment of any particular person as Minister she was exercising a prerogative which was well established under her predecessors. This was true, though whether the monarch had a right to exercise it in 1892 was a highly debatable question; and no monarch would presume to exercise it today.

With Labouchere successfully excluded, Gladstone's 'motley crew', as the Queen described them, arrived at Osborne, her house on the Isle of Wight, for their first Council. Sir William Harcourt, the sixty-four-year-old Chancellor of the Exchequer, looking 'rather awful ... like an elephant', assured her they were all most anxious to please her. She 'merely bowed'; and when, instead of rising from their knees after having been sworn in, they all crawled forward to kiss her hand, she thought how absurd they looked.

Throughout the next eighteen months her meetings with the 'deluded old fanatic' were strained and disagreeable, an ordeal to them both. Then at last Gladstone came to say that at his great age he could carry on no longer. It was not in the Queen's nature to pretend to be in the least sorry. Without asking for his advice as to a successor, she sent for Lord Rosebery.

Her relationship with Rosebery, though far from as strained as that with Gladstone, was never an easy one. She treated him as though he were an inexperienced child in constant need of her advice and admonition. She informed him immediately upon his appointment that while not objecting to Liberal measures which were 'not revolutionary', she did 'not think it possible that Ld. Rosebery [would] destroy well tried, valued, & necessary institutions [such as the House of Lords] for the sole purpose of flattering useless Radicals'. And when she learned that the Queen's Speech was to contain references to disestablishment bills for the Scottish and Welsh Churches she expressed her indignation so forcibly that Rosebery hinted that he might have to resign if she persisted in her objections to measures to which his party was committed.

Undeterred, the Queen continued to treat him as though she were *in loco parentis*. On the eve of his maiden speech as Prime Minister in the House of Lords she told him not to commit himself but to be 'as *general* & to a certain extent as vague as could be'. He need not say 'anything agst. what he [felt] himself pledged to'. He could 'do this & yet not commit himself too strongly'. 'What the Queen says here,' she added, making a rather unseemly reference to Rosebery's dead wife, Hannah de Rothschild, to whom he had been devoted, 'she does here in the *Name* of *one* who can no longer be a comfort & support to him & who also felt very anxious on this subject.'

From that day on Rosebery's speeches were frequently the subject of the Queen's criticism and reproach. He was urged to take 'a more serious tone', to be 'less jocular', to speak in a manner more 'befitting a Prime Minister'. A speech at Bradford, in which he referred to the House of Lords, that 'permanent barrier against the Liberal Party', as 'a great national danger', was particularly objectionable. She reprimanded him sternly for speaking in such tones without consulting her, without 'obtaining her sanction'. 'I did not think that this was a right position for my Prime Minister to take up,' she commented two years later, 'and I was not sorry when he was turned out.'

All the same, she was not altogether pleased to have to receive back the less manageable Lord Salisbury who was to remain Prime Minister until she died. He was far more adult than Lord Rosebery, to be sure; and he had been a great comfort to her in her quarrels with Gladstone. But, as she admitted after the resignation of Rosebery's Government: 'Personally I am vy. fond of Ld. Rosebery & prefer him (not his Politics) to Ld. S.' For his own part Salisbury often found the Queen a difficult mistress. In many ways he deeply admired her. 'I have always felt,' he said after her death, commenting on her instinctive rapport with her people, 'that when I knew what the Queen thought, I knew pretty certainly what view her subjects would take, and especially the middle class of her subjects.' Yet there were many occasions when, for all the respect and admiration he had for her, Salisbury, like the Queen's other Prime Ministers, had cause to be grateful for the sympathetic help afforded him by those remarkable men who served as her Private Secretaries.

2 Queen Victoria and her Household

The office of Private Secretary to the sovereign is not an ancient one. It came into existence when King George III began to lose his eyesight in 1805. His grandfather, King George II and great-grandfather, King George I, had been content to leave much of the business of government in the hands of their First Ministers, and to accept the constitutional theory that the Secretary of State for Home Affairs was the king's Private Secretary. But George III, whose views on the duties and responsibilities of a British monarch were quite different from his predecessors', undertook a great deal of business himself, writing letters and keeping copies of them in his own hand. And when he could no longer see sufficiently well to do this work, the appointment of a confidential secretary was, therefore, essential if he were to continue to carry it out. Besides, it was not only the King's eyesight that was failing. Some years before he had suffered a mental breakdown – which seems to have been caused by that rare metabolic disorder known as porphyria – and was supposed liable to the relapse which did, in fact, occur in 1811. The proposal to create the post of Private Secretary to the sovereign nevertheless aroused strong opposition, since it was considered both 'undesirable and irregular' for such a servant of the Crown to be so placed that he might become acquainted with the most confidential proceedings of the Cabinet.

The man chosen for the appointment of Secretary did much to allay the disquiet. He was Major Herbert Taylor, the son of a clergyman, formerly aide-de-camp to the King's second son, the Duke of York. Discreet, astute and trustworthy, Taylor soon gained the entire confidence not only of the King but also of those critics who had most strongly opposed his appointment. And when the King's mental derangement became so acute that he could no longer do any work at all, Taylor was appointed Private Secretary to the Queen. He was firm with her when he felt called upon to be so, calling her objections 'loose and ill-founded', for instance, when she protested against Parliament's decision not to grant her the separate establishment of a queen dowager on the establishment of the Regency. But the Queen trusted him as fully as the King had done. She made him one of the executors of her will

27

which she signed on her deathbed in his presence, bestowing on him 'a most affectionate look'.

Her eldest son, the Prince of Wales, who was to become King George IV on his father's death in 1820, also trusted Taylor. But few people trusted the man whom the Prince himself appointed his own Private Secretary, Colonel John McMahon.

McMahon's bustling little figure and red spotty face were to be regularly seen in London, as he hurried about on his master's more dubious errands, in his blue and buff uniform, his hat tilted at a rakish angle over one eye. He was said to be the illegitimate child of a chambermaid and a butler who later kept an oyster shop in Dublin. He had been a very bright child, and had become a clerk, then an actor, then a soldier in a regiment commanded by the Prince's friend Lord Moira who, recognizing his talents and artful resources, had helped him to buy a commission and had eventually introduced him to the Prince. McMahon was a loyal, hard-working and useful servant to his master. But when it was announced that he was to be confirmed in his office at a salary of £2,000 on the Prince's becoming Regent there was an outcry in the House of Commons against an appointment for which there was no precedent. One Member indignantly reminded the House that no monarch before George III had ever had a Private Secretary, and he only because he was blind. The office was both 'dangerous and unconstitutional', another Member protested, 'rendering the person holding it the secret adviser of the Sovereign with a degree of influence over his mind totally at variance with the forms of Government in England'.

The Regent ignored the protests, insisted on McMahon's also being appointed Paymaster of the Royal Bounty to Officers' Widows, a sinecure worth about £2,700 a year which was about to be abolished, and created him a baronet as well as a Privy Councillor, an honour never bestowed on Herbert Taylor by George III who, understanding 'these matters better than anyone', as Lord Liverpool, the Prime Minister said, decided that the sovereign's Private Secretary ought to be put on exactly the same footing as an Under-Secretary of State.

On his death in 1817, the wily *débrouillard* McMahon was succeeded by Major-General Sir Benjamin Bloomfield, another Irishman whom the Regent had met as a poor but socially accomplished horse-artillery officer on duty with the 10th Hussars at Brighton. It proved a far from satisfactory appointment. For, pleasant enough when young, Bloomfield became increasingly moody, sulky, bossy and petulant as he grew older. He also became a Methodist and took to hanging a great white placard outside his door with the words 'At Prayer' written on it. Moreover, being Keeper of the Privy Purse as well as Private Secretary,

Bloomfield was horrified by the sums which his master, having become King, lavished upon jewellery for the decoration of his mistresses, particularly upon the ample figure of the kindly, rich and rapacious Lady Conyngham. Bloomfield was indiscreet enough to confide in the King's friend, Charles Arbuthnot, that he thought that His Majesty would go mad such was his infatuation for Lady Conyngham, that it was 'quite shameful the way in which [she] was covered with jewels' which had been bought for her at a cost which Bloomfield estimated to be in the region of £100,000.

Bloomfield's persistent complaints about the King's expenditure on her naturally annoyed Lady Conyngham who urged the King to have him removed from his office. The King – who had himself more than once been so exasperated by the man that he had seized him by the collar and shaken him furiously – was only too willing to accede to her request. He accordingly wrote to Lord Liverpool to suggest that, as he was desirous that there should be 'no impediment or interruption' to the 'permanent tranquillity' that then existed between the King and his Government, 'it might be desirable to get rid of the office of Private Secretary'. This office had always been looked upon 'with a jealous eye', both by the Government and the country, and it would, in his opinion, be highly popular, therefore, if they were 'to break up the *thing altogether*'.

So Bloomfield was persuaded to relinquish his posts in the royal household in exchange for a sinecure worth £650 a year, his appointment as British Minister in Stockholm, and the promise of an Irish peerage. But no sooner had these arrangements been made than the King, despite his protest of wishing to abolish the post of Private Secretary, made it clear that he wished a more competent man to succeed Bloomfield, if not in name at least to take over his duties. The man the King proposed was Sir William Knighton who had already undertaken several confidential missions for His Majesty, including the collection of various compromising documents from the dying McMahon's country cottage near Blackheath.

Knighton was undoubtedly a remarkable man, industrious, conscientious, shrewd and discreet, yet so affected, staid and touchy that it was a cause of some astonishment in the Royal Household that the King was so attached to him. Born in Devon, the son of an impoverished country gentleman who had been disinherited and died young, Knighton had been sent by his widowed mother to study medicine under an uncle at Tavistock. For a time he had served as an assistant-surgeon in a naval hospital; but soon moved to London where he established himself in practice as a fashionable *accoucheur*. In this capacity he attended one of the several mistresses of Lord Wellesley who introduced him to the King. His Majesty, who found him 'the best mannered medical man' he had ever encountered, appointed him one of his Physicians-in-Ordinary, created him a baronet and took to consulting him not only as a doctor but as an adviser on all manner of private concerns. Their relationship was extraordinary. At times it seemed that they were the closest of friends, at others that the King detested the very sight of him. He took a peculiar delight in saying mortifying things about him. Once he cried out: 'I wish to God somebody would assassinate Knighton!' Charles Arbuthnot thought that the King not only hated but feared him, 'as a madman hates his keeper'. It seemed to others that they were less like madman and keeper than wayward charge and exasperated governess. Reliance led to resentment, resentment to outbursts of angry abuse against the person without whose help and encouragement unwelcome and distasteful duties could not be faced or performed. They quarrelled; Knighton complained of the King's ingratitude; the King insulted Knighton and told lies about him; the ill-used servant went away to sulk. But then the servant would be summoned back with a cry for help from his 'ever most truly attached and affectionate friend', the King, who could not, indeed, manage without him. For, despite his faults and affectations, his irritating assumptions of privileges, his constant hints at secret knowledge, his 'mysterious way of talking', and evident desire for advancement, Knighton was astute, patient and persevering; and he managed the royal finances with exemplary skill, keeping the extravagant King's expenditure within the limits of a private income – which Bloomfield had estimated at £90,000 a year – as well as anyone could have been expected to do. He was, however, a compulsive intriguer and for years did his best to undermine the influence of Lord Liverpool, whom Knighton never forgave for refusing him both the official title of Private Secretary and the office of Privy Councillor.

The Government were, therefore, infinitely relieved when this strange and profoundly influential man retired into the country after his master's death and when the more open, amiable and impartial Herbert Taylor became Private Secretary to the King's brother and successor, William IV. Taylor was an old-fashioned Tory but he assured the Government that, whatever his own private feelings and opinions were, these would be placed quite 'out of the question' when acting as their intermediary with the King. This was an undertaking which he never broke. As industrious and cautious as Knighton, he was neither personally ambitious nor in the least underhand. His influence was naturally very great but it was used, as he assured the Prime Minister, 'for the purpose of allaying the feelings of irritation created at times in His Majesty's mind, and of smoothing any difficulties that arise between him and his Ministers'. He was not above an occasional indiscretion: he was forced to admit that his tiresome master was sometimes obstinate, unpredictable, even obtuse, that he found it 'uphill work' keeping 'business in the regular Channels', that at times he failed to restrain the King who was inclined 'to be led away by the excitement of the Moment to [the] Use of language which [was] to be lamented'. But Taylor was essentially a model Private Secretary. Queen Victoria's were to follow his example.

During the first years of her reign Queen Victoria did not have an official Private Secretary. She had sought Taylor's opinion about the appointment and he had asked her, 'Is your Majesty afraid of the work?' She had told him she was not. He had, therefore, said to her: 'Then don't have a Private Secretary.' She had followed this advice, relying at first on Lord Melbourne to help and guide her, then upon Prince Albert and Stockmar, occasionally making use of the Prince's secretary, George Anson, and after 1849 of Anson's successor, Lieutenant-Colonel the Honourable Charles Grey, second surviving son of Earl Grey, Melbourne's predecessor as Prime Minister.

Grey, who was promoted General in 1865, became Private Secretary to the Queen after the Prince's death – though he was not officially gazetted for six years – and he continued in the office until his own death in 1870. He was a sound and sensible man, kind of heart though rather bluff in manner and of an independent mind. During Prince Albert's lifetime he had annoyed the Queen by loftily refusing to co-operate when she and her husband, together with some of her Ladies, decided one evening to carry out some experiments in table-turning. And after the Prince's death, while undertaking the duties of the sovereign's Private Secretary conscientiously, he firmly declined to perform any others which he did not regard as his proper business. Once, when a young Lady-in-Waiting appeared at Court with rather more make-up on her face than was normally tolerated there, the Queen said: 'Dear General Grey will tell her.' 'Dear General Grey', the General himself objected when her Majesty's message was conveyed to him, 'will do nothing of the kind.'

The Queen was deeply attached to him, though. Indeed, she displayed towards him a fondness which so put out Lord Clarendon, a former favourite of hers, that the jealous Clarendon became so irritatingly petulant that the Queen vainly endeavoured to prevent his becoming Foreign Secretary in Gladstone's first Cabinet.

Towards the end of his life Grey was much criticized by Ministers for not doing more to persuade the Queen to emerge from that seclusion into which she for so long withdrew in the passionate intensity of her grief at Prince Albert's death. Yet he did all that could have been expected of him. In fact, he marred the former happy relationship between himself and the Queen, so she complained, by pressing her too hard. Convinced that she needed to be reminded firmly and sharply of her duty, Grey advised Gladstone in 1869 to counteract the 'strong feeling' against the Queen's seclusion by ordering her in a *'peremptory'* tone to wake up to her responsibilities. The Queen would not, of course, have accepted such advice from Gladstone even had he felt up to offering it in the manner prescribed. It was to be left to the oriental subtlety of Disraeli and the bullying manner of the honest, rude, outspoken gillie, John Brown, to bring the Queen out of the past to which she had chosen to abandon herself. This had not been achieved by the time of Grey's death.

Grey was succeeded by his niece's husband, Colonel Henry Ponsonby, who had joined the Royal Household as Prince Albert's Equerry in 1856 after service in the Crimean War. He had often helped Grey with his work, and, as a reticent, intelligent man with a fluent pen and a bold clear hand, he had for some time been recognized as his most likely successor. Ponsonby's appointment was not made, however, without considerable opposition from the Queen's family who objected to what they supposed to be his 'extreme radical tendencies'. General Grey had been a Liberal and had once sat in the House of Commons in the Liberal interest for High Wycombe. But Ponsonby's views were supposed to be far more extreme than those of Grey, while his wife's political opinions were notorious. Mary Ponsonby was condemned as being 'clever', a dreadful failing – she actually wrote articles for the *Pall Mall Gazette* – and she had, as even her devoted husband had to admit, 'peculiar views on everything'. Consequently both the Duke of Cambridge, the Queen's uncle, and her son-in-law, Prince Christian, were rigidly opposed to Ponsonby's appointment. But the Queen, as Ponsonby wrote, 'disregarded the remonstrances and was pleased to appoint me, sending me at the same time a hint through the Dean of Windsor that I was to be cautious in expressing my opinions and not to permit my wife to compromise me in her conversation' – a hint which, when conveyed to Mrs Ponsonby, elicited the response that *she* herself had no intention of being compromised 'by being supposed to agree for an instant with the opinions of Court Officials'.

Although his untidy clothes and far too long trousers were a disgrace, and although she had occasion to rebuke him more than once for causing too much rowdy laughter in the Equerries' Room, the Queen liked Ponsonby from the beginning and recognized in him the kind of qualities which were to make him an exceptional Private Secretary. He had the ability to get at the root of a problem without wasting time with irrelevancies; he had a good knowledge of the world and of men; he was understanding, patient and industrious. While witty and possessed of a fine sense of the ridiculous, he was also capable of listening carefully to what was said to him by even the most tedious and stupid people without revealing a trace of irritation or boredom. He could not only express himself well in conversation but also in writing; and he had a lively sense of humour. He did not consider himself a gifted linguist, but he could converse and write letters in French, had a working knowledge of Italian and, though correspondence in German had to be left to the German Secretary, he was usually capable, as he used to admit with some pride, of starting a German visitor off in his own language and then receiving 'the resultant prolonged monologue with sufficiently appropriate interjections' to put him at his ease.

In his dealings with the Queen, Ponsonby required all the sense of proportion, stamina, ingenuity and patience at his command, for she was a most difficult, capricious and demanding employer, who, while she asked to be given advice, was frequently cross when it did not coincide with her own wishes. Disliking interviews in which her opinions, requests or orders might be called into question, she required that all matters, even those of a most trivial nature, should be committed to paper. Ponsonby accordingly had an enormous amount of paperwork to get through every day, some of it of the utmost importance to the successful conduct of the Government's affairs, much else of no importance at all. Documents, letters, memoranda, minutes and messages, all locked in despatch boxes, flowed in a seemingly endless stream between his room and hers, each particular point for her consideration having to be submitted on a separate sheet.

There were requests for her to accept books, to grant permission to copy pictures, to approve the details of Court functions, to confirm appointments and dismissals, to give her assent to Government policy, to select the names of clergymen suitable as preachers at Osborne, to decree the punishment to be inflicted upon a drunken footman at Windsor. There was one exchange of memoranda, which lasted for weeks, about the installation of a lift at Buckingham Palace; there was another, which continued for even longer, about the rights and duties of the Queen's band. The Queen's replies to Ponsonby's submissions came back either in the form of terse minutes at the foot of the document concerned or in letters, written hurriedly on the mourning paper which she used to the end of her life and into the broad, black edges of which many of the words, heavily underlined and often abbreviated, trailed indecipherably. One of the Queen's letters, in which she complained of the 'atrocious & disgraceful writing' of a young nobleman in the Colonial Office, took Ponsonby a quarter of an hour to get through. But at least, when they had at length been deciphered, her decisions were concise and definite. In 1886, for example, Sir Frederick Leighton, President of the Royal Academy, asked permission to have a copy taken of a portrait of the Queen by Sir Martin Archer Shee. The Queen's refusal ran: 'It is a monstrous thing no more like me than anything in the world.' Another artist asked leave to engrave one of the pictures he had painted for her: 'Certainly not. They are not good and he is very pushing.' A lady wrote to ask if her daughter might be granted permission to gain material for an article on the Royal Mews: 'This is a dreadful and dangerous woman. She better take the facts from the other papers.' Oscar Wilde sought leave 'to copy some of the poetry written by the Queen when younger': 'Really what will people not say & invent. Never cd. the Queen in her whole life write *one line of poetry* serious or comic or make a Rhyme even. This is therefore all *invention* & a *myth*.' Would the Queen graciously assent to the new medical school at Edinburgh being named after her: '*Yes*, on *one condition* viz: that *no* rooms for vivisection are included in it.'

So, day after day, the ebb and flow of paper ceaselessly continued: Canon Dalton must not repeat Grace in Latin. It was a mistake to say the chaplain at Hampton Court had given satisfaction; he never did so and was 'most interfering and disagreeable'. Neither the Dean of Westminster nor the Dean of Christ Church was to be allowed to preach at Osborne; the sermons of the first were far too long and of the second like lectures. With infinite care and patience Ponsonby transmitted the Queen's instructions, tactfully altering the wording so as to give the least offence, writing all the letters himself, for up till 1878 he had no assistant.

The paper-work, burdensome as it was, however, occupied only part of his time. He was constantly importuned by seekers after honours and titles, many of whose shameless petitions he did not trouble to pass on to the Queen. He was also constantly being called upon to take up the grievances and pass on the complaints of the numerous minor royalties who 'hovered at a distance round the Court', as well as to settle quarrels and to pacify the ruffled feelings of those within the Household who had been affronted either by their colleagues or rivals, or, as was often the case, by the Queen's selfishness and lack of consideration.

A characteristic letter came to Ponsonby from the Master of the Household, Sir Thomas Biddulph, who had felt constrained to complain before of the Queen's issuing arbitrary orders and of 'the unceremonious and inconvenient manner' in which she sometimes treated the wives of her officials. This subsequent letter was about the Marchioness of Ely, a Woman of the Bedchamber, a timid, nervous and perpetually flustered widow suffering from some form of speech defect which compelled her to convey messages from the Queen in a kind of 'mysterious whispering' which Ponsonby did not always 'strain his ears to hear'.

I saw Lady Ely [Sir Thomas Biddulph's letter ran]. She was ... principally taken up with her own health and waiting. She says she cannot go on as it is, that it is killing her and asked what to do. I said write plainly to the Queen what you can do, and make it clear that if H.M. cannot agree to your terms you must resign. I think this would bring the Queen to reason if firmly done. [Lady Ely] says six weeks [in waiting] at a time is the utmost possible, and that all the Doctors urge her to do less. She says what is true ... that the Queen will not allow Ely [her son] to come and see her. He was in the house and she asked me to see him ... Then she said, 'Oh, no, perhaps the Queen would not like it.' ... It shows her absurd fear of the Queen.

Ponsonby's services were required not only as a mediator between the Queen and her family and intimidated Ladies but also in the settlement of disputes occasioned either by the huffiness of the German Secretary, Herman Sahl – who was frequently so put out by some real or imagined slight that he refused to come down to meals – or by the squabbles of the Household doctors. One of these was described by Ponsonby as 'a very bad doctor' and 'a great gossip' who wearied his 'life out with grievances and quarrels'. Another, the celebrated Sir William Jenner, who was often in attendance on the Queen, was a Tory of the most extreme kind and given to outbursts of wild invective against Gladstone's Government which may well have been approved by the Queen but which seemed outrageous to Ponsonby. 'He is good at repartee and roars at his success,' Ponsonby told his wife after one particularly rowdy dinner at Osborne. 'He roundly abused Carlingford [Gladstone's Lord Privy Seal] and Lord Cairns [the former Lord Chancellor who was very deaf] because they could not understand him. I refuted an argument of his which he said he did not use. "Why," I exclaimed, "you said so just now." His eyes disappeared and in a calm voice he said, "I strongly advise you to consult an aurist, the first aurist in London, there is something extraordinarily wrong about your ears."'

Ponsonby was fond of Jenner, however, despite his loud cantankerousness and reactionary views. He also liked Dr James Reid, a sensible, humorous Scotsman who was appointed Resident Physician in 1881. On his first arrival at Court, Reid was informed that he could not, as an ordinary doctor, dine with the Household as this would be a breach of the Queen's instructions for the social acceptance of members of his profession. Not at all put out by this, Reid began to give dinners of his own to which many members of the Household preferred to go rather than to endure the dullness and constraints of their own dining-room.

The Queen was much annoyed when she heard of this practice, but not nearly so cross as she was when she learned that Reid had had the audacity to become engaged to one of her Maids-of-Honour, the Honourable Susan Baring, Lord Revelstoke's daughter. For, as was well known, the Queen disapproved of any members of her Household of either sex getting married. The Maids-of-Honour, in fact, were never allowed to receive any man, even their brothers, in their own rooms, being required to entertain them in the waiting-room downstairs. She was so angry when she was told what Reid had done that she refused to see him for three days, though she forgave him – having a far more lively sense of humour than her formidable appearance usually suggested – when he amused her by promising 'never to do it again'.

It was to men like Reid that Ponsonby turned as a relief from the appalling dullness of Court life. This dullness was never more oppressive than it was at Balmoral, to which the Queen was devoted because of its associations with her happy married days and which her Ministers abhorred, not only because they wasted so much of their time travelling there when they were required to attend upon the Queen, but also because they were so uncomfortable when they did get there. 'Carrying on the Government of a country six hundred miles from the Metropolis' doubled the labour involved in being Prime Minister, Disraeli complained, though not, of course to the Queen herself who was deaf to all appeals not to spend so much of her time there.

Ponsonby disliked Balmoral almost as intensely as Lord Salisbury who made no 'attempt to conceal his disgust with the place' and was always 'heartily glad' to get away from it. Ponsonby's opinion of it coincided with that of Lady Dalhousie, who had never been in a house she disliked more, and with that of Lord Rosebery, who said that he had thought the drawing-room at Osborne was the ugliest in the world until he had seen the one at Balmoral. 'Every private house strikes me as *so* comfortable', Ponsonby sadly lamented, 'after the severe dreariness of our palatial rooms *here*.'

It would not have been so bad had the members of the Household been allowed more freedom. But everything to do with the running of their lives was under the Queen's own strict control. She decided the precise time of their arrival and departure; she directed that they must never leave the house until she herself had gone out; when they did go out they must use only those particular ponies which, divided into five categories, were allocated to their use. Maids-of-Honour must not talk to the Gentlemen unless accompanied by a chaperone; on Sundays everyone had to go to church where the length and content of the sermons were regulated by the Queen's known wishes.

As well as the dinner for the Queen and her chosen guests, three separate meals were served each evening, those for the lower servants, the upper servants and the Household. The Household dinner was often an ordeal, particularly for the younger members, as the Queen's dislike of change meant that most of those in attendance on her were old and several were extremely deaf. Yet invitations to the Queen's dinners were dreaded; for although, as Ponsonby said, the Queen was occasionally in a jolly mood and 'seemed prepared for prattle' and to 'talk away on minor topics', more often she was not; and then the dinners were 'appallingly dull', the 'most depressing functions' he had ever known.

Ponsonby described one of the Queen's dinners in 1872 which was particularly and 'painfully flat'. Her Majesty, who had a cold, sat between her son, Prince Leopold, who 'never uttered', and Lord Gainsborough, who was deaf. The prolonged silences were broken only by various types of cough, 'respectable', 'deep', or 'gouty', and by 'all the servants dropping plates and making a clatteration of noises'.

The Countess of Lytton, widow of a former British Ambassador in Paris, who arrived at Balmoral in 1895 to fill a vacancy which had occurred among the Queen's Ladies-in-Waiting by the death of the Dowager Duchess of Roxburgh, found most of Her Majesty's dinners quite as irksome as Ponsonby did. On her arrival one bitterly cold October afternoon she was greeted by Harriet Phipps, the Queen's personal secretary, who, like all the Bedchamber Women and Maids-of-Honour who did not have titles, was given the rank of a Baron's daughter and was therefore known as the Honourable Harriet Phipps. Miss Phipps took Lady Lytton into a small room, formerly the Prince Consort's dressing-room which was used for receiving visitors upstairs. She was presented with the Victoria and Albert Order which all the Queen's Ladies wore, attached to a white ribbon, on their dresses. And, on returning to her room, she was told by a servant who knocked on the door: 'You are invited to dine with the Queen, miladi.'

At nine o'clock she went down to the dining-room where she waited with the other guests until the announcement, 'The Queen has arrived' drew them all to the door. The Queen hobbled into the room, leaning on the arm of Gholam Mustafa, her Indian servant, went through to the dining-room and took her place at the table. 'The beginning of the dinner was rather solemn,' Lady Lytton recorded in her diary. The Queen hardly spoke at all during the early courses; and it was not until she made some remark about the Spanish Ambassador having 'come in the afternoon and [being] expected to be received at once without making an appointment' that the atmosphere became more relaxed as the guests laughed 'for some little time' at this odd ignorance of protocol.

A subsequent dinner to which Lady Lytton was invited was much more easy as there were only four other guests. Two of these were the Queen's youngest daughter, Princess Beatrice, and her husband Prince Henry of Battenberg, a naturalized Englishman who had agreed to live at Court so as not to deprive the Queen of his wife's indispensable services. The Queen was quite communicative at these smaller, less formal dinners; and the conversation on this occasion was 'general and so easy'. The next evening, though, when Lady Lytton was again invited to dinner and there were far more guests, including Lord James of Hereford, the Minister in Attendance – there always having to be a member of the Cabinet on duty at Court – the evening once more was 'very solemn and the room so cold'.

After dinner the lady guests would usually play patience while the Queen would sit in her chair, sipping coffee from a cup whose saucer was held by a page, occasionally asking someone to be brought up to speak to her and giving that 'curious, nervous laugh' of hers when a person whom she did not know very well was presented. 'About eleven the [games of patience] stop,' Lady Lytton recorded, 'and looks are sent across to the Queen ... When she takes her stick, as if by magic the servants outside know it and open the door and Mustafa glides in but without a Salaam, seizes the Queen's arm and she rises slowly ... One feels very idiotic after this, and we either leave the drawing-room direct, or pass through the billiard-room where the Gentlemen of the Household remain.'

Most of these Gentlemen found the atmosphere in the billiard-room scarcely more relaxed than it was in the drawing-room, particularly when the Queen's second son, Prince Alfred, Duke of Edinburgh, was there. For the Duke was a most loquacious and boring talker whose monologues were endured only by those who were compelled to go to the billiard-room in order to smoke. 'The Duke of Edinburgh occupies the chair and talks about himself by the hour,' Ponsonby told his wife. 'Those who go are quite exhausted. Prince Henry has given up smoking in consequence.'

Tiresome as Ponsonby found the talk in the billiard-room and most of the Queen's dinners, the gillies' balls were even more of an ordeal for him. He did not enjoy the company of the Queen's gillies at the best of times. He found deer-stalking excessively boring and, when compelled against his will to take part in the sport, stuffed his pockets with newspapers and the *Fortnightly Review* so as to render the long waits less wearisome. At the end of the day there was sometimes a gruesome torch-lit dance round the slaughtered animals during which the gillies absorbed torrents of whisky and sang songs. Further quantities of whisky were drunk around the huge granite cairn which had been erected to the memory of Prince Albert and which still bears the legend: 'Albert the Great and Good, raised by his broken-hearted widow.'

At the rowdy, hearty gillies' balls the whisky flowed unchecked. Ponsonby endeavoured to spend as little time at them as possible. They were organized by the objectionably managing John Brown; and the Queen, who had always been an accomplished and graceful dancer and remained so into her seventies, attended them regularly, appearing to enjoy them to the full and even insisting that they were not cancelled when the Court was officially in mourning, though she usually had a quite obsessive predilection for its observances. Some time before the Prince Consort's death, when her relation, the Czar, died during the Crimean War, she had caused 'IMMEDIATE search to be made for precedents as to the Court going or not going into mourning for a sovereign with whom at the time of his decease England was at war'.

After the Prince's death everyone at Court had to wear full mourning for a year; the servants had to wear black crape bands on their arms for over eight years; and, while the other Ladies were permitted after 1864 to wear dresses of grey, violet, lilac or white, the Lady-in-Waiting was still required to wear mourning as deep as that of Her Majesty whose own widow's clothes were never discarded. Nevertheless, the Queen declined to postpone the gillies' ball for more than three days on the death of the Grand Duke of Hesse, her convenient yet unlikely excuse for not applying such strict rules to this occasion being that she did not 'regard it as gaiety'. Her Household agreed with her, Ponsonby especially. He sometimes stole away on the grounds that he had important work to do. But his absence was always noticed and remarked on 'with some asperity'. As a punishment he was obliged on his return to dance a particularly rowdy sort of reel which was one of John Brown's favourites.

Ponsonby was as dismayed as anyone by the rough, curt manner in which Brown, a former stable-boy, was allowed to treat the Queen and by the air of coarse importance which this indulgence led him to assume. He well understood how it was that her family and Ministers, whom Brown treated with no pretence of respect, came to dislike, even to detest the man. But like the calculating Disraeli, Ponsonby recognized his usefulness. Brown could persuade the Queen to do things which other men could not. Like most monarchs, she was liable to enter into close relationships with servants who do not share the kind of ambitions that some courtiers and nearly all politicians have. But the members of her Household, undignified and ludicrous as they found it, never really supposed that there was anything immoral in Brown's relationship with the Queen, though she obviously found him attractive as a man.

For all his other faults, Brown, so Ponsonby believed, was certainly not ambitious; and he made the Queen 'a most excellent servant' Ponsonby was, therefore, prepared to tolerate him without demur, even though the man was without question 'exceedingly troublesome'. One afternoon the Queen was kept waiting for a very long time in her carriage for Brown to take up his usual place on the box. Ponsonby saw her sitting there and, guessing why Brown had not appeared, went up to his room where he found him incapably drunk on his bed. Ponsonby locked the door, came down, got up on the box himself and drove off without a word. The Queen, too, remained silent.

It was, in fact, Ponsonby's understanding of the Queen's character that made him so useful, indeed so indispensable a Private Secretary. Like General Grey he knew just how far he could go on any particular occasion in persuading her to act against her own wishes, and he refused to jeopardize his influence over her by pressing her too hard when he well knew such pressure would merely result in her refusing to discuss the subject again. 'When she insists that 2 and 2 make 5,' he wrote, 'I say that I cannot help thinking they make 4. She replies there may be some truth in what I say, but she knows they make 5. Thereupon I drop the discussion. It is of no consequence and I leave it there, knowing the fact.' He contrasted this method with that of a colleague who pursued such controversies, bringing in proofs, arguments and, worst of all, former sayings of her own. 'No one likes this,' Ponsonby added. 'No one can stand admitting they are wrong, women especially; and the Queen can't abide it. Consequently she won't give in.'

Ponsonby's way of dealing with the Queen, in contrast to that of the unnamed colleagues, frequently did result in her giving in, or, more often, quietly allowing a matter to drop rather than admitting that she had been wrong.

One trivial, if time-consuming, incident well illustrates Ponsonby's way of dealing with a mistress to whom, he said, advice had always to be given 'in a most gingerly way'. It concerned the arrangements for a holiday, every trifling detail of which had to be submitted for the Queen's approval. Taking the register of servants who were to accompany her she struck all but one off the list of housemaids. Normally she travelled with an enormous suite. On trips abroad her staff numbered over a hundred. And, in a political crisis in 1866 when, for once, she agreed not to go to Balmoral in May but to borrow Cliveden instead so as to be within easy reach of her Ministers, she took ninety-one attendants with her including three doctors. But on this occasion she decreed that one housemaid would be quite enough. The staff objected and, as usual, asked Ponsonby to intervene. He did so, and thus recorded the result: 'Of course quite right that only one housemaid should go. I would send to her [another] girl from the Hotel. But stray girls were not always very honest. So I hoped the Queen would not leave things about to tempt her. [She was in the habit of taking with her an enormous number of pictures, photographs and treasured possessions whenever she moved from one place to another]. I got the answer that another housemaid should go from here.'

The Queen was obstinate, Ponsonby well knew, but she was rarely obtuse. If on many occasions unreasonable, she was essentially a woman of good sense. When far cleverer people were wrong she was often instinctively right. As Salisbury observed, she had a deeper understanding of the passing moods of her people than many politicians who spent far more time among them than she did. In dealing with her, as Ponsonby recognized, one had not only to try to understand her complex and contradictory character, but also to take advantage of her own mercurial moods and what she felt to be the state of her health.

While he accepted that his first duty was to serve her interests faithfully, to strengthen her position and to carry out her wishes, he recognized, too, that these interests were not always best served by obeying her orders or giving in quietly to her opinions. There were occasions when he had to write letters of whose contents he disapproved, to administer what he considered undeserved rebukes. But he rarely did so without making it clear to her what his own views were; and, though at the time she accused him of a lack of sympathy or unkindness for expressing them, she learned to respect him for doing so and occasionally on reflection modified her demands. She learned to rely upon him, also, to frame her communications in a concise and orderly manner without their losing that peculiarly vital and pungent style which came to her naturally as a diarist and letter-writer.

His fairness and impartiality were appreciated by Conservatives and Liberals alike. Although a Liberal himself he did not invariably agree with that party's policy; yet Gladstone, who knew how he endeavoured to counteract the Tory influences at Court to which the Queen was subjected – and was deeply appreciative of the services of a man who had vainly attempted to mitigate the Queen's dislike of him and had aroused her anger by praising his qualities – wrote in appreciation of Ponsonby's 'tact, discernment and constancy'. 'I have known and have liked and have admired all the men who have served the Queen in your delicate and responsible office,' wrote Gladstone in another letter, 'and I have liked most, probably because I knew him most... General Grey. But forgive me for saying so, you are "to the manner born". Such a combination of tact and temper, with loyalty, intelligence and truth, I cannot expect to see again.'

Gladstone's enemy, Disraeli, was equally grateful. 'I know you don't agree with me,' he said to Ponsonby in 1876, 'but I know you convey my messages accurately to the Queen.' 'We have passed five years', he added later, when informing Ponsonby that he had submitted his name for a Privy Councillorship, 'in the conduct of great affairs without a cloud between us.' 'I can only say that I could not wish my case stated to the Queen better than her Private Secretary does it,' Disraeli wrote to a friend. 'Perhaps I am a gainer by his Whiggishness, as it makes him more scrupulously on his guard to be always absolutely fair and lucid.'

When in 1878, Sir Henry Ponsonby became Keeper of the Privy Purse while still remaining Private Secretary, he was at last provided with assistance in his arduous duties. Fleetwood Edwards, a captain in the Royal Engineers, was appointed Assistant Private Secretary. An old Harrovian of great charm, Fleetwood Edwards had been private secretary and aide-de-camp to the Governor of Bermuda and had accompanied General Sir John Lintorn Simmons, the British delegation's military adviser, to the Congress of Berlin where he had attracted the favourable notice of Disraeli. Another Secretary, appointed in 1880, was Arthur Bigge, a lieutenant in the Royal Artillery. One of the twelve children of a Northumberland parson, Bigge had served in the same battery as the Prince Imperial, the son of Napoleon III and the Empress Eugénie; and, after the Prince's death in South Africa, he had escorted the body back to England. Having related the circumstances of the Prince's death to the Empress, he had been summoned to Balmoral to report to the Queen. She found him, as she told her eldest daughter, 'a charming person, of the very highest character, clever, amiable and agreeable, as well as good looking'. It was the beginning of a close and important relationship with the royal family which was to last for over half a century.

After the death of Sir Henry Ponsonby, worn out at the age of sixty-nine, in 1895, Bigge was appointed Private Secretary in his place; Fleetwood Edwards became Keeper of the Privy Purse; and Sir Henry's son, Frederick, reluctantly accepted the appointment of Assistant Private Secretary.

Frederick Ponsonby was a rather shy young man whose polite though blandly noncommittal responses to conversational gambits made him seem in later years at once intimidating and inscrutable. Educated at Eton, where he had rowed in the eight, he had been commissioned into the Duke of Cornwall's Light Infantry and, after transferring to his father's regiment, the Grenadier Guards, had become aide-de-camp to the Viceroy of India. He had not wanted to forsake his career in the Army; and when the summons to join the Royal Household as equerry had arrived, he had immediately despatched a telegram to his father asking if he could refuse. Sir Henry, who had not been consulted in the matter by the Queen, had replied that he could not very well do so. He had therefore felt obliged to return home.

Able and assiduous, Frederick Ponsonby had a gift for languages; and, despite the formality of his manner and his insistence on the strict observance of prevailing social customs and of the details of ceremonial etiquette, he was both imaginative and humorous. He was also a man of decided opinions which, as he grew older and more confident, he was always ready to express. The Queen once warned him about this: he was much too outspoken, she said; he must learn not to air views which no one wished to hear.

He had come to Her Majesty's notice at Osborne where he had taken part in a French play; and his evident mastery of the language, combined with his first-hand knowledge of India, persuaded Her Majesty to believe that he could be useful to her. The Indian connection was important at the time as the Queen, who, unlike many of her Household and Ministers, was quite devoid of racial prejudice, was being criticized for the confidence she reposed in one of her Indian servants, Abdul Karim, a Muslim *Khidmutgar* (waiter), whom she had promoted *Munshi* (secretary), receiving from him daily lessons in Hindustani and destroying all photographs of him handing dishes to her at table. The rest of the Household found him – as they had found John Brown – irritatingly pretentious, boasting of the number of clerks he had under him and the appearance of his name in the Court Circular. And when the Queen took to employing him as her Indian Secretary they became alarmed that he might pass on confidential information to undesirable friends in India, with whom he was believed to be in touch, and through them to Afghanistan. The matter was raised with the Secretary of State for India, Lord George Hamilton. But Hamilton refused to get involved with the 'Court's mud pies'; and so they felt obliged to take action themselves. Arthur Bigge, Fleetwood Edwards and James Reid all pointed out to the Queen, as tactfully as they could, the dangers of her reposing trust in a mischievous low-caste Hindu whose claim to be the son of a surgeon-general in the Indian Army appeared highly improbable. The Queen, declining to listen to their advice, protested angrily, 'To make out that the poor good *Munshi* is so *low* is really *outrageous* & in a country like England quite out of place ... She has known 2 Archbishops who were sons respectively of a Butcher & Grocer. ... Abdul's father saw good & honourable service as a Dr. and he feels cut to the heart at being thus spoken of.' The Queen also wrote to ask Frederick Ponsonby, then still in India, to go to see the *Munshi*'s father.

Ponsonby discovered that the old man, far from being a surgeon-general, was a prison apothecary; and on his return to England he imparted this unwelcome information to the Queen. She stoutly denied it; admonished Ponsonby for having stupidly seen the wrong man; and, to mark her displeasure, did not ask him to dinner for a year.

Determined to show her continuing faith in Abdul, the Queen announced her intention of taking him with her on her spring visit to Cimiez in 1897. Aghast at the prospect of having to sit at the same table with the 'repulsive and disagreeable' trouble-maker, the Household revolted. They would rather all resign than submit. Harriet Phipps was deputed to approach the Queen with this ultimatum which so enraged her that she lost her temper – an occurrence much rarer now than when she was young – and swept everything off the top of her desk on to the floor. Eventually it was decided to enlist the help of the Prime Minister, Lord Salisbury who, with his customary wiliness, told the Queen that the French were 'such odd people' that they would never understand the *Munshi*'s position and might 'mock *her* and be rude to *him*'. So the *Munshi* did not travel with the royal party to Cimiez. But soon after their arrival at the Hotel Regina, Princess May, who was one of the Queen's young companions, wrote to her husband, the Duke of York, 'Gdmama again spoke about the *M....i* who to the despair of the poor gentlemen arrived today. I was most guarded in my replies.'

The days of the *Munshi*'s influence were, however, now drawing to a close. On her return home Bigge once again braved the Queen's wrath by protesting about him. So did those whom Lord George Hamilton in a letter to the Viceroy of India described as the 'old Indian officers in her Court'. And in the end she was persuaded to have the *Munshi* put more into his 'proper place'.

Frederick Ponsonby's exclusion from the Queen's dinner table because of his revelation of the *Munshi*'s origins was no great hardship. But he did find life in the Royal Household hard to bear when he fell in love with a beautiful girl, Ria Kennard, whom the Queen strenuously opposed his marrying, protesting 'that a man always told his wife everything and therefore all her private affairs would get known all over London'. Her parents were also against the marriage; but even when they gave their consent the Queen remained obdurate. For three years they waited; and it was not until Harriet Phipps undertook to intercede on their behalf that her objections were at last overcome. Permission was granted, however, on the condition that they should not have – neither now nor later – the grace-and-favour house to which they might well have considered themselves entitled.

For the unmarried Ponsonby his life as Equerry was not in the least entertaining. There was, in fact, hardly anything for him to do. At Osborne, for example, he went to the Equerries' Room after breakfast to read the newspapers and write private letters while the Queen was having her own breakfast out in the garden in a green-fringed parasol tent, waited upon by her Indian servants and Highlanders, her dogs at her feet, a Lady-in-Waiting by her side and one or other of her daughters 'in nervous attendance'. At noon she went out for a drive. But it was only if she were going through one of the towns on the island that an Equerry was considered necessary. She usually contented herself with a slow drive in a pony-chair; and on these outings she was accompanied only by a Lady-in-Waiting or a Maid-of-Honour.

Having taken advantage of the Queen's absence from the house to go out themselves, the members of the Household then went in to have their luncheon at two o'clock. At this meal the Master of the Household carved a joint of meat at one end of the table, and the Equerry a second joint at the other. Ponsonby, who was twenty-seven at the time of his appointment to the Household, had never had much experience of carving; and at first, as he admitted, his slices of meat were 'only fit for the workhouse'. But eventually he gained 'a certain proficiency in the art'; and although the other men were so much older than himself, most over seventy and some over eighty, he began to enjoy these luncheons where, unlike the dinners in the Queen's dining-room, there was now a good deal of amusing conversation.

After luncheon the Queen went out for another drive; and so the men also left the house again, returning to their separate rooms to work until it was time for dinner for which they were always required to dress in black knee-breeches and silk stockings. After dinner they went to the billiard-room to play or to smoke.

Elsewhere in the house the Queen objected to smoking as strongly as she did to open fires in rooms except in the very coldest weather. Although she herself had been seen to smoke on a summer picnic to keep the midges away, her aversion to the habit being indulged indoors was so extreme that when two of her sons entered her room suddenly one day to offer their condolences upon some disaster, they thought it as well to apologize profusely for having dared to appear before her in their smoking jackets. Even Prince Albert had not presumed to smoke in her presence; and at Osborne his smoking-room was the only room with a lone A above the door instead of an A intertwined with a V. The Queen could always detect the smell of tobacco on documents which were sent up to her; and Frederick Ponsonby once received a sharp injunction not to smoke while decoding telegrams which made the smell of their official box 'most obnoxious'. He and his colleagues took to carrying peppermints in their pockets in case a summons to the Queen came at a moment when their breath was sure to offend her.

Once he had taken up the duties of Assistant Secretary, Ponsonby found his time much more fully occupied in cyphering and decyphering messages; dealing with a mass of correspondence which Bigge left for his attention; making notes of all the papers which were sent to the Queen in case an important document, which she might keep for as long as a week, did not return; copying out parts of despatches which the Queen wanted to keep for her files; learning shorthand; improving his German and studying the Almanac de Gotha so that he could make himself more familiar with the complicated ramifications of the royal family tree. He was also responsible for preparing the data on which the Queen based certain entries in her diary as she liked to be quite sure of the complete accuracy of her facts, though evidently she was not above allowing the occasional mis-statement to appear when it cast her in a favourable or flattering light. Thus it was that in recounting the Queen's review of her colonial troops in 1897, Ponsonby – while knowing it to be false – included a statement, which had appeared in the newspapers, to the effect that Her Majesty had spoken to the Indian officers in Hindustani. When this was read out to her she objected, 'That's not true. I did not speak in Hindustani, but in English.' She was therefore asked if this part of the account should be omitted. 'No,' she decided. 'You can leave it, for I could have done so had I wished.'

Another of Frederick Ponsonby's duties was to look after the Queen's birthday books by which she set great store, taking the latest volumes about with her wherever she went so that people on occasions mistook them for Bibles, and insisting that all the people who visited her should sign their names on the appropriate page. The German Secretary was nominally in charge of these books and was responsible for compiling their indexes. But he did not carry out his duties as well as he should have done, and the onus of keeping the books up to date fell upon Ponsonby. Once when the Queen was staying at Nice at the Hotel Regina it was suggested to her that Sarah Bernhardt, who was acting at the theatre in the town, should be invited to give a recital in the hotel. The Queen was at first reluctant, knowing that Bernhardt's morals were far from being above reproach. Later, however, she changed her mind, attended the recital of Theuriet's *Jean Marie* which she thought 'quite marvellous, so pathetic and full of feeling', and, much impressed by the virtuosity of the great actress whose cheeks were wet with tears, she asked Lady Lytton to present her to her so that she could compliment her. On leaving the room she sent to inquire if Sarah Bernhardt's autograph had been procured for the Birthday Book. Ponsonby was proud to have remembered to ensure that it was. He had watched with satisfaction mingled with astonishment as Bernhardt had taken the book from him, placed it on the floor, knelt in front of it, and scrawled across it, *'Le plus beau jour de ma vie'*, followed by a flamboyant signature. Ponsonby proudly sent up the book for the Queen to see. But, having done his 'duty nobly', as he thought, he got 'no marks'. First of all it was the wrong book: he ought to have used the artists' book. Secondly he should have prevented Miss Bernhardt from taking up the whole page.

Towards the end of her life the Queen became an increasingly trying mistress because of her failing sight, which not only further reduced the legibility of her own writing, but which also made it necessary for her Secretaries to write in larger, more clearly formed characters and, therefore, more slowly.* Ponsonby, resourceful as ever, bought some copy-books printed for girls' schools with the help of which he perfected a completely new hand. He also bought 'some special ink like boot varnish'; and, having used this to write his document, he dried it over a copper tray heated by a spirit lamp, an invention of Sir Arthur Bigge's. But this method did not satisfy the Queen. Since the thick black ink showed through the paper, only one side could be used which rendered the documents she had to read too bulky for her taste. She, therefore, issued instructions for Ponsonby to revert to his former practice of writing on both sides of the paper. So Ponsonby applied to the Stationery Office for a supply of paper the same size as the sheets then in use but very much thicker. At first the new paper was acceptable; but, as the Queen liked to keep all messages in her room for some time, she soon found that the accumulation of paper was inconvenient: would Captain Ponsonby kindly revert to the ordinary paper.

'I grasped then that it was hopeless', Ponsonby recorded, 'and I consulted Sir James Reid as to whether it would not be possible to explain all the difficulties to her, but he said he feared her sight was going and that any explanation would therefore be useless. So I went back to the ordinary paper and ordinary ink, and of course received a message to say would I write blacker, but as it was hopeless I didn't attempt to alter anything.'

In the end documents had to be read to her. Much of this reading was done by Princess Beatrice, her youngest child, which led to what Ponsonby called 'absurd mistakes'. Ponsonby wrote to his mother:

> The Queen is not even *au courant* with the ordinary topics of the present day. Imagine [Princess] B[eatrice] trying to explain ... our policy in the East. Bigge or I may write out long précis of [such] things but they are often not read to HM as [Princess] B[eatrice] is in a hurry to develop a photograph or wants to paint a flower for a Bazaar ... Apart from the hideous mistakes that occur ... there is the danger of the Q's letting go almost entirely the control of things which should be kept under the immediate supervision of the Sovereign ... The sad thing is that it is only her eyes, nothing else. Her memory is still wonderful, her shrewdness, her power of discrimination as strong as ever, her long experience of European politics alone makes her opinion valuable but

---

* Shortly after the introduction of the typewriter into England a machine was purchased for use at Windsor. But the Queen evidently did not like it. (*Behind the Throne*, Emden, p. 127.)

when her sole means of reading despatches, *précis*, debates, etc. lie in [Princess] B[eatrice], it is simply hopeless.

Ponsonby was later called upon to read to her himself. The summons would come unexpectedly at any hour; and he would have to rush away for his black frock-coat which it was necessary to wear in her presence even at Balmoral. Once he was called upon to read some papers to the Queen immediately, when he was going out fishing in country clothes and a red tie. He ran back to his room, changed into black trousers and put on a dark overcoat, hoping that the sombre colours would be enough to satisfy the Queen's dim eyes. On a later occasion he was summoned at breakfast time and found Her Majesty eating a boiled egg in a gold cup with a gold spoon. 'Two Indian *Khitmagars* in scarlet and gold remained motionless behind her chair, while outside a page and a Scotchman in a kilt waited till she rang.' Ponsonby also recalled his embarrassment at having to read to her a long telegram one evening after dinner while the Royal Marines band played Wagner: 'Although her hearing was good, I had to speak very loudly to make myself heard. Every now and then, however, the music stopped abruptly whilst I was left shouting at her, much to the amusement of the rest of the dinner party who were crowded at the end of the room.'

Exacting and exasperating as they often found her, most of the Queen's Household were nevertheless deeply attached to her. For she was still capable of exercising an undoubted charm which a Dean of Windsor described as 'irresistible'. And despite a habit of turning a conversation into a rigorous cross-examination, she could be as entertaining as, in her livelier moods, she was easily amused. She often told funny stories about herself and was fond of relating how one clear and starlit night at Windsor Castle she had opened her bedroom window to look out at the sky, and a sentry at the foot of the Castle wall, thinking she was a housemaid, 'began to address her in most affectionate and endearing terms. The Queen at once drew her curtains but was simply delighted at what had happened.' She was delighted, too, when the arch-reactionary Grand Duchess of Mecklenburg-Strelitz told her in shocked tones that a footman whom the Grand Duchess had instructed to conduct her up the Long Walk in Windsor Great Park to the statue of King George III, had asked her, 'Do you mean the old gentleman on the copper horse?' 'Imagine my royal and loyal feelings and horror at the modern servants calling the King and my Grandfather thus!' the Grand Duchess indignantly told her niece. 'But the Queen *roared*' with laughter.

Mohammed Shah, Aga Khan, who was a guest of the Queen three years before her death at the age of eighty-one, found her a far less forbidding personage than he had been led to expect. She had an odd accent, he thought, 'a mixture of Scotch and German' with 'the German conversational trick of interjecting "so" – pronounced "tzo" – into her remarks'.* But the 'facility and clarity' of her conversation was 'astonishing'. She was sometimes shy with young people, giggling apprehensively in their presence and giving diffident little shrugs of her shoulders when asking them questions. But she got on with them far better, particularly with most of her thirty-seven grandchildren, than she had with her own children. She enjoyed their company, and loved to watch them romping with the dogs on the lawns and to hear their 'little feet & merry voices' in the rooms above her own. 'Grandmama so kind and dear as usual,' wrote Princess Victoria of Prussia, of whom the Queen was particularly fond, after one of the Princess's frequent visits.

'Such was the majesty that surrounded Queen Victoria,' according to one of her numerous great-grandchildren, David, eldest son of the Duke of York, 'that she was regarded almost as a divinity of whom even her own family stood in awe. However, to us children she was "Gangan".' 'She wore', he added, then, as always, observant of people's clothes, 'a white tulle cap, black satin dress and shiny black boots with elastic sides.'

Watching her one day, shuffling along a garden path, grasping the handle of a walking-stick in a chubby, white, heavily beringed finger, followed by various dogs and several noisy children, one of her Ladies found herself astonished by the thought that this tiny, plump, old lady was one of 'the most influential, revered and powerful women in the world'.

She certainly enjoyed immense prestige. But was the Queen of England, others questioned, really powerful any more? The Queen herself would go no further than to say that at any rate she had been no 'mere puppet' in the formation of Governments. And she had good grounds to believe that her successors might not even be able to claim as much as that.

---

* Others, however, including Princess Alice, Countess of Athlone, could detect no trace of a foreign accent.

3 Edwardian Interlude

So strong was Queen Victoria's dislike of any change in her surroundings that at the time of her death most of the rooms at Windsor Castle and Buckingham Palace reflected the taste of those who had admired the exhibits at the Great Exhibition half a century before. Inside those dismal, shabby, ill-lit and vestigially heated apartments, cupboard after cupboard, wardrobe after wardrobe, drawer after drawer was stuffed with the accumulations of a long lifetime.

Disregarding all protests the Queen's eldest son, now King Edward VII, burst into the rooms and threw open the cupboards, intent upon reorganization and reform. A portly, energetic and impatient man with a grey beard, hooded, greyish eyes and a highly-coloured complexion, he strode down the corridors, puffing on an enormous Corona y Corona cigar, a dog at his heels, a hat on his head, giving orders to attendant courtiers and servants, emphasizing points with sharp jabs of his walking-stick. Case-loads of relics and ornaments were despatched to the Round Tower at Windsor; statues and busts of John Brown were destroyed; the papers of the *Munshi* were burned; the rooms of Prince Albert which had not been touched since his death were cleared and redecorated; other apartments were also renovated and refurnished; worthless pictures were removed and others rehung with the help of the Surveyor of the King's Pictures. New bathrooms and lavatories were installed; and the primitive telephone systems were improved and extended.

The work continued for several months; and it was not until the spring of 1902 that the King and Queen were able to move from Marlborough House to Buckingham Palace. Thereafter life at Court was transformed. The hush of the old Queen's days was gone for ever; and the spirit of the palace was caught not in the rustle of bombazine in a murky corridor but in the sound of the King's deep though penetrating voice, his gruff laugh, the barking of his spoiled little terrier, the smell of cigar smoke and women's scent, the sputtering of Mercedes motor cars in the courtyard outside.

There were those who did not welcome the change. Lord Esher, who was to become one of the King's most influential advisers, could not but regret the passing of 'the mystery and awe of the old Court', of the 'quiet, impressive entrance of the monarch' before dinner. King Edward was certainly 'kind and debonair and not undignified' but 'too *human*'. Others lamented that the entrée to Court no longer depended upon birth or rank or merit. Amongst the King's most intimate friends were several of whom his mother would have strongly disapproved. There was, for instance, Sir Ernest Cassel, the hospitable Jewish financier, who was as indefatigable in his pursuit of British and foreign decorations as he was in amassing money. There was the lively, swarthy, clever and stimulating Marquis de Soveral, the Portuguese Minister, whom nearly everyone found irresistible, even the husbands of his mistresses. There was the Honourable Mrs George Keppel, whose presence was accepted by Queen Alexandra – herself indulged and respected by the King – since she kept him entertained and therefore good-tempered.

But while there was much gaiety at Court there was little informality. For the King's taste for regularity and punctuality imposed upon it an almost immutable routine, while his insistence on the observance of proper etiquette in the matters of procedure and dress ensured that there was no relaxation in the strict rules he imposed. In the evenings ladies were always required to wear tiaras and gentlemen knee-breeches with full decorations.

The lovely Queen, exasperatingly unpunctual as well as deaf, was a law unto herself, capable of appearing with the star of the Order of the Garter on the wrong side if she felt it clashed with her other jewels. But her eccentricities were no excuse for anyone else's. The American Duchess of Marlborough, her beauty admired by the King though it was, was once sharply reprimanded for having appeared at dinner with a diamond crescent instead of the prescribed tiara. A *faux pas* by a man was certain to evoke an even sterner rebuke. Even foreign diplomats were not immune. The Swedish Minister, on appearing with his medals in the wrong order, was taken aside by the King who whispered in his ear – as though imparting a state secret of the utmost significance – the name of the Court jewellers.

It was generally agreed, however, that the King was an excellent and most generous host. His reforms of the Household included the pensioning off of many unnecessary servants including the Indians, whose sole duty it had been to prepare curry for luncheon whether anyone wanted it or not, and several of Queen Victoria's huge kitchen staff of nineteen chefs and numerous cooks, bakers, confectioners, pastrymen and apprentices. But no one could complain of the quality of the food, or of its quantity which was commensurate with the voracious appetite of the King himself, who could happily sit down to a twelve-course dinner at half past eight after a hearty lunch at half past two, and a tea of poached eggs, rolls and scones, *petits fours* and preserved ginger, and all manner of hot cakes, cold cakes, sweet cakes and Scotch shortcakes, at five o'clock.

After dinner the guests usually played cards. The King himself was very fond of bridge, which he nevertheless did not play well, soon losing interest when his cards were bad, yet never failing to criticize his partner's mistakes without the least equivocation or apology.

He soon recovered his temper, however, after even the most unsatisfactory game, accepting his winnings with complacent satisfaction and paying out his losses as though he were bestowing upon his opponent a most valuable present. And when he was ready to go to bed, between one o'clock and half past one, he was usually as affable as he had been during the day, making sure that everyone had a good supper, recommending the grilled oysters which were his own favourite refreshment at that time of night, going upstairs, as he had done in his youth, to escort the men guests to their rooms, to make sure that they had all that they could possibly require and to give a token poke to the fire in the grate.

Until they grew accustomed to them his staff found their master's sudden alternations between sharp temper and benign geniality highly unnerving. Fortunately most of them had known him for a long time. Francis Knollys, whom he appointed his Private Secretary, had been in his service since 1862. The Master of the Household, Lord Farquhar, was an old friend. So were the Comptroller, Major-General Sir Arthur Ellis, and the Keeper of the Privy Purse, Sir Dighton Probyn, a full-bearded veteran of the Indian Mutiny, who was a favourite butt for the King's rude banter. His two Assistant Private Secretaries were Colonel Arthur Davidson and Frederick Ponsonby, men of patience and understanding.

In his memoirs Ponsonby described several of the King's outbursts of uncontrollable anger, his 'boiling with rage', his 'breaking into a storm of abuse', 'shouting and storming', 'shaking the roof' of Buckingham Palace, his 'becoming more and more and more angry and finally exploding with fury'. Yet, although the King never troubled to conceal his annoyance at the most trifling grievances, most of his staff were devoted to him; some loved him; and all acknowledged that, dedicated as he was to a life of pleasure and comfort, he was conscientious in the fulfilment of his duty. 'Often I had to suggest a visit which I knew would be irksome to him, or that he should see somebody that I knew he would not want to see, and he would exclaim, "No, no, damned if I will do it!" ' recorded Charles Hardinge, Permanent Under-Secretary for Foreign Affairs. 'But he always did it, however tiresome it might be for him, without my having to argue the point or in fact say another word. He had a very strong sense of the duties which his position entailed and he never shirked them.'

At the beginning of his reign he had taken up his tasks and responsibilities with an obvious relish, conscious of the importance of his position, remarking to a friend who protested at his settling down to work at midnight, 'Yes, I must! Besides, it is all so inter-r-r-resting,' rolling his rs in that characteristic German way of his, then giving the friend 'one of his happy smiles'. Lord Esher described him as like a man who, 'after long years of pent-up action', had suddenly been freed from restraint and released to fulfil his mission. Enthusiastically he would ask question after question, interrupt the answers with his quickly murmured, 'Yes, yes, yes', give orders, scribble notes on bits of paper in his scarcely legible handwriting, and then stand in front of the fire 'looking wonderfully like Henry VIII, only better tempered'.

At first he had the four hundred or so letters which arrived at Buckingham Palace each day brought up to him unopened so that he could sort them all himself. But he found this work impossibly time-consuming; and soon delegated most of his desk-work to Secretaries whom he would tell roughly what to say, leaving the actual wording to them. He far preferred talking to people face to face or, failing that, on the telephone, to writing letters.

He was, in fact, far more effective as King outside the Palace than he was in it. His yearly programme was almost unalterably governed by his need to fulfil the social obligations of the London Season which began after Easter and ended with the races at Ascot in late June; by those other race meetings, including Epsom, at which his presence was expected as a matter of course; by the yachting at Cowes; by the opening of the grouse-shooting season on 12 August; by the autumn shooting at Balmoral; by his predilection for spending his birthday on 9 November as well as Christmas at Sandringham; and by those foreign travels, usually combined with some diplomatic mission, to which he was so devoted. But in between these pleasurable events he held himself ready to perform the many official duties and to fulfil those many public engagements which he felt it his responsibility to undertake, always being in London in January or February for the State opening of Parliament; in summer going to visit some industrial town, usually in the Midlands or the North; and at other times performing ceremonial functions, laying foundation stones, opening hospitals, inspecting museums and art galleries, visiting schools and colleges, attending dinners, reviewing troops, holding levees, and making those speeches which are the common burden – and, in his case it often seemed, the enjoyment – of royalty.

He was an excellent speaker with a pleasant, resonant voice and an easy, assured delivery. At his Accession Council he almost broke down on referring to the death of his mother, but recovered himself to speak with what Lord Carrington described as 'dignity and pathos' for nearly ten minutes, without references to a written script which his successors were to find indispensable. And thereafter he spoke at numerous functions both at home and abroad with complete success. Fluent in French, with a good command of German and a working knowledge of both Spanish and Italian, he was one of Europe's most effective diplomatists, certainly its most famous. And if his prodigious reputation as a decisive arbiter of foreign affairs was much exaggerated; if he was not, perhaps, as Whitelaw Reid, the American Ambassador in London, described him in a letter to President Roosevelt, 'the greatest mainstay of peace in Europe'; if he did not really deserve the credit, which was often accorded him, of being the sole originator of the *entente cordiale* between his own country and France, he did deserve to be recognized as having made a unique contribution to the creation of an atmosphere of trust and friendship in which that agreement could be reached.

Foreign affairs were his principal concern. He was interested in the Army and Royal Navy, too, in hospitals and medical research. But he found most domestic and colonial affairs extremely tedious; and with all matters that bored him he did not make the slightest effort to comprehend them. 'He had a most curious brain,' Frederick Ponsonby commented, 'and at one time one would find him a big, strong, far-seeing man, grasping the situation at a glance and taking a broad-minded view of it; at another one would be almost surprised at the smallness of his mind. He would be almost childish in his views, and would obstinately refuse to understand the question at issue.'

Yet, as H. H. Asquith, his last Prime Minister, said, if the matter were properly put to him, and if his severely limited patience was not exhausted by excessively verbose explanations, he understood everything perfectly well. He had 'an excellent head' and was 'most observant about people'.

It was a matter of constant irritation to the King that few Ministers other than Asquith – and Asquith himself not invariably – took the care to consult him or even to keep him informed of their policies. He was constantly having to complain of being 'completely left in the dark'. It was his constitutional right, he insisted, 'to have all dispatches of any importance, especially those initiating or relating to a change of policy, laid before him prior to their being decided upon'. It was a right that had always been observed during his mother's reign. Why was it not in his? He quite understood that there might well be some constitutional objection to his being allowed to see Cabinet papers while important

1 Queen Victoria, a year after her marriage. Lithograph by Emile Desmaisons, 1841.

2 Queen Victoria and Prince Albert holding a Drawing-Room at St James's Palace, 1861.

3 Queen Victoria and Prince Albert with King Louis Philippe of France in the royal train, 1844.

4 The Queen at a Gillies' Ball at Balmoral, 1882.

5 Queen Victoria's sitting-room at Osborne.

6 A nineteenth-century photograph of Balmoral Castle.

7 General Sir Charles Grey, Prince Albert's Secretary, who was appointed Queen Victoria's Private Secretary in 1867.

8 Sir Henry Ponsonby, who succeeded Grey as the Queen's Private Secretary in 1870 and remained in her service until his death in 1895.

9 The Queen with Disraeli during a visit to his home at Hughenden.

10 John Brown, Queen Victoria's 'Highland Servant'.

11 Queen Victoria with the Prince and Princess of Wales, 1883.

12 The Queen with the *Munshi* and her Private Secretary, Sir Arthur Bigge, later Lord Stamfordham. Watercolour by Begg.

13 A rare photograph of Queen Victoria in old age wearing glasses.

14 The future King Edward VII at his desk at Marlborough House c. 1895–1900.

15 The Prince of Wales's study at Marlborough House c. 1895.

16 The dining-room at Sandringham, 1889.

17 Sir Frederick Ponsonby,
Assistant Private Secretary to
Queen Victoria, King Edward VII
and King George V.

18 Francis, Lord Knollys, Private
Secretary to King Edward VII.

19 David Lloyd George, the Liberal
Chancellor of the Exchequer, later
to become Prime Minister, 1906.

20 King Edward VII, George, Prince of Wales, later King George V and Prince Edward, later King Edward VIII, *c.* 1909.

21 Nine sovereigns assembled at Windsor for the funeral of King Edward VII, 1910. *From left to right, back row*: King Haakon VII of Norway, King Ferdinand of Bulgaria, King Manoel of Portugal, Kaiser William II of Germany, King George I of the Hellenes, King Albert of the Belgians; *front row*: King Alfonso XIII of Spain, King George V, King Frederick VIII of Denmark.

matters were under discussion; and he was evidently not surprised to learn that it was considered 'impossible' to let him have access to these papers. But the perfunctory and uninformative reports of Cabinet meetings that *were* sent to him really made 'an absolute fool of the King', Francis Knollys protested. 'There is no use in ministers *liking* the King if he is treated like a puppet.'

If the Ministers did like the King he did not much like any of them. He got on well with Asquith's predecessor, Sir Henry Campbell-Bannerman in private; but, as Knollys confided in Lord Esher: 'I don't think the King ever will like "C.B." politically.' Undoubtedly he never did get to like Campbell-Bannerman's predecessor, the Conservative A. J. Balfour, with whom he had almost nothing in common. As for Asquith's Cabinet, there were very few of its members whom he took to, apart from John Burns, the ebullient working-class President of the Local Government Board, whose appearance at Court in knee-breeches was, in Esher's words, 'a revelation' and whose summary of his relationship with the King was expressed in the words: 'Me and 'im get on first rate together.' He quite liked the President of the Board of Trade, Winston Churchill, as a man, but Churchill was *'almost more of* [a] cad in office than he was in opposition'. So was the Chancellor of the Exchequer, David Lloyd George. Even Lord Haldane, the Secretary for War, who had studied philosophy at Göttingen University, though he had once been described as 'always acceptable', was dismissed as 'a damned radical lawyer and a German professor' when he felt obliged to reduce the Army estimates. Besides, Haldane wore such dreadful clothes. Once seeing him in a most unsuitable hat at a garden party, the King exclaimed in exasperated tones: 'See my War Minister approach in a hat he inherited from Goethe!'

The King's exasperation with his Ministers was much increased not only by their failure to keep him informed as he had a right to expect, but also by their evident intention to reduce him to a 'mere signing machine' and to erode by degrees those few prerogatives that still remained to the Crown. During his reign he was forced to accept that it was the right of Parliament not of the monarch to cede territory; that the Prime Minister could appoint and dismiss Secretaries of State without reference to the King; that the Cabinet had the right to take over the patronage of so-called 'Crown appointments', including the appointment of bishops; that the decisions of the Government were final in the matter of diplomatic appointments, too. The King did not give way without a struggle; but he always had to give way in the end. Often his inconvenient views were, if possible, ignored in the hope that he would – as he frequently did – not continue to press them once they had been forcefully stated.

Eventually the King decided virtually to abandon the practice of seeing his Ministers in audience at Buckingham Palace, talking to them instead when he happened to meet them socially elsewhere, or dealing with them through people he knew well and trusted, such as Admiral Lord Fisher, Sir Charles Hardinge, Cassel, de Soveral, Knollys and Ponsonby. In their turn Ministers took to consulting these men as well as Mrs Keppel who, circumspect, intelligent and completely loyal to the King, was used as a kind of invaluable and uniquely trusted liaison officer.

Towards the end of his life even Mrs Keppel lost her ability to entertain the King when he was afflicted by the moods of depression which increasingly overwhelmed him. These moods were deepened by his anxiety over foreign affairs, his consciousness that he had been able to do so little to disperse the threatening clouds over Europe or to come to any amicable agreement with his nephew, the Kaiser, above all by his concern about the constitutional crisis that had developed in consequence of the determination of the House of Lords to block the legislation of Asquith's Government. He had little sympathy with much of this legislation; for he was always 'a strong Conservative', as Sir Charles Dilke said of him, 'and a still stronger Jingo'. He read the reports of Lloyd George's inflammatory speeches with horror, instructing Knollys to 'protest in the most vigorous terms' against one of his Ministers delivering such addresses 'full of false statements, of socialism in its most insidious form and full of virulent abuse of one particular class'. The King could not understand how the Prime Minister could tolerate one of his colleagues making remarks which were 'in the highest degree improper' and which he looked upon as being 'an insult to the Sovereign'. Yet the King was not opposed to all change; he had always done his best to show his sympathy with social reform by identifying the monarchy with the awakening conscience of his people. He had shown a sincere concern for their welfare, particularly for their housing; and he had not hesitated to condemn the 'perfectly disgraceful' conditions in which so many of the poor were forced to live. And he strongly condemned the House of Lords' intransigence in threatening to reject Lloyd George's budget even though it provided for revolutionary land taxes as well as new income taxes and death duties. He told Knollys that he thought the peers 'were mad' to be so provocatively stubborn; and when, at the end of 1909, they played into Lloyd George's hands by rejecting the 'People's Budget', thus precipitating a general election, he confessed that he had never spent a more miserable day in his life.

While waiting for the election, members of the Government and their advisers discussed the possibility of either allowing the Prime Minister to assume the sovereign's prerogative of creating peers or of curbing the power of the Lords by framing a parliamentary Bill whose passage through the House would be guaranteed by giving a pledge that the King would create enough new peers favourable to it. The King, when informed of these discussions, was appalled by the thought that, if he were required to create several hundred Liberal peers in order to curb the power of the Lords, he would not only fatally debilitate the Upper House but also abandon the political impartiality of the Crown to the ultimate ruin of its reputation. He spoke gloomily of abdication.

A few months later, the critical problem still unresolved, the King was dead. He died believing his son would be the last king of England.

4 The Grandfather: King George V

'I feel that I am getting a down on George V just now,' Harold Nicolson, the King's biographer, told his wife in the middle of writing his book. 'He is all right as a gay young midshipman. He may be all right as a wise old King. But the intervening period when he was . . . just shooting at Sandringham is hard to manage or swallow. For seventeen years he did nothing at all but kill animals and stick in stamps.'

The life of the King as Duke of York and, after his elder brother's death, as Prince of Wales, was certainly uneventful. That suited him very well. He would have been quite happy to spend all his time at York Cottage, the small, cramped house on his father's estate at Sandringham, leading a quiet, country life with his family, shooting, pottering about in the garden, playing a game of billiards with an equerry in the evening before going early to bed, or perhaps staying up to read to his wife. 'Georgie is a dear,' Princess May told her old governess soon after her marriage. 'He adores me which is touching. He likes reading to people so I jumped at this & he is going to read me some of his favourite books . . . I am very glad I am married & don't feel at all strange, in fact I feel as if I had been married for years & quite settled down.'

Her husband shared neither his father's taste for foreign travel nor his passion for female society. 'England is good enough for me,' he once said. 'I like my own country best, climate or no, and I'm staying in it . . . There's nothing of the cosmopolitan in me.' As for his father's foreign friends and beautiful, witty women, he also had nothing in common with them. Nor had his wife, who strongly disapproved of what she called '*leurs* goings-on'. The Princess was a shy, reserved and competent woman before whom, as Augustus Hare observed, scandal sat dumb. A traditionalist like her husband – who was utterly devoted to her in his undemonstrative way – she nevertheless had more sympathy than he with those whose tastes differed from her own, and more originality of mind. But whenever he expressed disapproval of her opinions, her attempts to wear less unfashionable clothes, or her efforts to learn dance steps, she did not argue with him, accepting his rebukes with quiet submission. He himself was the least quiet of men. Short and slight, he had an alarmingly loud voice and an extremely hearty laugh. Voluble and noisy, he was also emphatic, banging the table with his fist to stress a point. He had an unfortunate fondness for practical jokes and rude banter; and, while emotional and susceptible himself, he lacked the imagination to appreciate how those who shared these characteristics would react to his boisterous, insensitive gusto. He loved his children, but he told Lord Cromer that he believed princes ought to be brought up in fear of their fathers. 'I was always frightened of my father,' he said. 'They must be frightened of me.' He teased them all unmercifully, making his favourite, Mary, his only daughter, blush scarlet with embarrassment and contributing to the onset of the painful stammer which his second son never completely overcame.

This bluff, vehement, insistently jovial manner may well be seen as compensating for an innate diffidence. For he was highly conscious of his own inadequacies, plagued by doubt that he could prove a worthy successor to his father whose death saddened him immeasurably. 'I am heartbroken and overwhelmed with grief,' he wrote in his diary in his slow, laborious, childish hand on the evening of King Edward's death. 'I have lost my best friend and the best of fathers ... But God will help me in my great responsibilities and darling May will be my comfort as she always has been. May God give me strength and guidance in the heavy task which has fallen upon me.'

The thought that he was deprived for ever of his father's advice appalled him. He had fallen into the habit of consulting him about every aspect of his life, 'even as to whether his footmen ought to wear black or red liveries at dinner', and 'complaining terribly', when his father was not available, that he had no one else to go to. He was never more aware of the extent of his loss than in the early months of his reign when the constitutional problem which had so disturbed the last days of King Edward's life, and which was left unresolved at his death, now returned to harass the inexperienced son.

His father, unsure himself of how to deal with the problem, had not been able to bequeath him any guidance; and the advice he did receive from his friends and the members of his Household was confusing and conflicting. Sir Arthur Bigge, who had been appointed his Private Secretary after his grandmother's death, urged him in one direction. Lord Knollys, his father's Private Secretary, who, at Bigge's suggestion, had been appointed joint Private Secretary on his accession, pressed him to pursue a quite different course. He himself was anxious to act only in accordance with constitutional propriety. Yet what was the constitutionally proper attitude for the monarchy to adopt in 1910 was extremely difficult to decide.

The Liberals had lost over a hundred seats in the House of Commons in the general election in January. But they were still in power under their leader, Mr Asquith, and could look for general support to the Irish Nationalists and the Labour Party. They regarded it as intolerable, therefore, that their measures, in particular their Parliament Bill which sought to curtail the powers of the House of Lords, should be blocked by a second chamber composed mainly of Conservative peers. So Asquith wanted the King to agree, if necessary, to swamp this Conservative opposition by the creation of as many as five hundred new peers sympathetic to the Liberal cause. Asquith, while doing his best to keep the King's name out of the controversy in his public statements, believed that His Majesty was in duty bound to accept the advice given to him by the Government in power.

Lord Knollys, a strong Liberal himself, was entirely in sympathy with Mr Asquith. He believed that the King ought to agree to a dissolution of Parliament, which would entail another general election, and to give the Liberals a secret undertaking that, were they to be returned to power, he would use his royal prerogative to transform the composition of the House of Lords so that Liberal policies could be carried through. 'I feel certain that you can safely and constitutionally accept what the Cabinet propose,' Lord Knollys wrote to the King, '& I venture to urge you strongly to do so.' He assured the King that should the Cabinet's proposals be rejected and Asquith be therefore compelled to resign, the Leader of the Conservative Opposition, A. J. Balfour, would not be willing to form an alternative administration. This was not the case: on 29 April at a meeting at Lambeth Palace, Balfour had made it 'quite clear that he would be prepared to form a Government to prevent the King being put in the position contemplated by the demand for the creation of peers'.

Sir Arthur Bigge's view, in sharp contrast to Lord Knollys's, was that the King should on no account give the secret undertaking which the Cabinet required. It would, by bestowing an advantage on the Liberals, bring the Crown into party politics. It was 'not His Majesty's duty to save the Prime Minister from the mistake of his incautious words on the 14th April' when Asquith had declared in the House of Commons: 'In no case shall we recommend dissolution, except under such conditions as will secure that in the new Parliament the judgement of the people, as expressed in the election, will be carried into law.'

'What is the object of the King giving the Cabinet to understand that, in the event of the Government being returned with an adequate majority in the new House of Commons, he will be ready to exercise his constitutional powers, *if his intentions are not to be made public until the occasion arises?*' Bigge asked in an indignant letter to his master. 'Why should the King not wait until the occasion arises . . . Is it straight? . . . Is it English?'

The King was instinctively inclined to answer, 'No.' A man of the utmost integrity and straightforwardness, he deeply resented being asked to make a secret promise. 'I have never been accustomed to conceal things,' he said. 'I have never in my life done anything I was ashamed to confess.' Yet the continued pressures of the Prime Minister, the Liberal Leader of the House of Lords and, above all, Lord Knollys, proved too much for him. When Knollys assured him that the advice he was giving would have been given to his father and that he was convinced that his late Majesty would have followed it, the King was persuaded. Bigge thought this 'quoting what a dead person' might have done, particularly a person whose memory the King so much revered, was 'most unfair, if not improper'. He himself might have urged that he was 'perfectly certain' that Queen Victoria would have preferred Bigge's advice to Knollys's. The King, however, felt that if his father would have been guided by Knollys, he must give way. He wrote in his diary on 16 November:

After a long talk I agreed most reluctantly to give the Cabinet a secret understanding that in the event of the Government being returned with a majority at the General Election, I should use my prerogative to make Peers if asked for. I disliked having to do this very much, but agreed that this was the only alternative to the Cabinet resigning, which at this moment would be disastrous. Francis [Knollys] strongly urged me to take this course & I think his advice is generally very sound. I only trust and pray he is right this time.

As it happened the King was, in his own words, 'spared any further humiliation by the creation of peers'. The general election of December 1910 did little to alter the balance of power in the House of Commons; but the Parliament Bill was passed with a narrow majority. The King was profoundly relieved. If he had been forced to create peers merely to enforce its passage, he told Bigge, now raised to the peerage as Lord Stamfordham, he would 'never have survived' the humiliation, never have been 'the same person again'.

This constitutional crisis was no sooner resolved, however, than the King was plunged into the passionate disputes over the principle of Home Rule for Ireland. Asquith introduced his Home Rule Bill in the House of Commons in April 1912; and by the end of the year the controversy over it had reached such a pitch that civil war seemed possible and the King was forced to consider the advice that, in order to avoid this calamity, he should exercise his prerogative by refusing royal assent to the Bill when it had eventually been forced through Parliament.

This dangerous interpretation of the King's duty was pressed upon him not only by the diehard Lord Halsbury, the former Conservative Lord Chancellor, but also by Bonar Law, who had succeeded Balfour as Leader of the Opposition; and the King, as Lord Esher noted, was 'properly disturbed by it'. It was Lord Esher's own opinion that Halsbury and Bonar Law were quite wrong, that the King was constitutionally bound to follow the advice of his Ministers in all cases. Later, however, Esher changed his mind, averring that the danger of civil war imposed upon the King the duty of dismissing Asquith and entrusting the Government to some responsible statesman like Lord Rosebery until a general election could be held. The King evidently responded to this unwelcome and unexpected advice with some asperity, whereupon Esher told him he 'ought not to worry himself to death but put the matter aside. The King turned abruptly away with some emotion'.

He could not stop worrying. Distressed by the prospect of civil war, he was also deeply disturbed by the savage bitterness of the political conflict which led to violent scenes in the House of Commons where books and insults were hurled across the floor and the Speaker, before threatening to resign, was twice obliged to adjourn the House. Outside the House, members of the opposing parties refused to speak to each other. The American Ambassador was reminded of the 'intense days of the slavery controversy, just before the Civil War'.

The King himself, already much upset by the letters which streamed into Buckingham Palace from Northern Ireland begging him not to hand these predominantly Protestant provinces over to the Roman Catholic South, was appalled to hear that an Ulster Volunteer Force had attracted the services of 84,000 armed men and that an Irish Citizen Army was being raised in Dublin to oppose them. He believed that there should be a general election before the Home Rule Bill became law. But he thought that Asquith would resign rather than agree to a dissolution of Parliament; and, although Asquith was not, in his opinion, facing the crisis with sufficient urgency, he did not want him to resign. He liked him and respected him; and was, in any case, already as averse to change as his grandmother had ever been. Besides, he foresaw that in an election 'many Liberal candidates would seek to divert attention from the threatened coercion of Ulster by accusing the Crown of interference in party issues'. He therefore concluded that the only solution was 'an agreed settlement between the leaders of the two parties'; and with this end in view he wrote an enormously long letter to the Prime Minister.

Without much hope of its success, the Cabinet consented to an inter-party conference on the subject, but declined to initiate the proposal. Nor would Bonar Law agree to initiate it; but he did hold out the hope that the Conservative Party would attend such a conference if the King were to propose it formally himself.

The need for a settlement seemed to the King more urgent every day, and never more urgent than when he heard that, faced with an ultimatum from Sir Arthur Paget, the forceful General Officer commanding the troops in Ireland – who had told his officers there that they must be prepared either to take part in 'active operations' in Ulster or to resign their commissions – nearly sixty officers, including Brigadier-General Hubert Gough, commander of the 3rd Cavalry Brigade, had decided to send in their papers. It subsequently transpired that Paget had misunderstood the instructions he had received from the Government in London who were, at that time, concerned only to secure military and naval installations in Northern Ireland. But the morale of the Army had been badly shaken; and the King's reputation had not been enhanced by Paget's telling his officers that the orders he was passing on to them came direct from their Sovereign and not 'from those dirty swine, the politicians'.

Soon after this the King approached the Speaker of the House of Commons to ask if he would be prepared to preside over a conference between the various parties. The Speaker said that he would. And on 21 July the conference was convened at Buckingham Palace. As Asquith had foreseen the conference soon broke down; but the King was satisfied that his efforts in arranging it had not been entirely wasted. He was sure that 'a more friendly understanding' had been created; and was considering what he could do to build on that understanding when news reached London of Austria's ultimatum to Serbia which was to lead to the First World War.

Throughout the war the King was sadly conscious of how little he could do to influence its course. Occasionally the Prime Minister would ask for his help, as Asquith did, for example, when it was felt that a personal appeal by the King to his cousin the Czar might persuade the Russians to hold up mobilization and thus induce the Kaiser to restrain Austria. 'The poor King was hauled out of bed,' Asquith recalled, '& one of my strangest experiences ... was sitting with him – he in a brown dressing gown over his night shirt & with copious signs of having been aroused from his first "beauty sleep" – while I read the message and the proposed answer. All he did was to suggest that it should be more personal & direct by the insertion of the words "My dear Nicky" and the addition at the end of the signature "Georgie"!'

But the King's help and counsel were not often sought; and when advice was offered it was usually ignored. Despite his justified protests at the 'petty and undignified' preoccupation of certain Members of the

House of Commons at the beginning of a potentially disastrous war with the titles of various foreign princes who were related to the royal family, a committee was set up which deprived some of these princes of their titles. He equally deplored the campaign against the gifted and completely trustworthy German-born Prince Louis of Battenberg, his cousin, who was First Sea Lord. But Prince Louis was forced to resign all the same. The King did all he could, on his own admission, to prevent the appointment of the aged and controversial Lord Fisher, who 'was not trusted by the Navy', as Prince Louis's successor.* On this occasion as well he had to give in with great reluctance. He also tried to prevent the banners of enemy emperors, kings and princes being removed from their traditional places above their stalls in St George's Chapel, Windsor, on the reasonable ground that they were symbols of past history. Yet, although he was able to prevent the simultaneous removal of the brass plates bearing their names which were fixed to the wall behind the stalls, he had to agree, on the advice of the Prime Minister, to the removal of the banners. In one case at least, however, his protests were effective. When the German Zeppelin raids on London began there was an outcry for reprisals. Lord Fisher characteristically proposed that batches of German prisoners should be shot for every raid that took place. Others suggested the sinking of unarmed enemy vessels on sight, a proposal which the King found 'simply disgusting'. The Cabinet themselves came forward with the proposition that captured German submarine crews should be submitted to 'differential treatment'. The King, who maintained that these sailors merely obeyed orders, considered this idea as ill-advised as it was inhumane; and he deprecated it with what Mrs Asquith called the same 'real moral indignation' as he was later to condemn the indiscriminate internment of all aliens, and as he had earlier condemned the forcible feeding of imprisoned suffragettes, though, needless to say, he was wholly out of sympathy with both their methods and their aims. In the case of the submarine crews, the Cabinet gave way. They did so, though, not because, as the King pointed out to them, prisoners of war had a right not to be treated like criminals, but because, as he had foreseen might happen, the Germans, in retaliation for the ill-treatment of their captured submariners, took reprisals against British prisoners, placing several officers in solitary confinement.

Yet, while the King felt that he could contribute little of real importance to the winning of the war, it was during its course that his great

* At dinner at Balmoral the King grew red in the face with anger when talking of Fisher who disappeared for a time after handing in his resignation as First Sea Lord in 1915. 'If I had been in London when Fisher was found,' he declared furiously, 'I should have told him that he should have been hanged from the yard-arm for desertion of his post in the face of the enemy.' (Robert Rhodes James, *Memoirs of a Conservative: J. C. C. Davidson's Memoirs and Papers*, p. 108.)

and enduring popularity with his people began to be established and his lack of confidence in himself as a worthy successor to his father to diminish. This increasing self-assurance and surer touch were demonstrated in 1916 when Asquith was obliged to resign as Prime Minister. The King, in accordance with constitutional practice, sent for the Conservative leader, Bonar Law, who, so His Majesty supposed, would agree to become Prime Minister only on the condition that Parliament was dissolved. The King, strongly opposed to an election in wartime which this dissolution would entail, asked Lord Haldane, as a former Lord Chancellor, whether or not he could 'constitutionally refuse' to grant it if it were to be made 'a condition of anyone undertaking to form a government'. Haldane replied that the only Minister who could 'properly give advice' as to a dissolution was the Prime Minister, and that it followed that the sovereign could not 'entertain any bargain for a dissolution merely with a possible prime minister before the latter was fully installed'. Armed with this expert opinion, the King told Bonar Law that if he were asked for a dissolution he would refuse to grant it.

Disappointed by this refusal, Bonar Law was forced to the conclusion that he could form a government only if Asquith joined it. But Asquith refused to do so; and at a conference at Buckingham Palace, summoned by the King, it proved impossible to change his mind. He would not serve under Law or anyone else. 'What is the proposal?' he asked. 'That I who have held first place for eight years should be asked to take a subordinate position.' In face of this obstinacy, Law felt that he had no alternative but to return his commission. The King then sent for David Lloyd George, the Secretary for War, who thus became Prime Minister and brought the war to its successful conclusion.

The King's relationship with Lloyd George was not always easy. He had been touched and grateful when Lloyd George, alone of all his Ministers, broke down and cried when he came to offer his sympathy on the death of King Edward VII. Previously he had not much liked the dynamic little Welshman but he had then decided that he was perhaps 'both more loyal to the Throne and more sincere' than he had formerly supposed.

All the same, since his father had never held Lloyd George in very high regard, the King – though he recognized his outstanding talents – never altogether trusted him either. Nor did the Palace staff, whom the new Prime Minister's secretaries, in the words of J. C. C. Davidson, a future Chancellor of the Duchy of Lancaster, 'treated like dirt'. 'They did not get up from their chairs when Stamfordham – who, after all, was the King's Private Secretary and adviser – came into the room to ascertain some fact for the King,' Davidson said. 'Lloyd George was ... not a monarchist at heart ... He disliked any show of pomp and dignity on the part of the Crown and its servants ... I often wonder why the King stood the humiliating treatment handed out to him by Lloyd George and his minions without giving him a piece of his mind.'

At the beginning of his premiership there was little doubt that Lloyd George considered the King – as he considered several of the generals, particularly Haig and Robertson – almost as an enemy. Certainly the King was inclined to support the generals in their differences with the politicians over the conduct of operations. When it was suggested to him that 'the soldiers were all wrong', he 'expressed his entire disagreement', so Stamfordham wrote, 'and said that the politicians should leave the conduct of the war to experts'. He strongly supported Haig, an old friend who had been the first man not of royal blood ever to have been married in the private chapel at Buckingham Palace. And, although he disapproved of Haig's writing personal and highly critical letters behind his superiors' backs – 'if anyone acted like that, and told tales out of school,' he once remarked, 'he would, at school, be called a sneak' – he insisted on promoting him field marshal on New Year's Day 1917, much to Lloyd George's annoyance. He also staunchly supported Lloyd George's *bête noire*, General Sir William Robertson, an officer, risen from the ranks, whose plain speaking and blunt manner had always appealed to the King's taste. And it was not until Lloyd George said firmly to Stamfordham: 'If His Majesty insisted upon Robertson's remaining in office ... the King would have to find other Ministers,' that the King agreed to Robertson's enforced resignation.

Lloyd George was not, of course, the King's only critic. At the time of the Russian Revolution of 1917, for instance, there was much talk of republicanism. H. G. Wells declared that the time had come for the country to rid itself of 'the ancient trappings of throne and sceptre' and referred to the sad spectacle of England struggling through adversity under 'an alien and uninspiring court', a remark which provoked the King angrily to exclaim: 'I may be uninspired, but I'll be damned if I'm alien.' Such attacks, to which he was peculiarly sensitive, wounded him deeply; and when it was rumoured that he must be pro-German because he had a German name, he 'started and grew pale'. He immediately decided that the family must have another name; and after numerous proposals had been mooted from Plantagenet to Lancaster, and Tudor-Stewart to D'Este, Stamfordham's happy suggestion of Windsor was gratefully adopted.*

* Queen Elizabeth II's marriage to Prince Philip in 1947 placed the continuance of Windsor as the Royal Family's name in doubt. Prince Philip's father, Prince Andrew of Greece, was of the family of Schleswig-Holstein-Sonderburg-Glücksburg. His mother, Princess Alice, was the daughter of Prince Louis of Battenberg, who had married Princess Victoria of Hesse, a granddaughter of Queen Victoria. Prince Louis of Battenberg had in 1917 changed his name to Mountbatten – which appropriately enough for the First Sea Lord happened to be the name of a small naval fort in

Despite the Prime Minister's early criticism of the King, he finally came to recognize his worth. 'There can be no question', Lloyd George wrote when the war was over, 'that one outstanding reason for the high level of loyalty and patriotic effort which the people of this country maintained was the attitude and conduct of King George ... In estimating the value of the different factors which conduced to the maintenance of our home front ... a very high place must be given to the affection inspired by the King and the unremitting diligence with which he set himself in those dark days to discharge the function of his high office.'

His diligence was undoubtedly remarkable. He visited hospitals and factories; he carried out innumerable inspections; he went to France five times to see the armies there; every few months he went to spend some time with the sailors of his beloved Navy; he toured industrial areas; he personally conferred some 50,000 decorations. His mother told him he was trying to do too much; but he protested that he had to go about to 'see as many people as possible'; they appreciated it. He was quite prepared to sacrifice himself so long as the war was won; besides, he was not too tired. As early as August 1916, however, the American Ambassador thought he looked exhausted, 'ten years older'.

Much to his annoyance Lloyd George had persuaded him to give up alcohol. Full employment and high wages, he had been assured, had led to a worrying increase in the amount of drink consumed in the country: a declaration of total abstinence by the King would set a marvellous example. Under Lloyd George's pressure, the King felt that he could not very well do other than promise not only to give up alcohol himself but also to issue orders against its consumption by everyone else in the

Plymouth Sound – and he was at the same time created first Marquess of Milford Haven. His son, Prince Philip's uncle, therefore, became Lord Louis Mountbatten. Although the College of Heralds suggested Oldcastle, an Anglicization of Oldenburg, an ancestral name in his father's family, the Home Secretary preferred Mountbatten as a suitable name for Prince Philip. This proposal was adopted. On her marriage, the Queen accordingly became a Mountbatten; and both her eldest children were born Mountbattens. Two months after her accession, however, as a result of great pressure, so it was said, from Winston Churchill, and much to the delight of Lord Beaverbrook whose newspapers had long been running a press campaign against Lord Louis, now Lord Mountbatten, the *London Gazette* announced: 'The Queen today [9 April 1952] declared in Council Her Will and Pleasure that She and Her Children shall be styled and known as the House and Family of Windsor, and that Her descendants, other than female descendants who marry, and their descendants shall bear the name of Windsor.' Eight years later, though, the Queen announced that she had 'always wanted, without changing the name of the Royal House established by her grandfather, to associate the name of her husband with her own and his descendants'. These, other than female descendants who married and their descendants, were to 'bear the name Mountbatten-Windsor'. The Queen, it was added, had had this in her mind for a long time and it was 'close to her heart'. It was argued by some constitutional lawyers and genealogical authorities, that, as princes and princesses have no surname, the name Mountbatten-Windsor would not come into use until the time of the Queen's grandchildren. But, in fact, her daughter, Princess Anne, signed her name in the register at Westminster Abbey on the occasion of her marriage beneath the words Anne Elizabeth Alice Louise Mountbatten-Windsor.

Royal Household. It was a brave gesture, but hardly anyone – except Lord Kitchener, and, for a time, Lord Haldane – followed his example, not even Lloyd George and certainly not Asquith. Indeed, according to his eldest son, the King himself did not observe the rules he had laid down with too pedantic a strictness. Guests at his table were offered a variety of soft drinks, including ginger beer which Lord Rosebery reluctantly chose as the nearest thing to alcohol and which induced a fearful attack of hiccups. But the Queen's jug of fruit juice was mixed with champagne; and the King himself, when the meal was over, retired to his study to attend to a 'small matter of business which was tacitly assumed to be a small glass of port, and this no one would grudge him'. In public, however, he stuck to what became known as 'the King's pledge' manfully. He was also rigorous in his instructions that the Royal Household should not eat more than ordinary rations permitted, and should always be in the dining-room to the very second of the appointed time. Frederick Ponsonby remembered:

Those who were late got nothing. When I say late, the ordinary meaning of the word hardly conveyed the wonderful punctuality of the King and Queen. One was late if the clock sounded when one was on the stairs ... Godfrey-Faussett [an equerry] was kept on the telephone one day and came into the dining-room after everyone else had sat down. He found nothing to eat and immediately rang the bell and asked for a boiled egg. If he had ordered a dozen turkeys he could not have made a bigger stir. The King accused him of being a slave to his inside, of unpatriotic behaviour, and even went so far as to hint that we should lose the war on account of his gluttony.

At the end of the war the King found himself once more in disagreement with Lloyd George who wanted to make political capital out of victory by dissolving Parliament and calling a general election. The King strongly urged Lloyd George not to demand a dissolution at such a time when the electorate were in no mood to express a considered judgement and when many soldiers would be practically disfranchised because there would not be enough time to issue them with their voting papers. But the Prime Minister insisted; and the King felt constitutionally bound to give way.

He was much displeased by what he took to be Lloyd George's opportunism and disregard of his own wishes; and he was even more annoyed when, without consulting him, Sir Maurice Hankey, the Clerk of the Cabinet, agreed on behalf of Lloyd George's Government that the Kaiser, who was arraigned under the Treaty of Versailles 'for a supreme offence against international morality', should be put on trial in England. The King had already expressed strong disapproval of the Kaiser being tried at all. 'The majority of people appear to have lost their balance about the Kaiser,' Stamfordham had written, expressing the King's own views. 'We shall land ourselves in hopeless difficulties if a so-called International Tribunal is embarked on. It certainly will not be "international" if only the allied countries find the judges who will themselves be the accusers ... Cooler heads advocate the Falkland Islands and no trial.'

On learning that permission had been given for the Kaiser to be tried in England, Stamfordham wrote a letter of protest on the King's behalf: 'The King feels aggrieved that ... a decision of such supreme import-ance, and one so especially affecting His Majesty personally, was not communicated to him in some other way than through the medium of the Press.' It was the sharpest rebuke ever received by Hankey who was much relieved when the matter was resolved by the refusal of the Dutch to extradite the Kaiser from their country.

After the fall of his Government in 1922, Lloyd George was suc-ceeded by the Conservative, Bonar Law, who, suffering from cancer of the throat, was himself obliged to resign a few months later. The King was thus faced with the problem of choosing a new Prime Minister from the Conservative Party. The leading contender was Lord Curzon, Foreign Secretary in Law's Cabinet, a former Viceroy of India, and a man, in the words of Lord Lee of Fareham, 'pompous beyond belief'. Law himself expected Curzon would be his successor. But, although he never underestimated Curzon's great talents, he found it difficult to take him quite seriously. 'He never said anything of Curzon which could be regarded as at all derogatory,' Law's biographer, Robert Blake, has written. 'Yet when the name of Curzon came up in conversa-tion there would be a twinkle in his eye, just a hint that there was something slightly, very slightly, comical about the whole character of Curzon.' So, without actually refusing to give the King advice, Law let it be known that he would prefer not to be consulted, and suggested that the King talk to Lord Salisbury, Lord President of the Council, instead. His Majesty 'properly and naturally respected the wishes of a very sick man'.

Lord Salisbury, however, when summoned to the Palace, strongly recommended Curzon as 'the only acceptable Prime Minister', and intimated that Law himself was 'disinclined to pass Curzon over'. But Stamfordham also consulted Sir Ronald Waterhouse, Law's Private Secretary, who brought with him a memorandum which, he said, 'practically expressed the views of Mr Bonar Law'. This memorandum, which had been drafted by J. C. C. Davidson, proposed a rival candi-date, Stanley Baldwin, Law's Chancellor of the Exchequer and Leader of the House of Commons, a more approachable man – nine years younger than Curzon – who had a strong following in the Party. Two days later Waterhouse called at the Palace again; and, on this occasion, told Lord Stamfordham that Law had said: 'On the whole I think I should advise [the King] to send for Baldwin.'

This was the advice which was additionally and decisively given by the former Conservative Prime Minister, A. J. Balfour, who left a memorandum of the recommendations which he had made:

The King should follow the obvious, though not inevitable course and, in the first instance, ask the Leader of the House of Commons to form a Government ... The apparent difficulty was that Curzon was a man of greater age, greater experience and greater position than Baldwin whose experience was relatively insignificant and who, so far as I was aware, had no special capacity as a Parliamentarian. But undoubtedly there were several difficulties at the present time in having a Prime Minister in the House of Lords ... I understand from Stamfordham that these views were probably in very close proximity with those already held by His Majesty.

So, although he hated the idea of disappointing Curzon, whom he regarded 'as an old friend', having known him for thirty-five years, the King felt obliged to send for Baldwin. J. C. C. Davidson, who had had dinner with Baldwin the evening before, wrote:

Baldwin was alarmed at the prospect and when I told him ... that I thought it almost inevitable he would be Prime Minister ... he was genuinely frightened. I think that Baldwin thought that his promotion to premiership would be put off, and that Curzon would succeed Law. He realized that Curzon, for all his foibles, had an immense amount of experience. He was conscious that he [himself] was ill-equipped in experience for the higher atmosphere of politics ... I told him that the choice was not his, and that if he was sent for by the King he must accept as a duty for the country and to his party.

Baldwin, of course, did accept. But, a few months later, in January 1924, the Conservatives were defeated in the House of Commons and he had to resign. The King again acted with constitutional propriety in sending for the leader of the next largest party in the House, although this, the Labour Party, had won no more than 191 seats at the recent election against the Conservatives 258 and the Liberals 158. Several schemes were discussed in the hope that the supposed catastrophe of putting Labour in power might be averted. It was proposed that Balfour or Austen Chamberlain, a former Chancellor of the Exchequer, should replace Baldwin as Prime Minister; that Asquith should lead a coalition of Liberals and Conservatives; even that Reginald McKenna – who had once been Chancellor of the Exchequer but, no longer in Parliament, was now chairman of a bank – should form a non-parliamentary Government of 'national trustees'. But the King disregarded all these impractical solutions. He felt that the Labour Party ought to be given a 'fair chance'. 'They have different ideas to ours as they are all socialists,' he told his mother, 'but they ought to be treated fairly.' So, without consulting Baldwin, he sent for their leader, Ramsay MacDonald, the handsome Scottish son of an unmarried maidservant.

Naturally the King viewed the prospect of the first Labour Government in the country's history with some misgiving. He had no reason to doubt that he would get on well enough with MacDonald himself who was unlikely to have any desire to demand unwelcome breaks with ceremony or tradition, who, on the contrary, had a marked predilection for ritual and dressing up. But, having heard with dismay of the recent singing of 'The Red Flag' and the 'Marseillaise' at the Labour Party meeting in the Albert Hall, he could not be so sure of MacDonald's colleagues, particularly of George Lansbury, the Member for Bow and Bromley, who had spoken darkly of intrigues at Court – where pressure, so Lansbury alleged, was being brought to bear on the King to keep Labour out of office – and of a previous English King who had 'stood against the common people and lost his head'. Yet King George v – who got on perfectly well with Lansbury when he met him – was determined to do all he could to put the new Ministers at their ease and to gain their confidence. When asked how he regarded the forthcoming change he replied: 'My grandfather would have hated it; my father could hardly have tolerated it; but I march with the times.'

It could hardly be said that he did so with any enthusiasm. But he certainly had no patience with those at Court who commiserated with him for having to deal with such low-born people as Labour politicians. Already he had demonstrated, as Lady Cynthia Colville said, that 'he had no intention of allowing his Ministers to be rebuffed, at any rate in his presence'. When Lady Cynthia's father, as Lord President of the Council, accompanied the King and Queen on a visit to Derbyshire, the arch-Conservative Duchess of Abercorn refused to sit next to him at dinner at Chatsworth. The next day the King invited his Lord President to travel back to London with him in the royal train 'and noticeably avoided asking the Abercorns to do the same'. By such means he made it clear that no one was to slight his Labour Ministers any more than his Liberal ones. When a courtier, 'whose roots were firmly planted in the Edwardian age', commiserated with him on his having to deal with these 'tiresome people', he declined to answer, turning his back on him.

MacDonald recorded how, having been sworn a member of the Privy Council – this was the first time that a Prime Minister had not been one already – he was alone with the King for nearly an hour: 'He talked so steadily that I could hardly thank him. Most friendly. Referred to Lansbury's King Charles speech & Albert Hall songs. I pointed out that, if there had been any counter demonstration, effect would have

been serious & very uncomfortable for both of us. He agreed ...
Referred to Russia. Hoped I would do nothing to compel him to shake
hands with the murderers of his relatives.'*

MacDonald's Ministers found the King as pleasant and easy as did
MacDonald himself. One of them, J. R. Clynes, who was to be Lord
Privy Seal, recalled:

As we stood waiting for his Majesty, amid the gold and crimson
magnificence of the Palace, I could not help marvelling at the strange turn of
Fortune's wheel, which had brought MacDonald the starvling clerk, J. H.
Thomas the engine driver [Colonial Secretary], Henderson the foundry
labourer and Clynes the mill-hand to this pinnacle beside the man whose
forbears had been Kings for so many generations ... We were, perhaps,
somewhat embarrassed, but the little, quiet man whom we addressed as 'Your
Majesty' swiftly put us at our ease. He was himself rather anxious ... I have no
doubt that he had read the wild statements of some of our extremists, and I
think he wondered to what he was committing his people ... I had expected to
find him unbending; instead he was kindness and sympathy itself.†

Clynes later became Home Secretary and, as he grew to know the King
better, the more he liked and respected him. Their talks together –
during which the King often pleaded for leniency for criminals, except
for those guilty of crimes against women and children – were 'made
easy by the genial, kindly, considerate personality of George v, a truly
constitutional monarch who always put the will of his people nearest his
heart'.

J. H. Thomas, the Colonial Secretary and trade union leader,

---

* Of all the evils of the post-war world, the King ranked Bolshevism the worst. When Sir Robert
Bruce Lockhart, who had headed the Special Mission to the Soviet Government, returned to
England in 1918, having been arrested and exchanged for Maksim Maksimovich Litvinov, the
Russians' diplomatic representative in London, who had also been arrested for engaging in
propaganda activities, the King was 'very nice', Bruce Lockhart recorded in his diary, 'and
showed a surprising grasp of the situation. He, however, did most of the talking and during the
forty minutes I was with him I didn't really get much in ... He has a wholesome dread of
Bolshevism.' (*Diaries of Sir Robert Bruce Lockhart*, I, p. 47.) The King steadfastly refused to receive
the Russian Ambassador personally and the Prince of Wales was required to do so on his behalf.
The King did, however, have to accept the presence of Sokolnikov at a levee with the other
ambassadors. The King 'bitterly resented' this, Lady Airlie wrote. 'I was sitting next to His
Majesty at dinner one evening ... when someone rather tactlessly referred to the new appointment. The King burst out with ... "What do you think it means to me to be forced to shake hands
with a man of the party that murdered my cousin? Neither Ramsay MacDonald nor Snowden [the
Chancellor of the Exchequer] or even Henderson [the Foreign Secretary] would receive him in
their houses, yet they let me in for it."' (Mabell Airlie, *Thatched with Gold*, p. 182.)

† When the King handed Clynes the ancient seal of his office in a battered leather case, Clynes
remarked that the case looked almost as old as the historic royal seal itself. The King apparently
took this comment to heart. 'Being in reality a formal private seal of the Sovereign it is never
actually used,' Clynes explained. 'And having put it into the safe in my room I did not see it again
until, at the end of my term of office, I had to get it out and hand it back to the King. Then I
discovered that the seal was enclosed in a clean new leather case. It was typical of George v that he
had not forgotten my idle words at our talk.' (J. R. Clynes, *Memoirs*, II, pp. 21–2.)

admired the King quite as much as Clynes did, while the King for his part rejoiced in the company of the blunt, jovial and commonsensical Welshman whose rude stories, told in 'a peculiarly pungent working-class accent with a defiant avoidance of the aspirate', never failed to amuse him. On their first meeting the King was evidently a little shocked by Thomas's strong language. 'Really Mr Thomas!' he rebuked him, 'I thought you were representing a sanctimonious Government.' 'Yes, your Majesty,' Thomas replied. 'But I'm the relief.' Certainly thereafter he often proved himself a relief to the King who, valuing his insight, consulted him on all manner of subjects, whether connected with Thomas's office or not; and he always received an honest reply. Once, for example, he asked Thomas for his opinion of a fellow trade union leader. 'Between ourselves, your Majesty,' Thomas promptly replied, 'I think 'e's a 'ell of a 'ound.'

With MacDonald – who tactfully omitted Lansbury from his first Government – the King's relations remained as friendly as they had been from the beginning. Naturally there were certain difficulties. In the first place there was the question of nominations to those senior offices of the Court which had long been regarded as political appointments and for which MacDonald had no suitable or willing candidates. He proposed that these appointments should, therefore, be left to the King. But both the King and Stamfordham – mindful of the trouble caused in 1839 when the Queen had refused to change any of her Whig for Tory Ladies – believed it would be better if some at least of the Household appointments were made by the Prime Minister. It was agreed, therefore, that three of the Lords-in-Waiting and the three officers of the House of Commons who are nominally members of the Household should be chosen by the Prime Minister. For these latter posts MacDonald selected Thomas Griffiths, Member for Pontypool, as the Treasurer of the Household, J. A. Parkinson, Member for Wigan, as Comptroller of the Household and John Davison, Member for Smethwick, as Vice-Chamberlain. The appointments of Lord Chamberlain, Lord Steward, Master of the Horse and the three other Lords-in-Waiting were to be made by the King, with the Prime Minister's approval, on condition that those appointed did not speak or vote in Parliament. This compromise was accepted by all parties and remains the practice at the Court of St James's today.

Other problems that arose were dealt with by the King and MacDonald in an equally amicable way; and when the Government was defeated and MacDonald went to the Palace to ask for a dissolution of Parliament, the King obviously viewed the prospect of losing him with deep regret. He did not want to grant a dissolution, 'being aware', as he put it himself, 'how strongly the country deprecates another General

Election within less than a year'; and he was under no constitutional obligation to grant it to a Prime Minister not possessing a majority in Parliament, as Asquith had said in public only a few months before. But, having ascertained that the leaders of both the Conservative and Liberal Parties were unable or unwilling to form an Administration themselves, he acceded to MacDonald's request.

The King was most cordial & interview at times almost touching as we assured each other that we had done the best we could for each other [MacDonald recorded in his diary]. I did not have to ask for the dissolution. He had been prepared & he talked as though I had asked for it. He regretted the reason & hoped we might have found it possible to remain, but understood if we accepted this defeat or even avoided it, we should only be worried for a few weeks more & then have to go ... He remarked that no other Party could form a Government that would last. He would protect himself by sending me a memorandum saying that he granted the election with great reluctance, and hinted that I might say so. I warned him that that would bring him into politics, but that I should receive a memorandum if written for historical purposes and perhaps send him one in turn ... He remarked: 'You have found me an ordinary man, haven't you.'

To the King ordinariness was a kind of virtue. Years later he told the Archbishop of Canterbury with a hint of pride that he was, after all, 'a very ordinary fellow'. This did not, though, in any sense imply that he considered himself a fool. 'I am not a clever man,' he once said, 'but if I had not picked up something from all the brains I've met, I should be an idiot.' He felt that he had picked up a good deal from MacDonald.

Baldwin's second Conservative Cabinet, which came into power after the general election, lasted longer than the King had expected. But in June 1929 MacDonald returned to office, to the evident pleasure of the King who confided in Lady Cynthia Colville that he found him much easier to get on with than Baldwin and much readier to listen to his advice. On a later occasion, the King told MacDonald himself: 'You have been the Prime Minister I have liked best; you have so many qualities; you have kept up the dignity of the office without using it to give you dignity.'

The King was, therefore, much chagrined when, two years after its creation, MacDonald's Government was obliged to resign at a time of economic crisis. The atmosphere when his Ministers came to the palace to hand back their seals was 'solemn and funereal', Clynes recorded. 'There was no talk. We entered His Majesty's study one by one, carrying our seals in small red boxes. The King stood beside a table, one hand resting upon it. His face looked grey and lined.'

Not long before, his devoted and resourceful Private Secretary, Stamfordham, had died at St James's Palace at the age of eighty-two;

and the King felt the loss of him sorely. 'Dear Bigge passed peacefully away at 4.30 today,' he had recorded in his diary at the time. 'I shall miss him terribly. His loss is irreparable.' His successor, Clive Wigram, had been Assistant Private Secretary since 1910 when he had given up a military career of great promise. Educated at Winchester, where his skill at games was legendary, Wigram was a tall, good-looking man, more approachable than Stamfordham, but less acute. Direct, genial, honest and open, shrewd but unintellectual, he was much like his master who grew to trust him implicitly, though in 1931 both of them felt the need of Stamfordham's experience and subtle mind.

Having discussed the crisis not only with Wigram and MacDonald but also with the Conservative and Liberal leaders, the King came to the conclusion that he would have to contrive to bring about a National Government in which MacDonald would remain Prime Minister with the support of the other two parties. Assured that Baldwin and the Liberal leader, Sir Herbert Samuel, approved of the idea of a National Government and were prepared to serve in one, he told MacDonald that he believed him to be 'the only person who could carry the country through'. MacDonald was at first reluctant to agree to the King's suggestion, but at length, persuaded by repeated urgings, that it was his duty to the country and to his own self-respect to remain, and flattered by the intimation that no one else could save Britain, he agreed to lead the National Government which the King had in mind. So, at four o'clock on the afternoon of 24 August 1931, MacDonald drove to Buckingham Palace. He 'arrived looking worn and weary and was received by the King,' Wigram recorded. 'The King invited him to form a National Administration. Mr Ramsay MacDonald accepted the offer, and kissed hands on his appointment as the new Prime Minister.' The next evening the King left for Balmoral, relieved beyond measure that the latest crisis of his reign was over.

He was now sixty-six years old, and far more confident than he had been in the early years of his reign. Consequently both his Household and his Ministers began to find him more difficult to deal with. 'It's not for me to have opinions or to interfere,' he would say, passing his right hand across his body in a well-known and apparently deprecatory gesture. But his opinions were well enough known and volubly expressed all the same. 'When he saw Ministers,' so Lord Cromer, his Lord Chamberlain, said, 'he would never allow them to talk. He had mugged up the papers very conscientiously and would give them his own ideas.' Several Ministers confirmed this themselves.

Also, as Frederick Ponsonby, his Assistant Private Secretary recorded, he was 'so accustomed to people agreeing with him' that he grew to dislike those who ventured to express opinions contrary to his own. He 'hated all insincerity, and flattery', but he did not care for 'the candid friend business' either, and was liable to fly into sudden, explosive rage if contradicted, making full use of what Lord Lee called his 'good working knowledge of the language of the forecastle'. These rages were soon overcome, however, and the culprit soon forgiven. 'He would call me every name under the sun,' the Honourable Sir Derek Keppel, Master of the Household, recalled. 'But always as I was leaving the room after an explosion, he would call me back and make his peace with, "Derek, did you ever hear this story. . .?"'

Nevertheless, few members of his Household cared to risk the explosion in the first place. One of these few who did not hesitate to speak his mind was Captain Charles Cust, an old naval friend who had been his Equerry since 1892. Frederick Ponsonby recalled an occasion at Balmoral when Cust was sitting in the billiard-room going through a pile of books on the floor which had been sent to him from London. The King came in and said, 'I say, Charles, is that the way you treat my books?'

'*Your* books!' Cust protested. 'Why, you haven't in the whole of this house got a book that's worth reading. Your so-called library is nothing but beautifully bound piffle.'

Later the King asked Ponsonby if what Cust had said was true. Ponsonby said that it was, the Balmoral library having long ago been the repository of all the presentation copies of books, 'usually quite unreadable', which had been given to Queen Victoria and Edward VII. So the King told Ponsonby to set aside a certain sum each year for buying interesting Scottish books and to weed the worthless ones out.

Even Cust got into trouble, though, when he suggested – as Stamfordham had done more tactfully – that it was absurd for the old widowed Queen Alexandra to live alone with her daughter, Princess Victoria, in the big house at Sandringham while he as King with a family and a Household, numbering some forty people in all, should be crammed into York Cottage.

The King's decision not to disturb his rather selfish mother – to whom it never seems to have occurred to offer to move – stemmed quite as much from his devotion to her as from his dislike of any change. This dislike, which naturally grew more pronounced as he grew older, extended to almost every innovation of the post-war years from bobbed hair, short skirts and painted finger nails, to jazz, cocktails, polo-necked sweaters, female Members of Parliament, and men who did not believe, as he implicitly believed, 'in God, the invincibility of the Royal Navy, and the essential rightness of whatever was British'. He was not an obtuse man and certainly not an unkind one: when, during his serious

illness, the unmarried daughter of one of his servants became pregnant
he was heard repeatedly murmuring in his delirium that the girl's
father must be told not to be too hard on her, to treat her gently. Nor
were all his expressions of prejudice and abrupt commands always
intended to be taken seriously: 'Go on and do it, you obstinate devil,' he
would shout angrily at some intrepid member of his Household who
hesitated to carry out some ill-considered instruction; but when he
discovered that the command had not been obeyed he might well let the
matter drop.

Yet, even in his most benign moods, the appearance of anything
unfamiliar was liable to arouse his wrath rather than his curiosity.
'What!' he cried in horror when his eldest son ordered him an avocado
pear as a special treat. 'What in heaven's name is this?' Any suggestion
that there should be an alteration in the routine of Court life was
greeted with scepticism and distrust. 'Well, we never did *that* in the
olden days,' he would say doubtfully, or he would settle a problem by
announcing, 'It has always been done that way.' So at the dinner table,
for instance, forks were still laid with their prongs facing downwards, as
they had been thus placed in the days when the prongs might otherwise
have caught in the frills of the gentlemen's cuffs. He used the same
collar-stud for more than fifty years, reinforcing it with a gold filling
when it showed signs of decay; and had the same hairbrushes for quite
as long with only one rebristling.

Particularly conservative in matters of dress, he continued throughout his life to wear the kind of expensive cloth-topped boots, curly-
brimmed bowler hats and well-cut stiff collars that he had worn as a
young man. His trousers – without turn-ups, of course – were creased
down the sides. Those who dressed in the modern manner, who, for
instance, went riding in jodhpurs, were dismissed as 'cads'. Once when
Derek Keppel was seen entering the palace in a bowler hat during the
London Season, the King assailed him roughly: 'You scoundrel, what
do you mean by coming in here in that rat-catcher fashion? You never
see me dressing like that in London.'

'Well, Sir,' Keppel replied, 'you don't have to go about in buses.'

'*Buses*! Nonsense!'

After the war he was obliged to acknowledge the relaxations of the
rule that, when the monarch was in London, Guards officers must not
appear in the streets in daytime without top hat and morning-coat, nor
at the dinner table without a white tie. But the Prince of Wales was still
required to wear his morning coat when calling upon his father and to
wear the Garter Star on his tailcoat whenever he dined with his parents,
even if there were no other guests.

His own Household were allowed to wear short coats in the daytime, instead of frock-coats; but this was one of the few relaxations permitted in the etiquette of the Court where the routine was as regular and unchanging as it had been in the days of Queen Victoria, and the protocol quite as exacting.

Lady guests invited to Windsor Castle for Ascot week were expected to arrive with two new dresses for the mornings, four new *ensembles* for the races, and five evening dresses which were to be worn, as Lady Hardinge said, with long white gloves reaching almost to the armpits. Before dinner they were lined up in the Green Drawing Room by the Lady of the Bedchamber, in order of precedence, forming a quarter-circle. The Master of the Household arranged the men, also in a quarter-circle and all wearing knee-breeches, opposite them. Exactly at half past eight the King and Queen and various other members of the royal family appeared at the door; and a short ceremony of chor-eographic precision was then enacted: the Queen came forward towards the gentlemen and shook hands with them in turn; the King approached the curtsying ladies to shake hands with them; the gentle-man instructed to sit on the Queen's right detached himself from the male quarter-circle, bowed low, offered her his arm, and led the parade of about thirty guests into dinner. A string band, sweating in a confined space concealed by a grille in the dining-room wall, played the National Anthem.

Throughout the dinner – a quite simple meal, promptly and quickly served on gilt or silver services by pages in blue livery and footmen in scarlet – the band continued to play. As soon as he saw that everyone had finished the King looked at the Queen who stood up immediately. The ladies, following suit, curtsyed to the King as they left the room. Evidently relieved by their departure, the King then beckoned to two men to occupy the vacated chairs on either side of him. But although, in striking contrast to his father, he preferred their company to that of the women – enjoying their jokes, particularly the oldest chestnuts – he did not remain in the dining-room for more than twenty minutes at the most: 'There was barely time', the Prince of Wales later complained, 'to smoke even the shortest cigar.'

The Queen, having returned to the Green Drawing Room, had taken up her crochet as a sign for the Lady of the Bedchamber to bring up the first of the ladies whom she had been instructed to bring into Her Majesty's presence. On the return of the King, however, these conver-sations came to an abrupt halt; and the company sat down to play cards until eleven o'clock when the quarter-circles were re-formed for the ceremony of wishing the royal family goodnight.

On less formal occasions the King and Queen sometimes conducted their guests around the castle, showing them its treasures upon which the Queen, a museum director *manquée*, was an expert, though not, as some people supposed, an infallible connoisseur, being more interested in royal iconography than in art. The King, who had an extremely retentive memory, listened carefully to what his wife said and often referred to the little notebooks in which she – a determined not to say avaricious collector – listed her own and his private collections. He was, therefore, capable of reciting the history of their possessions with almost as much fluency as the Queen. Sometimes, however, 'flaming "howlers" crept into the text of his discourse', and, aware of this, he would turn to her and say in his gruff voice, and with his hearty laugh, 'May, now you know all about this.' There were times, too, when he became much exasperated by his wife's absorption in their own possessions and those for which she felt herself responsible as custodian for the nation. Once when he overheard her asking a dinner guest if he had bought any interesting pieces lately, he angrily thumped the table and cried out, 'There you go again, May – always furniture, furniture, furniture!'

The King much preferred those days when there were no guests to entertain other than friends whom he had known well for years. Then he could follow his usual routine of rising early; doing some work before breakfast for which he appeared on the stroke of nine, with his beloved and indulged parrot, Charlotte, on his finger; reading *The Times* from cover to cover; then going out to see what the weather was like, a dog, usually a wire-haired terrier, at his heels, smoking a cigarette. Then he would either return to work, go for a walk round the farms or gardens, or for a ride in the park. Sometimes, when at Windsor, he would play golf on the course his father had made in the grounds below the East Terrace, or go shooting. On fine afternoons he liked to stroll away for a quiet picnic tea with the Queen and in the evenings to look at his stamps, to listen to Gilbert and Sullivan, to read some undemanding biography or detective story, or to watch an adventure film or an English comedy. At precisely ten minutes past eleven he went to bed. It was a simple life but it was never a Spartan one. His eldest son said of him: 'I knew no one who liked his comforts more, save perhaps myself. Everything about him was always of the best – his clothes, his fine hammer guns by Purdey, his food, his stationery, his cigarette cases by Fabergé ... the presents he gave to his friends.'

Also the King never stinted himself of servants. Frederick Ponsonby remembered going down to Sandringham one day in 1934.

Before I left London I received a curious message that I was to come in time for tea, as the film *Lives of a Bengal Lancer* was to be shown at six; also did I like oysters? I duly arrived in time for tea, but was mystified by the query about oysters. It turned out that the King strongly objected to plates of oysters being wasted and that on the first night three of the Household had refused to eat them. Therefore it was necessary to ascertain beforehand whether everyone ate them.

The King had explained to me that he had brought very few servants, but when the cinema took place and the servants were allowed to come I found there were forty-five.

As the years passed and his old-fashioned beard grew grey and his voice familiar to his people by means of the newly invented wireless, his distrust of which he was prevailed upon to overcome, the King became one of the best loved people in the country, reliable, honest, steady, stern yet kindly, a man who stood resolutely for the traditional virtues of a bygone age yet who in the General Strike pleaded for moderation, recognizing that the strikers were just as much his people as were those who had employed them – and good people, too – resisting all attempts to penalize them. In a speech he made at the Guildhall to both Houses of Parliament in the year before his death he expressed admirable Whig sentiments, though this, as A. J. P. Taylor has observed, was hardly surprising, as it had been written for him by G. M. Trevelyan, a great-nephew of Lord Macaulay.

His dutiful Queen – that stately figure in her long skirts and what felt like iron stays to those who danced with her, in those familiar toques that covered her grey hair and the folds of pale blue and mauve brocade that concealed her ample bosom – was quite as loved as her husband. At the time of their Silver Jubilee in 1935 the crowds that came out in their hundreds of thousands to welcome them, causing them as much surprise as gratitude, were cheering her as much as him. He understood this perfectly well himself. In one of the speeches he was obliged to make his voice broke at the mention of her name as he knew it would. When going through the draft his Secretary had prepared for him he had told him to place that part at the end. 'I can trust myself,' he had said, 'to speak of the Queen when I think of all I owe her.' To those who did not know her well she could appear utterly intimidating: she was said to be the only person of whom the formidable Lady Astor stood in awe.* But to her more intimate friends she presented a far less awesome persona.

---

* A characteristic story of Queen Mary is told by Brigadier Stanley Clark: 'I remember being present at a Fakenham, Norfolk, antique shop when she was there. A bullock from the market broke away from its captors and raced through the streets. Balked by the line of men, the fear-crazed animal swerved to one side and charged in through the door of the shop, scattering the antique china and furniture. The occupants of the shop, including myself, dived for cover – except one, Queen Mary. I saw her raise her lorgnettes to her eyes, and her hand held her parasol stiffly before her. It did not quiver and was like an imperious sword. The animal stopped, pawed the floor, and was seized and secured by the market men and led away. We all came sheepishly from our hiding-places, and Queen Mary, voice steady and untroubled, continued with her inspection of the pieces on display.' (Stanley Clark, *Palace Diary*, p. 100.)

She had an eager enjoyment of life, [wrote Lady Airlie, one of her Ladies-in-Waiting] and a sense of fun, carefully controlled like all her emotions, but always rippling beneath the surface. I can remember her laughing over the jokes in *Punch* and even in *La Vie Parisienne*; learning the words of 'Yes, We Have No Bananas' – the silly song hit – and singing it with me at the tops of our voices for the joy of shocking a particularly staid member of the Household . . . She was not always the dignified Queen Consort known to the world.

Nor was the King as stodgily hidebound as he sometimes liked it to be supposed. 'He was a symbol but he was a person as well,' wrote one of his contemporaries. 'The symbol inspired awe, and he never did anything which could mar his symbolic dignity; but only the person could inspire affection and we liked to think of him as a very homely person. Mr [Walter Hines] Page, the American Ambassador, and no admirer of the King species, was delighted and half surprised to find that King George and he could "chat like two human beings".' Lord Lee also praised the King's 'complete naturalness'; while Lord Cromer said, 'He had more than a sense of fun, even a sense of humour. He could say very acute and amusing things.'

Ramsay MacDonald, during the Silver Jubilee celebrations, remarked on his happy combination of grandeur and homeliness. The King displayed the demeanour and status of his regal rank at a 'glittering State Banquet' at which the twenty-four pipers – who traditionally appeared, their tartans swinging and their pipes askirl, to march twice round the room 'much to the astonishment and occasional alarm of foreign guests' – made a particularly fine show. At a reception for the Diplomatic Corps the atmosphere was once again one of 'great dignity'. This was followed by a reception of the Dominion Premiers, another most dignified occasion, yet at the same time a triumph both 'touching and homely'. 'The King's reply was a perfect expression of sovereign affection and solicitude. When he came to references and reminiscences personal to himself and the Queen his voice broke and tears stood in his eyes. Everyone deeply moved. Here the Empire was a great family, the gathering a family reunion, the King a paternal head. We all went away feeling that we had taken part in something very much like a Holy Communion.'

For the common people the Jubilee was more like 'a family party', wrote Harold Macmillan, then Member of Parliament for Stockton-on-Tees: 'And nowhere were the celebrations more notable than in the poorer streets of every town. I remember very well driving round Stockton with my wife on that day. Flags were hung across all the streets from one side to the other. Men and women of every class and of every political complexion joined together in common rejoicing.'

Not long after this the King held his last Privy Council meeting. 'He had changed greatly,' MacDonald wrote; 'his voice was fairly firm but his body weak. He seemed detached from us all and weary.' He sat in a chair with three pillows propping him up. His doctor, Lord Dawson, was with him, endeavouring to help him sign the Order appointing a Council of State.

His right hand was plainly useless [MacDonald recorded in his diary]. Dawson knelt by the table in front of him & helped him to manipulate his left, the fingers of which he kept drumming upon the warrant in front of him. 'I cannot concentrate,' he said with a sighing smile. Dawson suggested he should help him by supporting the pen which seemed to be difficult for him to do. He said 'No I shall sign myself.' We waited looking on. At length he began, Dawson supporting the pen. The first mark on the paper is his abortive attempt to write 'George', & second is the usual mark which he then made with Dawson's help. Watching the struggle . . . moved me to tears. Then we began to walk out of the bedroom. At first the King took no notice but was told that we were going. He looked at us and smiled. I was the last out & I shall never forget the look illuminated by affection (his eyes looked rather large) which he gave me & continued it as I went & bowed a second time – my final farewell to a gracious & kindly friend and a master whom I have served with all my heart.

5 The Uncle: King Edward VIII

The day after his father's death, on 21 January 1936, King Edward VIII flew from Sandringham to London in his own aeroplane for the Accession Council at St James's Palace. Looking pale and unhappy, 'very nervous and ill at ease', he read his declaration to the Councillors from a sheet of paper which he held first in one trembling hand, then in the other before placing it on the table in front of him.

He had never wanted to be King. As a child he had been seen looking through a weekly paper with his brother. They had come across a picture of himself captioned 'our future King'. His brother had pointed this out to him; but he had hastily brushed his finger aside and turned over the page.

Later on, during the war, when allowed to go to France he had seemed to take a perverse pleasure in putting himself in the way of enemy fire. 'It was common gossip in those days', Lord Lee recorded, 'that one reason why he exposed himself so needlessly was that he had a morbid dread of succeeding to the throne and when begged to be more careful, his reply always was, "But why should I? My brother would love the job and would make a much better King."' After the war in the hunting field the Prince was equally reckless, riding headlong at hedges without regard to the best places to jump over them and frequently falling off his horse.

These mishaps and this recklessness added to his great popularity. There was no doubt, indeed, that in the 1920s he had been as popular as anyone in England. Boyish, spontaneous, eager to please and wanting to be liked, he had displayed a remarkable capacity for handling crowds, for drawing individuals under the spell of his almost irresistible charm, captivating them by that sudden, disarming smile which transformed the usually rather sad expression of his handsome features. Though ill-educated and unintellectual, he was quick-witted and responsive, possessed of an extremely retentive memory which enabled him to flatter people by instantly recollecting their names and never forgetting their faces. Immature and affectionate, impulsive, unstable and indiscreet, he was as instinctively generous as he was emotional, delighting in the giving of presents, reduced to tears before a tour of

New Zealand by the prospect of having to be parted so long from his friend, Mrs Dudley Ward, with whom he was deeply in love. Renowned for his lavish tips, he is reported to have handed out £5 notes to men who opened gates for him when out hunting and to have tossed over a cheque for £300, back payment for his services as a Guards officer in the war, to his cousin, Lord Louis Mountbatten, knowing that the then comparatively impecunious young naval officer would have more urgent need of it than himself.

Yet there were those who even then did not find the Prince in the least attractive; who believed his character to be sadly flawed; who noticed – as Lady Hardinge did – that his 'almost overwhelming charm [was] not a natural charm, but could be switched on and off at will'; who had to admit – as did Mrs Dudley Ward – that he was, indeed, 'very spoilt'; who agreed with Lord Davidson 'that he was an obstinate, but really a weak man'. Certainly he was self-indulgent and opinionated, with more capacity for feeling than for thought, given to sudden enthusiasms and discordant ambitions which were likely to die as quickly as they had been born, subject to bouts of profound depression and to occasional fits of moody selfishness. Ready to assure acquaintances that he hoped they would feel no constraint in his presence, he was quick to snub those who took what he felt to be undue advantage of the freedom he accorded them. Although he fulfilled most of his public duties with grace and panache, there were times as he grew older when he displayed a sullen reluctance to go through with ceremonies that bored him, or even to assume an agreeable manner towards people he did not like or did not want to meet. A resident of Bermuda which he visited in 1931 remembered how, having reluctantly consented to be driven about the island for the pleasure of the crowds that had assembled beside the roads, he passed along 'with a face like thunder, refusing to look right or left'. His unpunctuality was notorious, and the despair of his mother and father.

He would have found unwelcome obligations easier to fulfil had he met with less discouragement from his father. But just as his mother, shy and inhibited with her sons, was quite incapable of showing them the affection they needed, so his father, demanding and critical, rebuffed his desire for approbation with a stubborn refusal to notice the talents which the Prince undoubtedly possessed. Successes usually went unremarked; failures were invariably followed by angry reprimands. Conversations between father and son frequently ended with the Prince being rebuked for some past fault or recent *faux pas*. Once the Prince, thinking to please his father, congratulated him on having done something which was 'good propaganda'. The King turned on him angrily, ordering him never to make such a remark again: he never in his life had done anything as propaganda; he did things because it was his duty to do them.

Of his own duties in life the Prince was never fully aware. His mother thought he ought to spend more of his time in England, learning how to govern, as she put it, making up for the gap in his constitutional experience caused by the war. But the King and the Prime Minister both thought he would be better employed abroad as a kind of roving diplomat. He himself, while professing to prefer the idea of visits overseas to engagements at home, seems to have been driven less by a desire to strengthen England's relations with foreign countries than by the need to escape from his parents' watchfulness, to lead his own life. His mother's Lady-in-Waiting, Lady Airlie, has described him at the age of twenty-five in her drawing-room one morning, sitting on a stool in front of the fire, smoking constantly as he talked of his future, 'nervous and frustrated, pulled this way and that'.

His father discouraged him from talking to politicians; but there was little evidence that he would have chosen to do so had the decision been left to him. There were certain questions of the day that aroused his interest; but he showed no particular curiosity about the machinery of government. He felt a sincere concern for the welfare of working men and their families, especially of those who had fought in the war; but he was as innately conservative as his father, in some ways more so, even reactionary. During the General Strike of 1926 he lent his car and chauffeur to transport the Government newspaper to Wales – though the King had told his sons to keep well out of the conflict – and he afterwards maintained that by putting down something they felt was 'terribly wrong, something contrary to British traditions', the upper and middle classes had put on 'a first class show'. No one who knew him well was in any doubt where his political sympathies lay. His well-known impatience with the stuffy conventions of his parents' Court; his slangy talk and the kind of nasal, sub-Cockney accent which the fashionable rich then affected; his loud clothes which were worn with what the more staid of the upper class considered vulgar rakishness and which led to so many scenes with his father, all combined to give the impression of a young man in revolt. And so he was in revolt. But it was not a revolt against the organization of society so much as a personal protest against the limitations and restrictions which his birth had imposed upon his own life.

Yet it was widely expected that on his father's death he would transform the Court, modernize the monarchy and begin a new and exciting era in the history of English kingship. As his father's life moved 'peacefully to its close', in the well-remembered words of the official bulletin, the English people not only, therefore, mourned the passing of a much loved monarch but looked forward with eager anticipation to the reign of his popular son. Their expectations were not to be realized.

Although they did not know it yet, the new King had already met and fallen helplessly in love with Mrs Ernest Simpson, who had been introduced to him by his friend, Lady Furness. She was a handsome, well-dressed, amusing, though at this time rather quiet and subdued American woman with what Cecil Beaton described as 'extremely utilitarian looking hands'. Beaton, who renewed his acquaintance with her towards the end of 1935, 'liked her immensely'. He found her 'bright and witty, improved in looks and chic ... She looked immaculate, soignée and fresh as a young girl. Her skin was as bright and smooth as the inside of a shell, her hair so sleek she might have been Chinese ... She spoke amusingly, in staccato sentences punctuated by explosive bursts of laughter that lit up her face with great gaiety, and made her eyebrows look attractively surprised.' Later Beaton recorded in his diary his impression that she loved the King but was 'not *in* love with him'. Of his utter devotion to her and complete reliance on her, there could be no doubt.

Like her husband, Mrs Simpson had been married before and was soon to obtain a divorce for the second time. The King's overwhelmingly intense passion for her, combined with his determination to marry her, and if possible to make her Queen, was to influence his every action throughout his short reign. It explains what to one observer at least seemed his 'frantic and unreasonable grief' at his father's death, a grief that 'far exceeded that of his mother and his three brothers'. It explains the wild, almost hysterical shout of 'I'll fix those bloody clocks!' in reaction to some trivial mistake which had been brought about while the old King was dying – because the clocks at Sandringham were still kept half an hour fast in accordance with an order given by Edward VII – and the insensitive instructions given there and then for the clockmaker to come to the house to alter them. It explains the anxiety and shaking hands at the Accession Privy Council when he himself claimed to be not nearly so nervous as his father had been, merely fulfilling a duty like any other.

The day after this Accession Council he stood with Wallis Simpson in another room in St James's Palace, looking through the window as Garter King of Arms proclaimed his accession.

Since his mother had her immense collection of china, souvenirs, relics, furniture and objects of art and vertu to deal with at Buckingham Palace, the King decided for the time being to remain at York House, St James's Palace, which had been his home since August 1919. He had always intensely disliked Buckingham Palace himself. 'The vast building,' he wrote years later, 'with its stately rooms and endless corridors and passages ... seemed pervaded by a curious, musty smell that still assails me whenever I enter its portals. I was never happy there.'

So he was perfectly content to remain at York House which he had described on moving in as 'a rambling, antiquated structure, a veritable rabbit warren, with passages interrupted by unexpected flights of steps leading to unsymmetrical rooms full of ugly Victorian furniture, brass beds, and discarded portraits of former monarchs', but which he had since made pleasantly informal. With the help of Mrs Dudley Ward he had selected the most attractive pieces of furniture, relegating the heavy Victorian items to store rooms in attic and cellar. As his drawing-room he had chosen a well-shaped room on the first floor whose walls were covered with maps of the world with the British Empire coloured red and the rest kept rigorously up to date in accordance with the dictates of political geography rather than with an eye to pleasing decoration or design. A bedroom and a bathroom led off this drawing-room. The dining-room was downstairs but was used only on occasions when the need for space or a more formal atmosphere made a table laid by the fireplace in the drawing-room inappropriate.

The King hoped that life at St James's would remain as informal as possible, that he would not be called upon to make any unwelcome changes in his entourage. There was no question of his having to take over his father's Private Secretary, as Lord Wigram asked leave to resign as soon as the period of mourning for King George V was over. But some changes in his Household were inevitable, for when he asked his own Private Secretary, Sir Godfrey Thomas, to remain in the post, Thomas declined on the grounds that he was not really qualified for it. Thomas, who had succeeded his father as tenth baronet in 1919, had been with the King since the end of the war, having left the Foreign Office to take up the appointment; and, though more quiet, unassuming and intellectual than most of the men to whom the King was instinctively drawn, he and his master became good friends. Too modest to accept the post of Private Secretary, he agreed to stay on as Assistant when the senior position was offered to Major the Honourable Alexander Hardinge.

Hardinge, who had been awarded the Military Cross as adjutant in the Grenadier Guards in 1918, looked very much like a soldier, 'though his secret longing had always been to be an architect'. Handsome and erect with neatly brushed hair and a well-clipped moustache, he was a great grandson of both Field-Marshal Viscount Hardinge and Field-Marshal the Earl of Lucan and the son of Edward VII's indispensable attendant, Charles Hardinge, who had become the first Baron

Hardinge of Penshurst and Viceroy of India. Educated, like his father (and like Sir Godfrey Thomas) at Harrow, and afterwards at Trinity College, Cambridge, he had married a granddaughter of Queen Victoria's Prime Minister, Lord Salisbury, and had become Assistant Private Secretary to King George v in 1920. Rather rakish in his youth, he was now a man of calm judgement, orderly mind, reserved manner and the utmost integrity. Thoughtful, old-fashioned, aristocratic, and devoted to his family, he had soon settled into life at the late King's Court. 'Chips' Channon, that egregiously fashionable, amusing, well-informed but sometimes insensitive and often prejudiced diarist, had written on 6 December the year before: 'I think the Court is dead and out-of-date. Emerald [Cunard] told us how she had lunched today with Alex Hardinge who, though quite young [forty-nine] has already taken on the Court "colour". He very much criticized the Prince of Wales and his entourage. It is high time such dreary narrow minded fogies were sacked, as, indeed, they will be, in the next reign.'

Channon might well have written in similar terms of Captain Alan Lascelles who became Sir Godfrey Thomas's colleague as Assistant Private Secretary. Seven years older than Hardinge, 'Tommy' Lascelles had also won the Military Cross and, as the son of Commander the Honourable Frederick Canning Lascelles, came from the same sort of background. Educated at Marlborough and Trinity College, Oxford and married to a daughter of Lord Chelmsford, he had served in the Bedfordshire Yeomanry and had been appointed Assistant Private Secretary to the Prince of Wales in 1920. He had not been happy in the appointment and had requested permission to leave the Prince's service in 1929 after a tour of Africa during which, although accompanied by Lady Furness, the Prince brought safaris in Kenya and Tanganyika to a halt in various places where he met other women who attracted him. Some months later Lascelles found a more congenial master in the Governor-General of Canada whose Secretary he became before being appointed Assistant Private Secretary to George v. He was a clever, scrupulous, rather sardonic and drily witty man with a thin, pale face, steel-rimmed spectacles, and clothes of resolutely old-fashioned cut. Harold Nicolson found him 'gay and agreeable' and 'most helpful' when he was writing his biography of King George v, 'so quick in his replies, so certain, so humorous and so friendly'. Others, however, including King Edward viii, thought him austere and aloof. Indeed, in later years the King grew to dislike him intensely – the feeling was reciprocated – and even now there was a wariness in their relationship which often rendered the atmosphere at Court strained and embarrassing. It caused much surprise, therefore, when after the traditional six months' period during which his predecessor's Household remained in office, the King reappointed Lascelles his Assistant Private Secretary.

By that time, though, there was little else he could have done for the King's haphazard business methods had made an experienced staff essential. Before his resignation, Lord Wigram had been exasperated by the King's unpredictable temper, his lack of method, and selfish insensitivity, his habit of interrupting the meals of his staff or even of getting them out of their baths or beds whenever he felt in the mood to do some work. Wigram would have been even more exasperated had he known that on at least one occasion when he went to see the King at Buckingham Palace, in order to avoid him, and to keep an appointment with Mrs Simpson instead, His Majesty climbed out of one of the windows and ran away across the garden.

At first the King had been quite conscientious with his work, reading his papers with attention and initialling them at the foot of the page. But he soon grew tired of this boring labour; and for days on end would not attempt to do any work at all before noon. Men summoned for interview would be sent away without having seen him. He became alternately irritable and exhilarated, morose and excited, but rarely seemed happy. His servants, to whom he had in the past behaved with consideration, now found him not only thoughtless but petty.

Many of his old friends, too, were dismayed by his changing attitude towards them. For this Mrs Simpson was held largely to blame. 'It was scarcely realized at this early stage', wrote Hardinge, 'how overwhelming and inexorable was the influence exerted on the King [by Mrs Simpson]. As time went on it became clearer that every decision big or small, was subordinated to her will ... It was she who filled his thoughts at all times, she alone who mattered; before her the affairs of state sank into insignificance.'

In his anxiety to please her, the King now chose his companions with her in mind: people she liked were invited to St James's or Fort Belvedere in Windsor Great Park, that 'castellated conglomeration' as the King himself described it, which, begun by William, Duke of Cumberland, and enlarged by Sir Jeffrey Wyatville for George IV, he had modernized and redecorated for his private use. Here, her friends were his welcome guests; those she had cause to dislike or distrust were no longer invited. Brigadier-General G. F. Trotter, formerly the King's Assistant Comptroller and, although much older, one of his closest friends, was dismissed. Rear-Admiral Sir Lionel Halsey, another former member of his staff, once known as 'the old Salt', was deemed 'a bore' and, after trying to talk to the King about Mrs Simpson, was not asked to Fort Belvedere again. Even his intimate friend Major Edward Dudley [Fruity] Metcalfe, who had been with him during his tours and who had been promised a place in his Household was not given one.

When Hardinge and Lascelles and the other members of his Household went to Fort Belvedere it was because they were required there for business. They were frequently kept waiting about and were not asked to stay for a meal. And when the King did eventually appear, the negligent way in which he conducted his business combined with the slapdash manner in which the Fort was run, disturbed them all deeply. Lady Diana Cooper, a guest at the Fort before the King's accession, has described the casual atmosphere there, the way in which the guests served themselves with what little food was provided at luncheon – 'American-style (therefore favoured, bless him)' – how, when Lady Diana asked for white wine rather than champagne, he went off and fumbled 'about for too long looking for it himself'; and how the Prince, wearing a kilt and a Scottish bonnet, marched round the table playing bagpipes after dinner. A year later, when the Prince was King, life at the Fort, Lady Diana discovered, had hardly altered at all. 'Unchanged in manners and love,' he still played his bagpipes after dinner; he still doted upon Mrs Simpson and attended to her every wish. His servants, Lady Diana added, were still 'a bit hobbledehoy'.

The King was well aware of this himself and would exclaim, when one of them had behaved in a peculiarly offhand way, what on earth his father would have thought about it. Yet the few reforms which he carried out at Fort Belvedere and at the other royal residences and palaces were mostly financial rather than disciplinary, and accordingly caused much resentment, particularly when his petty economies were contrasted with the lavishness of his presents to Mrs Simpson, who was constantly being given furniture for her flat, and who – so Mrs Belloc Lowndes was informed – received well over £100,000 worth of jewels from him, and who certainly came into possession of several royal heirlooms, including the emeralds that Queen Alexandra had bequeathed him for his future wife as Queen of England. These jewels, she is said to have since told several friends, she is leaving in her will to the French Government.

While the royal family were naturally deeply distressed by the King's gifts of valuable heirlooms to Mrs Simpson, the Government were far more concerned about her attitude towards the Fascist states of Europe. Known to have sympathetic feelings towards Nazi Germany, she was believed also, on no very reliable evidence, to have important German contacts. She was accordingly kept under surveillance by security officers.

That the King shared her opinion of the German and Italian Governments was not in doubt. Indiscreet and well satisfied of the soundness of his opinions, he made no secret of them. Like many opinionated men who are susceptible to flattery and move in influential circles, he was inclined to suppose himself more capable and discerning than he really was, and had no hesitation in unconstitutionally propounding arguments at variance with the views of his Ministers. As Prince of Wales he had, to the great annoyance of his father, spoken publicly in favour of the hand of friendship being stretched out to the Germans by those who had fought them and had 'now forgotten all about it and the Great War'. It was a speech which, expressing views which were contrary to Foreign Office policy, provoked much comment abroad, particularly in Germany where the limited powers of the English crown were little understood. Yet the Prince had not been in the least contrite, and had evidently told the German Ambassador that, although his words had aroused some adverse comment, particularly in France, he was not going to retract them because he was 'convinced he had said the right thing'.

With this Ambassador, Leopold von Hoesch, he was on the closest terms, confiding to him that, in his opinion, the attitude of the Foreign Office was 'too one-sided', that, while he believed wars were 'no longer a means for solving political problems', he was far from a pacifist and, therefore, fully understood that – just as he desired his own country to remain strong and command respect – 'the Reich Government and the German people were inspired by a similar desire'. He had, in fact, a 'complete understanding of Germany's position and aspirations'.

The King apparently said as much, and more, to the Duke of Saxe-Coburg-Gotha, an old Etonian member of the Nazi Party who was a grandson of Queen Victoria, a brother of Princess Alice, Countess of Athlone, and a first cousin once removed of the King. In a conversation with the Duke, which was reported to Berlin, the King evidently described the League of Nations as 'a farce', complained 'about Russia and Litvinov, with whom he had, "unfortunately", just had to shake hands and spoke of an alliance with Germany which was *for him* an urgent necessity'. When asked whether a discussion between Baldwin, the Prime Minister, and Hitler would be desirable, 'he replied in the following words: "Who is King here? Baldwin or I? I myself wish to talk to Hitler, and will do so here or in Germany. Tell him that please".'

Whether or not the King used these words or, indeed, expressed himself so openly at all to the Duke, he certainly held the views ascribed to him. As 'Chips' Channon said, he was 'pro-German, against Russia and against too much slipshod democracy'.

You are aware from my reports that King Edward, quite generally, feels warm sympathy for Germany [von Hoesch confirmed to Berlin]. I have become convinced during frequent, often lengthy talks with him that these sympathies are deep-rooted and strong enough to withstand the contrary influences to which they are not seldom exposed ... I am convinced that his friendly attitude towards Germany might in time come to exercise a certain influence on the shaping of British foreign policy.

According to the admittedly unreliable evidence of Fritz Hesse, a press attaché at the German Embassy, Germany was able to benefit from this influence a few weeks later when a German army, in contravention of both the Treaty of Versailles and the Locarno Pact of 1925, reoccupied the left bank of the Rhine, an action which seemed for a time to threaten war. Von Hoesch immediately went to see the King, so Hesse maintained, and persuaded him to send for Baldwin. Hesse was with the Ambassador when the King telephoned to report the outcome of the interview. 'I sent for the Prime Minister and gave him a piece of my mind,' Hesse heard the King say on an extension of von Hoesch's telephone. 'I told the old so-and-so that I would abdicate if he made war. There was a frightful scene. But you needn't worry, there won't be a war.'

Improbable as the conversation which Hesse reported sounds, there can be little doubt that von Hoesch, as he himself reported, did get in touch with the King and was assured that there was 'understanding for the German point of view' and that 'complications of a serious nature [were] in no circumstances to be allowed to develop'. Nor can there be much doubt that von Ribbentrop, who succeeded von Hoesch as Ambassador, would not have come to England had not the Nazis believed that the death of King George v made a final attempt to persuade the British to join an Anglo-German alliance worthwhile. 'I was sceptical about the likelihood of success,' wrote von Ribbentrop in an attempt to vindicate his failure, 'but, because of Edward viii, it seemed that a last effort should be made. Today I no longer have faith in any understanding. England does not desire in close proximity a paramount Germany, which would be a constant menace to the British Isles. On this she will fight ... Baldwin realized this at the time, and Edward viii had to abdicate, since it was not certain, because of his views, he would co-operate in an anti-German policy.'

The King had, indeed, already demonstrated his unwillingness to co-operate in a policy directed against Fascist Italy. In a conversation with the Italian Ambassador, Count Grandi, he had allegedly 'expressed profound regret that such serious tension should have developed in Anglo-Italian relations ... Although under the parliamentary system the government was not in the King's hands, he would continue to do what appeared to him to be possible and necessary.'

When Italy's conquest of Abyssinia was complete, the Foreign Minister, Anthony Eden, endeavoured to persuade the King to receive the exiled Emperor, Haile Selassie. It would, Eden said, be a popular gesture. On his own admission, the King replied, 'Popular with whom? Certainly not with the Italians.' His Ministers, he later commented, 'had embarked on a futile policy of coercing Mussolini, which had utterly failed in its purpose and was only forcing him into ever closer relations with Hitler ... It was more important in my eyes at this stage to gain an ally than to score debating victories in the tottering League of Nations.'

While it can certainly be argued that the King's views on foreign policy were realistic and were widely held by others at the time, it cannot be denied that he was acting without regard to constitutional propriety in airing them so openly and against the known wishes of the Government. It is not surprising that Foreign Office papers were carefully sifted before being dispatched in their red boxes to him, nor that there were members of the Government – not to mention of the Opposition – who were not sorry to see the King depart when a different issue precipitated his abdication.

In the lengthy negotiations which led up to the abdication, the King's Private Secretary, Major Hardinge, played a leading part. Throughout the summer of 1936 Hardinge made repeated attempts to persuade the Prime Minister to give the most serious attention to the dangerous position in which the monarchy was being placed by the King's involvement with Mrs Simpson which was now well known in America and on the Continent though not yet in England. But Baldwin, at once a kindly, tolerant, understanding man and a shrewd politician, was never in a hurry to solve a problem which might, given time, solve itself. He was, accordingly, reluctant to interfere, making the excuse that no constitutional issue could arise as long as Mrs Simpson remained married to Mr Simpson. Baldwin was worried all the same. Numerous letters had been sent to him from abroad, protesting about the conduct of the King who that summer went on a widely publicized cruise with Mrs Simpson aboard a chartered yacht; and Baldwin feared the time would soon come when he would have to raise with him the distasteful subject of his private life. There was talk that the King might actually be intending to marry Mrs Simpson after her second divorce which was now impending. Certainly, it had not gone unnoticed that in lengthy discussions about the financial provisions to be made for the monarchy which had to be settled at the outset of each reign, the King had shown keener interest in the allowances which would be made to a future Queen than in any other aspect of the Civil List. So, when in the middle of October, Hardinge pressed Baldwin yet again to see the King, to try to stop the divorce proceedings and to persuade His Majesty to be more discreet with Mrs Simpson in public, Baldwin eventually consented.

Hardinge then telephoned the King who expressed himself shocked that it should be considered that either he or the Prime Minister could interfere with Mrs Simpson's divorce. He agreed, however, to see Mr Baldwin at Fort Belvedere at ten o'clock the next morning. The interview which then took place has been described as often, perhaps, as any other in modern times. Each man provided his own account on which numerous other accounts have been based. Harold Nicolson's version, written in his diary under the date 7 September, is probably quite close to the truth:

Oliver Baldwin came to see me this morning. He told me that his father and the King walked round and round the garden at Fort Belvedere discussing the business, and then returned to the library ... Stanley Baldwin was feeling exhausted. He asked for a whisky-and-soda. The bell was rung: the footman came: the drink was produced. S.B. raised his glass and said (rather foolishly to my mind), 'Well, Sir, whatever happens, my Mrs and I wish you happiness from the depths of our souls.' At which the King burst into floods of tears. Then S.B. himself began to cry. What a strange conversation-piece, those two blubbering together on a sofa.

When he had recovered himself, Baldwin, according to his own account, addressed the King in these terms:

The British Monarchy is a unique institution. The crown in this country through centuries has been deprived of many of its prerogatives, but today, while that is true, it stands for far more than it has ever done in its history ... But while this feeling largely depends on the respect that has grown up in the last three generations for the monarchy, it might not take so long, in face of the kind of criticisms to which it was being exposed, to lose that power far more rapidly than it was built up, and once lost I doubt if anything could restore it.

Having said this, Baldwin produced a folder containing a representative selection of the letters he had received. He placed this folder on the table and left it there; and a conversation on the following general lines seems then to have taken place:

BALDWIN The American papers are full of it ... The effect of such comment would be to sap the position of the throne unless it were stopped ... I don't believe you can get away with it ... I think you know our people. They'll tolerate a lot in private life but they will not stand for this kind of thing in the life of a public personage and when they read in the Court Circular of Mrs Simpson's visit to Balmoral they resented it.

THE KING The lady is my friend and I do not wish to let her in by the back door, but quite openly ... I hope you will agree that I have carried out my duties with dignity.

BALDWIN I do agree and all the more as I know that the duties of royalty are not much to your liking.

THE KING I know there is nothing kingly about me but I have tried to mix with the people and make them think I was one of them.

BALDWIN Cannot you have this coming divorce put off.

THE KING Mr Baldwin! That is the lady's private business. I have no right to interfere with the affairs of an individual. It would be wrong were I to attempt to influence Mrs Simpson just because she happens to be a friend of the King.

BALDWIN But these proceedings are a dangerous matter. If a verdict were given which left the matter in suspense everyone would start talking. Then the newspapers would start printing stories. There might be sides taken and factions grow up in this country in a matter where no factions ought to exist. Could not Mrs Simpson be asked to leave the country for six months?

THE KING Mrs Simpson is the only woman in the world for me and I cannot live without her ... You and I must settle this matter together. I will not have anyone interfering.

When he heard what had passed at this interview Major Hardinge was most disappointed that nothing had been said about the most crucial aspect of the matter – the King's apparent wish to marry Mrs Simpson. He discussed this problem with some of the heads of the Civil Service who agreed with him that Mrs Simpson should be approached herself. Her solicitor, Theodore Goddard, was asked to go to see her. He did so, and came back with Mrs Simpson's assurance that any idea of her marrying the King was absurd.

A few days after Baldwin's conversation with the King at Fort Belvedere, the editor of *The Times*, Geoffrey Dawson, went to see Major Hardinge at Buckingham Palace with a long letter he had received from an Englishman living in America who had strongly protested about the incalculable damage being done to the prestige of Britain and the British monarchy in the United States by the 'poisonous publicity attending the King's friendship with Mrs Simpson'. The writer of this letter had expressed the hope that the King would abdicate in favour of his brother who could be expected to carry on 'the sterling tradition' established by their father. Hardinge agreed that this letter – which Dawson received on the same day as that on which the *New York Journal* published an article stating categorically that the King would marry Mrs Simpson – should be shown to the King. Hardinge also decided that, as his Private Secretary with a duty to keep the King fully informed of public opinion in the country, the time had now come for him to write a letter to him himself.

He had had this in mind for some days. He knew that newspaper editors were becoming increasingly restless and that before long a damaging story was bound to be printed. He knew, too, that the Prime Minister had discussed the crisis with the Leader of the Opposition and with the General Secretary of the Trades Union Congress both of whom agreed that the King ought to be left in no doubt that working people in the country would be horrified by the idea of Mrs Simpson becoming Queen. 'Our people won't 'ave it,' said Ernest Bevin categorically. And, in talking to Harold Nicolson of his great affection for King George v, J. H. Thomas added, 'And now 'ere we 'ave this little hobstinate man with 'is Mrs Simpson. Hit won't do 'arold, I tell you that straight. I know the people of this country. I know them. They 'ate 'aving no family life at Court.'

'The plain truth is', wrote Hugh Dalton, 'that the great mass of British men, and still more British women, especially outside London, which is in every sense an abnormal city, were from the start anti-Mrs Simpson.' Aneurin Bevan agreed with him. When asked what he thought would be the reaction of the Parliamentary Labour Party to the King marrying Mrs Simpson, Bevan replied 'that his own feelings were entirely neutral, but if the King wished to understand the feelings of the members of the Party, he could not do better than ask himself what would be the reaction of "a typical middle-class woman in Surbiton"'.

Informed of these views of the Labour Party leaders, Hardinge was also aware that various senior civil servants had expressed similar views. Indeed he had been shown a draft memorandum prepared for the official head of the Civil Service and the Permanent Secretary of the Treasury which would have had the King presented with a warning as strongly worded as this:

Unless steps are taken promptly to allay the widespread and growing misgivings among the people, the feelings of respect, esteem and affection which Your Majesty has evoked among them will disappear in a revulsion of so grave and perilous a character as possibly to threaten the stability of the nation and the Empire ... In Mr Baldwin's opinion there is but one course which he can advise you to take, namely to put an end to Your Majesty's association with Mrs Simpson.

Hardinge thought this was putting the case far too bluntly and made several suggestions for its amendment. Neville Chamberlain, the Chancellor of the Exchequer, on the other hand, thought it did not make the gravity of the matter sufficiently clear and suggested that the King should not only be bluntly advised that his 'association with Mrs Simpson should be terminated forthwith', but also that, if this advice were to be refused, 'only one result could follow in accordance with the requirements of constitutional monarchy, that is, the resignation of ... the Government. If Mrs Simpson left the country forthwith, this distasteful matter could be settled in a less formal manner.'

As it happened Baldwin declined to send such a message, but, aware of the strength of feeling that had brought it into existence, Hardinge was more than ever convinced that some sort of communication would have to be placed before the King. Time was running short. The editor of the *Morning Post* had warned that he could not stay silent much longer. Hardinge had also received a reply from Lord Tweedsmuir, Governor-General of Canada, to a letter he had sent asking if there were any evidence there of damage to the prestige of the monarchy due to the unfortunate publicity it was receiving in the American press. 'The condition of Canadian opinion', Tweedsmuir had told him, after emphasizing how respected the monarchy had become in Canada during the time of the late King, 'seems to me to be most anxious and disquieting.'

Australians did not hear as much about Mrs Simpson as Canadians did, but they, too – so Hardinge was informed by Stanley Bruce, the High Commissioner for Australia, with whom he had lunch on 13 November – would not countenance the idea of Mrs Simpson as their Queen. 'If there was any question of marriage with Mrs Simpson,' Bruce said, 'the King would have to go, as far as Australia was concerned.' Bruce urged the need for a speedy solution: the time to act was 'at once'.

Hardinge thought so, too. 'Give him time,' he had often said in the past in loyal answer to his master's critics. 'He hasn't found his feet yet.' But now there was no time left. He wrote his letter to the King and, in his own words, feeling that he 'desperately needed an outside opinion' as to the general wisdom and propriety of its contents 'as well as its accuracy', he showed it to Geoffrey Dawson. Dawson said it was 'an admirable letter, respectful, courageous and definite'. So Hardinge had it delivered to Fort Belvedere. This is what it said:

Sir,
  With my humble duty.
  As Your Majesty's Private Secretary, I feel it my duty to bring to your notice the following facts which have come to my knowledge, and which I *know* to be accurate:
  (1) The silence of the British Press on the subject of Your Majesty's friendship with Mrs Simpson is *not* going to be maintained. It is probably only a matter of days before the outburst begins. Judging by the letters from British subjects living in foreign countries where the Press has been outspoken, the effect will be calamitous.
  (2) The Prime Minister and senior members of the Government are meeting to-day to discuss what action should be taken to deal with the serious situation which is developing. As Your Majesty no doubt knows, the resignation of the Government – an eventuality which can by no means be excluded – would result in Your Majesty having to find someone else capable of forming a government which would receive the support of the present House of

Commons. I have reason to know that, in view of the feeling prevalent among members of the House of Commons of all parties, this is hardly within the bounds of possibility. The only alternative remaining is a dissolution and a General Election, in which Your Majesty's personal affairs would be the chief issue – and I cannot help feeling that even those who would sympathize with Your Majesty as an individual would deeply resent the damage which would inevitably be done to the Crown, the cornerstone on which the whole Empire rests.

If Your Majesty will permit me to say so, there is only one step which holds out any prospect of avoiding this dangerous situation, and that is for Mrs Simpson to go abroad *without further delay*, and I would *beg* Your Majesty to give this proposal your earnest consideration before the position has become irretrievable. Owing to the changing attitude of the Press, the matter has become one of great urgency.

I have the honour, etc., etc.,

Alexander Hardinge

P.S. I am by way of going after dinner to-night to High Wycombe to shoot there to-morrow, but the Post Office will have my telephone number, and I am of course entirely at Your Majesty's disposal if there is anything at all that you want.

On reading this letter, so the King afterwards maintained, he was at first shocked by its suddenness, then angered by its suggestion that he should tell the woman he intended to marry to go abroad, then hurt by the cold formality of its tone. He was conscious of having performed his recent public duties conscientiously. Because it was pouring with rain he had cancelled the State procession for his opening Parliament ten days before and had driven from Buckingham Palace to Westminster in a closed car. But in the House of Lords he had behaved impeccably, making the traditional declaration to uphold the Protestant faith and reading his speech with confident grace. Although he was forty-two he looked to Harold Nicolson 'like a boy of eighteen', wearing, as the coronation had not yet taken place, the cocked hat of an Admiral of the Fleet instead of the crown usually worn by the monarch on this important occasion. Nicolson, whose ear was peculiarly sensitive to the faintest nuances of a man's accent, thought that there was already now a trace of that American in the King's speech which was later to become so pronounced; but he was not alone in thinking that his demeanour was assured and dignified.

A week or so later the King visited the Royal Navy at Southampton with the First Lord of the Admiralty, Sir Samuel Hoare. On this occasion he ignored the pouring rain, refusing to wear a macintosh and scoring a personal triumph which, as Hoare said, demonstrated 'his surpassing talent for managing great crowds'.

He seemed to know personally every officer and seaman in the fleet. On one of the evenings there was a smoking concert in the aircraft carrier *Courageous* ... The vast underdeck was packed with seamen. In my long experience of mass meetings I never saw one so completely dominated by a single personality. At one point he turned to me and said, 'I am going to see what is happening at the other end.' Elbowing his way through the crowd, he walked to the end of the underdeck and started community singing to the accompaniment of a sea-man's mouth-organ. When he came back to the platform, he made an impromptu speech that brought the house down. Then, a seaman in the crowd proposed three cheers for him, and there followed an unforgettable scene of the wildest and most spontaneous enthusiasm.

There was no denying his enormous skill and the beguiling charm of his personality on such occasions. 'He had it in him', Mohammed Shah, Aga Khan claimed to have been told by Lord Wigram, 'to be the greatest King in the history of our country.' It was not an uncommon opinion. He may well have believed it himself; and it seems reasonable to suppose that bitter consciousness of a supreme opportunity lost was, in the future, to prejudice his interpretation of the events which led to his abdication and the motives of those who played a leading part in them. Certainly his own published version of the crisis, which presents it as a kind of plot with Baldwin, in league with the Archbishop of Canterbury, Geoffrey Dawson and Hardinge, intent on bringing him down, is at once disingenuous and misleading. It even misrepresents himself; for, as his most skilful and understanding biographer, Frances Donaldson, has written:

The King was in every way more sympathetic, more considerate of the feelings of others, more honourable and more likeable than the picture he painted of himself. Throughout the crisis he behaved with a sincerity and straight-forwardness which forced the respect of those who worked for him. In the notes other people made of their dealings with him there is never any trace of the self-satisfied sarcasm which so mars his later account.

Yet while he gives the impression that he saw Baldwin as an enemy from the beginning – which may well have been the case with the Archbishop of Canterbury, but was certainly not so with the Prime Minister – the King's distrust of his Household, particularly of Hardinge and Lascelles, was not a subsequent distortion. Even with Sir Godfrey Thomas, whom he had no cause to distrust as a member of his late father's Household, he would not discuss the implications of his love for Mrs Simpson. Sir Godfrey wrote him a letter, less formal and more affectionate than Hardinge's, pointing out the unpleasant consequences of his abdication; but the King did not reply to it. Nor did he reply to Hardinge whose services as the King's intermediary, Hardinge was given to understand, were no longer required.

99

For a time he considered dismissing Hardinge from his Household altogether; and, although he seemed quite friendly towards him when they were obliged to meet, it was clear that he would not find it easy to forgive him. Walter Monckton, yet another old Harrovian with the Military Cross, a highly successful barrister who had become a friend of the King at Oxford and who was now asked to become his representative in Hardinge's place, said that the King 'bitterly resented' Hardinge's attitude. The King showed Monckton the offending letter which, Monckton agreed, was 'too emphatically' expressed and which resulted in the King's being 'confirmed in his policy of not confiding his feeling and his ideas on this subject to any of his staff'. However, having agreed to act for the King temporarily himself, Monckton dissuaded him from dismissing Hardinge and advised him not to make any hasty decisions about Mrs Simpson whom he could not, in any case, marry until 27 April when her decree *nisi* became absolute.

The King also showed Hardinge's letter to Mrs Simpson, describing it as 'an impertinence'. She herself professed to having been stunned by it, and said that the only thing for her to do now was to leave the country as Hardinge had suggested. The King refused to consider such an idea. He was going to send for Baldwin, he told her, and to tell him that if the country did not approve of their marriage he was 'ready to go'.

The next evening he did so at Buckingham Palace. 'I understand that you and several members of the Cabinet have some fear of a constitutional crisis developing over my friendship with Mrs Simpson,' the King said straight away; and, when the Prime Minister admitted that this was so, he went on to say that he was intent upon marrying her. Baldwin, who was satisfied that constitutionally the sovereign's choice of consort required the Government's approval, replied that this particular marriage 'would not have the approbation of the country', and pointed out to him that 'the position of the King's wife was different from the position of any other citizen in the country; it was part of the price which the King had to pay'. 'His wife becomes Queen,' Baldwin said, 'the Queen becomes the Queen of the country; and therefore, in the choice of a Queen, the voice of the people must be heard.'

'I want you to be the first to know', the King now stated unequivocally, 'that I have made up my mind and nothing will alter it. I have looked at it from all sides – and I mean to abdicate to marry Mrs Simpson.'

'Sir, this is a very grave decision and I am deeply grieved.'

The King, looking quite exalted, Baldwin thought, 'like a young knight who had caught a glimpse of the Holy Grail', repeated his determination to marry Mrs Simpson. He wanted to marry her as King and, with her as Queen, he would be all the better a King. But if the

Government refused to countenance the marriage, he had resigned himself to abdication. Stretching out his hand, he held the Prime Minister's in his own 'for a long time and there were almost tears in his eyes when he said goodbye'.

The next day the King told his three brothers of the decision which he had reached. According to his own account, the eldest, the Duke of York, who was to succeed him, appeared too shocked to speak. The Duke of Gloucester seemed to be preoccupied with his own position. The Duke of Kent, who was closer to him than the other two and who had been helped by him to overcome an addiction to drugs some years before, disguised the feelings that he had elsewhere expressed that his brother was 'besotted on the woman', and gave the impression of being 'reconciled'. Their mother, to whom the King had already spoken, also expressed more sympathy than she could truly feel for him. Miserable, ashamed and angry, she could never forget that a son of hers had behaved selfishly. She had not wanted to talk to him about the matter earlier because, as she put it herself, 'in the first place I don't want to give the impression of interfering in his private life, and also because he is the most obstinate of all my sons. To oppose him over anything is only to make him more determined to do it. At present he is utterly infatuated, but my great hope is that violent infatuations usually wear off.'

It distressed her to the end of her life that this infatuation never did wear off. In fact, it was far more than an infatuation. The King's love for Mrs Simpson, Winston Churchill assured Lady Airlie, 'is one of the great loves of history. I saw him when she had gone away for a fortnight. He was miserable – haggard, dejected, not knowing what to do. Then I saw him when she had been back for a day or two, and he was a different man – gay, debonair, self-confident. Make no mistake, he can't live without her.'

His mother, however, thought that he should at least have made the effort to do so. Over two years later she wrote to him:

You did not seem able to take in any point of view but your own. I do not think you have ever realized the shock, which the attitude you took up caused your family and the whole Nation. It seemed inconceivable to those who had made such sacrifices during the war that you, as their King, refused a lesser sacrifice ... My feelings for you as your Mother remain the same, and our being parted and the cause of it, grieve me beyond words. After all, all my life I have put my Country before everything else, and I simply cannot change now.

Although he professed himself intent upon abdication if the Government would not agree to accept Mrs Simpson as Queen, the King still harboured the hope that he might, to use one of his own favourite expressions, 'get away with it'. During the second week of November he went on a well-publicized tour of South Wales, in the course of which he

demonstrated a genuine and deep concern for the plight of the un-
employed, and made the widely quoted remarks, 'Something must be
done. You may be sure that all I can do for you I will.'

The Government were annoyed by these comments which were
generally taken to be a condemnation of their inadequacy. Nor did the
Labour Party welcome them. Herbert Morrison disapproved of the
'Sovereign expressing views on matters which were the subject of
political controversy'. Ernest Bevin was 'sorry that the King [had] been
brought into the business'. And Aneurin Bevan, as Member for the
Ebbw Vale division of Monmouthshire, refused to be associated with a
visit which would 'appear to support the notion that private charity has
made, or can ever make, a contribution of any value to the solution of
the problems of South Wales'. But the popular press was enthusiastic in
its praise of the King's positive approach. The *Daily Mirror* contrasted
the indolence of Baldwin with the reaction of 'our beloved King', 'a
wisely unconventional monarch', to the tragedy of unemployment. The
Daily Mail printed a long leader warmly commending 'the King
Edward touch' and denigrating the record of his Ministers.

Esmond Harmsworth, son of the *Daily Mail*'s proprietor, Lord
Rothermere, now invited Mrs Simpson to lunch at Claridge's where he
asked her whether she and the King had ever considered a morganatic
marriage in which the wife retained her lower rank and any offspring
were debarred from the succession. The idea appealed to Mrs Simpson
as a reasonable compromise, though it did not at first do so to the King.
However, as Mrs Simpson liked the idea, he grew to like it too. 'I'll try
anything in the spot I'm in,' he said. But as Baldwin told Harmsworth,
'a morganatic marriage would mean a special Bill being passed in
Parliament; and Parliament would *never* pass it'. And so, on 2 December
when the Cabinet met to discuss the problem, having consulted the
Prime Ministers of the Dominions, it was decided that the King should
be told a morganatic marriage – which Chamberlain suspected would
only be 'a prelude to the further step of making Mrs Simpson Queen
with full rights' – was impracticable.

By then the famous speech of the Bishop of Bradford criticizing the
King's behaviour had broken the Press's uneasy silence about Mrs
Simpson; and the King was taken aback by the hostility of much of the
comment. After reading a particularly stern leader in one provincial
paper, he remarked sadly: 'They don't want her!'

Lord Beaverbrook, owner of the *Daily Express*, who with Esmond
Harmsworth, had approached the other newspapers on the King's
behalf in October to 'regulate publicity', now urged the King to allow
those newspapers still friendly towards him to attack the Government,
to 'strike back vigorously' at Baldwin and his supporters who were

endeavouring to deprive him of his throne. But the King was reluctant to do so. He wanted to 'dampen the uproar', as he put it, 'to avoid the responsibility of splitting the nation and jeopardizing the monarchy on the issue of [his] personal happiness; and to protect [Mrs Simpson] from the full blast of sensationalism'.

Deeply disturbed by the unfavourable publicity which she had already received, Mrs Simpson made up her mind to leave the country; and, accompanied by the King's personal detective and his friend Lord Brownlow, she left for Cannes, closely pursued by numerous newspaper reporters. Before she left, however, she suggested to the King that he should make a broadcast to the nation, putting forward his own point of view. The King enthusiastically took up this idea, settling down to write the draft of a speech which he sent to Lord Beaverbrook and to another of his supporters, Winston Churchill, for their comments. Both Beaverbrook and Churchill agreed that the Cabinet would be sure to object to a broadcast by the King on the grounds that it would constitute an appeal to the people over the heads of the Government. And this of course, was exactly how the Cabinet did view it.

What I want, Sir, is what you told me you wanted [Baldwin said to the King]. To go with dignity, not dividing the country, and making things as smooth as possible for your successor. To broadcast would be to go over the heads of your Ministers ... You will be telling millions throughout the world – among them a vast number of women – that you are determined to marry one who has a husband living. They will want to know all about her, and the Press will ring with gossip, the very thing you want to avoid. You may, by speaking, divide opinion; but you will certainly harden it. The Churches are straining at the leash; only three papers would be on your side, the *News Chronicle*, the *Daily Mail* and the *Daily Express*.

When the Cabinet gave their formal opinion that to make the kind of broadcast which he had in mind would be unconstitutional, as they were responsible for his words, the King admitted defeat. For a time he hesitated, encouraged by Churchill to believe that he would get strong support if he insisted on a morganatic marriage, and urged by Mrs Simpson, to whom he spoke by telephone every day, to stand firm and 'fight for his rights'. 'She kept up that line until near the end, maintaining that he was King and his popularity would carry everything,' said the King's Canadian-born friend Sir Edward Peacock, senior partner in Baring Brothers and Receiver General of the Duchy of Cornwall, who was often at Fort Belvedere during the crisis. 'With him this lasted only a very short time; then he realized the falsity of the position, and put it definitely aside, saying that under no circumstances would he be a party to a constitutional crisis, or any other move that would weaken the constitution or cause trouble between the Crown and its Ministers.'

All the same, he did not tell his brother the Duke of York that he had definitely decided on abdication until 7 December. Four days before, he had called on his mother whom he had not been to see for nearly a fortnight. She had implored him to reconsider his decision to marry Mrs Simpson; but he had replied that all that mattered was their happiness, he could not live alone as King and *must* marry her.

When [the King who was] in a great state of excitement ... left after making this dreadful announcement to his mother he told me to come & see him at the Fort the next morning [the Duke of York recorded in his diary]. I rang him up but he would not see me and put me off till Saturday. I told him I would be at Royal Lodge [in Windsor Park] on Saturday ... But he put me off again ... Sunday evening I rang up. 'The King has a conference & will speak to you later' was the answer. But he did not ring up. Monday morning December 7th came. I rang at 10 p.m. and my brother told me he might be able to see me that evening ... He rang me at 10 minutes to 7 p.m. to say 'Come & see me after dinner.' I said 'No, I will come & see you at once.' I was with him at 7 p.m. The awful suspense of waiting was over. I found him pacing up & down the room & he told me of his decision that he would go.

Now that the King had irrevocably made up his mind to abdicate, he seemed to have cast all care aside. The next evening he presided over a dinner party at Fort Belvedere. The Prime Minister was there with his parliamentary Private Secretary, Major Thomas Dugdale. So were the Dukes of York and Kent, Peacock, Monckton, George Allen, the King's solicitor, and Sir Ulick Alexander, Keeper of the Privy Purse. All the guests were in gloomy mood, Baldwin in particular, his heavy face 'pasty and lifeless under the candlelight'. But their host, so the Duke of York noted in his diary, was 'the life & soul of the party'. He appeared 'happy and gay', Baldwin remarked at a Cabinet meeting the following morning, 'as if he were looking forward to his honeymoon'.

According to the King's own account the conversation never flagged, but he 'saw to it that the topic that was responsible for bringing us together was never once mentioned'. 'Although I never saw Baldwin again,' the King added, 'I believe that he took from the Fort, that evening, the recollection of an unbowed, unresentful if somewhat whimsical Sovereign.'

If the King seemed perfectly happy, the Duke of York was becoming more and more upset as his own accession became imminent. On the day after the strange dinner party at Fort Belvedere, he went to see his mother with whom he 'broke down and sobbed like a child'. While he was still with her a message came from 10 Downing Street that he would be required the following morning, 10 December, to witness the signing of the Instrument of Abdication. After this brief formality was completed in the octagonal drawing-room at Fort Belvedere he wrote:

I was present at the fateful moment which made me D[avid]'s successor to the throne. Perfectly calm D[avid] signed 5 or 6 copies of the instrument & then 5 copies of his message to Parliament, one for each Dominion Parliament. It was a dreadful moment & one never to be forgotten by those present. One or two curious incidents happened later re the servants. I was there all the morning & afternoon. I went to R[oyal] L[odge] for a rest as the tension was getting unbearable at the Fort. But I could not rest alone [the Duchess was in bed with influenza in London] & I returned to the Fort . . . I later went to London where I found a large crowd outside my house cheering madly. I was overwhelmed.

The documents which, as Lord Templewood confirmed, the King signed without 'the least emotion', were taken back to London in the official despatch box by Walter Monckton who, now that his duties as negotiator were over, passed them on to Major Hardinge at Buckingham Palace. Hardinge took them to 10 Downing Street; and a few hours later the Prime Minister rose in the House of Commons to make one of the most effective speeches he had ever delivered there. Harold Nicolson wrote a vivid description of it in his diary:

The House is crowded and rather nervous and noisy. The Prime Minister comes in pushing past the encumbered knees of his colleagues, and finds his place. He has a box with him, and on sitting down, at once discovers that he has lost the key. He probes and rummages for a bit and then finds the key. He unlocks the box, extracts some sheets of paper with the royal monogram in red, and with it some flimsy notes of his own, more squalid than a young Labour candidate would dare to produce at a Wapping bye-election. He [then] walks firmly to the Bar, turns round, bows, and advances to the Chair. He stops and bows again. 'A message from the King', he shouts, 'signed by His Majesty's own Hand.' He then hands the papers to the Speaker.

The latter rises and reads out the message of Abdication in a quavering voice. The feeling that at any moment he may break down from emotion increases our own emotion. I have never known in any assemblage such accumulation of pity and terror.

The Prime Minister then rises. He tells the whole story. He has a blue handkerchief in the breast-pocket of his tail-coat. The 'Hear, Hears!' echo solemnly like Amens. His papers are in a confused state and he hesitates somewhat. He confuses dates and turns to Simon, 'It was Monday, was it not, the 27th?' The artifice of such asides is so effective that one imagines it to be deliberate. There is no moment when he overstates emotion or indulges in oratory. There is intense silence broken only by the reporters in the gallery scuttling away to telephone the speech paragraph by paragraph. I suppose that in after-centuries men will read the words of that speech and exclaim, 'What an opportunity wasted!' They will never know the tragic force of its simplicity. 'I said to the King . . .' 'The King told me . . .' It was Sophoclean and almost unbearable. Attlee felt this. When it was over he asked that the sitting might be adjourned till 6 p.m. We file out broken in body and soul, conscious that we have heard the best speech that we shall ever hear in our lives. There was no question of applause. It was the silence of Gettysburg.

The next evening the new King went to Fort Belvedere to see his brother who was busy packing his personal possessions. It had been agreed the day before that the King would buy from him both Balmoral and Sandringham and that he would make him a yearly allowance of – so it is supposed – £60,000. There was, however, one important matter still to be decided. Later the former King was to recall how his brother dealt with this matter:

Words do not come easily to Bertie on occasions of great emotion. But without his having to tell me so, I knew that he felt my going deeply. At the same time he can be extremely practical. 'By the way,' he asked me, 'have you given any thought as to what you are going to be called now?' This question took me aback. 'Why no, as a matter of fact, I haven't.'

The new King had. So had several members of the Government, as the question was a more important one than the former King had realized. Lord Wigram, now deputy Constable and Lieutenant Governor of Windsor Castle, together with Sir Claud Schuster, Permanent Secretary to the Lord Chancellor, had been to see King George to discuss the subject with him. The matter was urgent as Sir John Reith, Director General of the BBC, who was going to introduce the former King on the air that night – when he was to make the broadcast which the Government could not now prevent – would have to know what to call him. It was thought that 'Mr Edward Windsor' would be appropriate. 'That is quite wrong,' King George said immediately, and then asked Schuster for his opinion as a lawyer what exactly his brother was giving up by his abdication. When Schuster replied that he was not sure, the King displayed one of those sudden flashes of impatient acerbity which were later to startle others who had been led to believe him always as mild and unassuming as he was shy and retiring. He retorted sharply, 'It would be quite a good thing to find out before coming to see me.'

'Now, as to his name,' he continued with assurance. 'He cannot be *Mr* E[dward W[indsor] as he was born the son of a duke. That makes him Lord E[dward] W[indsor] anyhow. If he ever comes back to this country he can stand and be elected to the House of Commons. Would you like that?'

'No,' said Schuster.

And if he were to be created an ordinary duke he could sit and vote in the House of Lords. Would Schuster like that? Schuster said he would not.

'Well,' the King concluded, 'if he became a royal duke he cannot speak or vote in the House of Lords* and he is not being deprived of his rank in the Navy, Army or Air Force . . . I suggest His Royal Highness, the Duke of Windsor.'†

So it was settled. King George would announce his intention of creating his brother Duke of Windsor at his Accession Council the next morning. In the meantime Reith would be authorized to announce him as 'His Royal Highness Prince Edward'.

This Reith did in his deep, solemn Scottish voice; and Prince Edward read the text – which Winston Churchill, who had parted from him with tears in his eyes, had improved by the addition of a few sonorous phrases – at first rather uncertainly, then more assuredly and finally with confidence:

At long last I am able to say a few words of my own.

I have never wanted to withold anything, but until now it has been not constitutionally possible for me to speak.

A few hours ago I discharged my last duty as King and Emperor, and now

---

* The King was mistaken about this. Royal dukes can speak in the House of Lords. King George III's sons did. So did King Edward VII as Prince of Wales. Prince Charles has also spoken there.

† The Letters Patent, which subsequently conferred this title upon Prince Edward, expressly precluded the Duchess and any descendants they might have from using the title 'Royal Highness'. This had been decided by King George VI in consultation with the Cabinet who had in turn consulted the Dominion Cabinets. Baldwin, if the matter had been left to him, would probably have agreed to the Duchess being granted the title. But the Dominion Prime Ministers were strongly against it. The reaction of Mr Savage of New Zealand was characteristic of them all. 'On being informed that on her marriage Mrs Simpson would henceforth be known as "Her Grace the Duchess of Windsor", Mr Savage observed to Baldwin: "And quite enough too!"' (H. Montgomery Hyde, *Baldwin: The Unexpected Prime Minister*, p. 518.)

The unwelcome news was received by the Duke in a letter from King George VI a few days before his marriage. 'This is a nice wedding present!' he exclaimed indignantly. 'I know Bertie – I know he couldn't have written this letter on his own.' Nevertheless, the decision, which rankled with him for the rest of his life, created a coolness between the brothers thereafter. 'When he had been King he was told he could not marry Mrs Simpson because she would have to take his status and become Queen,' wrote Walter Monckton who naturally sympathized with his disappointed friend. 'So he gave up his Empire to make her his wife. He could not give up his royal birth, or his right to be called "His Royal Highness" which flowed from it. It was a little hard to be told, when he did marry her, that she would not have the same status as himself.' (Birkenhead, *Walter Monckton*, p. 166.) Monckton, who advised the Duke to take legal advice in the matter, afterwards told Diana Mosley – another friend of the Duke and, incidentally, one who considered him much maligned, 'an unusually sweet and lovable man' – that, in his opinion, if the Duke had brought an action in the English courts against the decision not to allow his wife the style and dignity of a royal duchess he would have won it. (Diana Mosley, *Life of Contrasts*, p. 267.) In any case, the Duke saw to it that the Duchess was always referred to as 'Royal Highness' in their Parisian household. (John Dean, *H.R.H. Prince Philip Duke of Edinburgh*, p. 21.) The Duke's sister-in-law, Queen Elizabeth, found it difficult to forget that his passion for Mrs Simpson had forced her husband to undertake duties which were to contribute to his premature death. But her daughter, Queen Elizabeth II, did her best to heal the breach between her mother and the Duke who had been her favourite uncle. She went to see him and the Duchess when they came to London on private visits; and in 1967 invited them to attend officially the unveiling of a commemorative plaque to Queen Mary.

that I have been succeeded by my brother, the Duke of York, my first words must be to declare my allegiance to him. This I do with all my heart.

You all know the reasons which have impelled me to renounce the Throne. But I want you to understand that in making up my mind I did not forget the country or the Empire which as Prince of Wales, and lately as King, I have for twenty-five years tried to serve. But you must believe me when I tell you that I have found it impossible to carry the heavy burden of responsibility and to discharge my duties as King as I would wish to do without the help and support of the woman I love.

The Ministers of the Crown, and in particular Mr Baldwin, the Prime Minister, have always treated me with full consideration. There has never been any constitutional difference between me and them and between me and Parliament. Bred in the constitutional tradition by my Father, I should never have allowed any such issue to arise ...

I now quit altogether public affairs, and I lay down my burden. It may be some time before I return to my native land, but I shall always follow the fortunes of the British race and Empire with profound interest, and if at any time in the future I can be found of service to His Majesty in a private station I shall not fail.

And now we all have a new King. I wish him, and you, his people, happiness and prosperity with all my heart. God bless you all. God save the King.

'Self in tears,' wrote Lady Hardinge in her diary when the broadcast was over, 'but everyone else thinks it very vulgar.' Perfectly satisfied with it himself, Prince Edward left immediately for Royal Lodge where his brothers were waiting to say goodbye to him. 'Dickie, this is absolutely terrible,' the eldest of them had said earlier to Lord Louis Mountbatten in a voice almost choking with emotion. 'I never wanted this to happen; I'm quite unprepared for it. David has been trained for this all his life. I've never even seen a State Paper. I'm only a naval officer; it's the only thing I know about.' To these often quoted words, Lord Louis consolingly replied: 'This is a very curious coincidence. My father once told me that, when the Duke of Clarence died, your father came to him and said almost the same things that you have said to me now, and my father answered: "George, you're wrong. There is no more fitting preparation for a King than to have been trained in the Navy."'

The diffident young naval officer was now George VI. As such, having kissed him and parted from him as fellow Freemasons, Prince Edward bowed to him in the doorway. Watching him do so, the Duke of Kent 'cried out almost fiercely, "It isn't possible! It isn't happening!"' 'But it had happened,' Prince Edward commented. 'It was all over.'

And most men and women in the country seemed glad that it was so. 'What is so tragic is now that the people have got over the first sentimental shock, they *want* the King to abdicate,' Harold Nicolson had told his wife two days before. 'Opinion in the Commons is now almost wholly anti-King. If he can first betray his duty and then betray the woman he loves, there is no good in the man. Thus although he may keep his throne if he "renounces" Mrs Simpson, he will have lost the respect of his subjects.' Outside the Commons, Nicolson found that the people were not angry with Mrs Simpson but possessed by 'a deep and enraged fury against the King himself. In eight months he had destroyed the great structure of popularity which he had raised.' Lady Hardinge agreed with him. 'If one says, "I hear he is going to stay,"' she had noted in her journal, 'everyone's face falls.'

'Opinion in the country settled down now steadily behind the Government,' Leo Amery, the former Secretary of State for Dominion Affairs, confirmed. 'The country as a whole [had become] progressively more shocked at the idea that the King could hesitate between his duty to them and his affection for a woman.' As Brian Inglis pointed out in his detailed study of the whole abdication affair, the public's 'first instinct had been to assume that the King, whom they liked, was being got at by his Ministers, whom they did not like. Not until Baldwin's Commons speech was the nature of the constitutional crisis formally clarified. But as soon as it was, people began to realize that Baldwin had a case ... The King, people felt, was behaving out of character. He had stepped out of his fairy tale; Prince Charming might marry a princess, or he might marry Cinderella; but he certainly could not marry a Mrs Simpson.' There was sympathy for him, of course; but there was more – if little initial enthusiasm – for his unwilling successor.

6 The Father: King George VI

A few hours after the Duke of Windsor left Portsmouth for Boulogne, his brother King George VI entered St James's Palace for his Accession Council. He looked pale, tired and drawn and was obviously even more nervous than his brother had been eleven months before. He read his prepared statement slowly and carefully, frequently hesitating over a word. He had 'a really beautiful voice', Harold Nicolson thought, but his stammer made it 'almost intolerably painful to listen to him'. It was 'as if one read a fine piece of prose written on a typewriter the keys of which stick from time to time and mar the beauty of the whole. It [made] him stress the wrong words.'

He had been afflicted with this stammer since the age of eight. Several causes might be held responsible for its onset other than an intimidating father whom the shy and anxious child had tried desperately and often vainly to satisfy. He had been made to wear painful splints by day, and for a time in bed at night, to straighten his knock-kneed legs, a slight physical deformity from which his father also suffered. He had been forced to write with his right hand when naturally left-handed. Later he had been bullied by the naval cadets in whose rowdy company he had continued his rather sketchy education, rarely rising very far from the bottom of the class.

But, although prone to outbursts of anger, to weeping and to moods of silent depression, he was never a difficult child. He tried hard to succeed. Conscientious, persevering and thorough, he firmly set his mind to overcome difficulties and disadvantages which would have overwhelmed a less resilient and resolute spirit. He had no originality of mind and little curiosity: he shared most of his father's tastes; and, while more sympathetic to the prevailing ideas and fashions of his times, he was innately and unalterably conservative. Had his birth permitted it he would have chosen – as his father would have chosen – to lead the quiet life, untroubled by ambition, of a country gentleman.

As it was, he became a midshipman, then a sub-lieutenant who saw active service at the battle of Jutland in 1916. But his days afloat were rendered miserable by sea sickness and then by acute pains from a duodenal ulcer. Obliged to admit that he was wholly unsuited for a life at sea, he joined the Royal Air Force and, though he hated flying, he became a qualified pilot. After an unrewarding year at Trinity College, Cambridge, he began to undertake a growing number of official engagements, painful ordeals for him because of his stammer. Then, after a pertinacious courtship of a girl who had little desire to take on the responsibilities of royalty, he persuaded her to become his wife. He married her in Westminster Abbey in 1923. The marriage was to transform his life.

Lady Elizabeth Bowes-Lyon was the youngest daughter of the fourteenth Earl of Strathmore, a pretty, appealing and lovable girl, whose rather diffident charm was rendered all the more alluring by a ready and often earthy sense of humour. He could not have made a better choice. His mother praised her 'engaging and natural' manner; his father adored her, and could even find it in his heart to forgive her when Bertie's 'dear little wife' was late for a meal. 'You are not late, my dear,' he once said to the astonishment of everyone present, accepting her apology in words which have probably been quoted more often than any others he ever uttered, 'I think we must have sat down two minutes too early.' Few people who met her subsequently were not captivated by her extraordinary charm. In a flattering tribute no more adulatory in tone than many others that have been paid to her Cecil Beaton asked:

If she were anyone other than she is would one come so readily under her spell? Would one admire quite so much those old-fashioned dainty movements? The sweetly pretty smile, with tongue continually moistening the lower lip? Yes – whoever she were, she could not be faulted. As it is, everything about her adds to her fascination. Even her professed enjoyment of good Scottish oatcakes only adds to her comeliness ... She has such style, subtlety and humour, but it is her empathy and her understanding of human nature that endears her to everyone she talks to ... She manages to disperse anxiety and care, even makes it seem impossible that people should ever behave badly, or that things could go wrong. Of course there is something of the great actress about her, and in public she has to put on a show that never fails, but it is her heart and imagination which guide her. She will always say just the one thing that puts people at ease and makes them feel a glow of happiness, because she understands and appreciates the reality of any situation – whether it be tragic or gay.

At 145 Piccadilly and at the Royal Lodge at Windsor Great Park, the Duke and Duchess of York settled down to a life of complete domestic happiness. Their first child, Princess Elizabeth, was born in 1926 – the year in which a skilful speech therapist, Lionel Logue, helped the Duke to begin to overcome the worst aspects of his stammer – and their second, Princess Margaret Rose, in 1930. A few years later their life was suddenly disrupted by King Edward VIII's abdication; and in May 1937 the new King and Queen had to face the ordeal of the coronation.

The coronations of the kings and queens of England, whose ancient ritual and tribal elements have remained almost unchanged for more than a thousand years, used not to be conducted with the skilful, well-rehearsed precision which we have now come to expect. Even the coronation of George IV, a master impresario who had become 'perfectly absorbed in all the petty arrangements' and had succeeded in extracting the immense sum of £243,000 from the Government to ensure that it was an occasion of the most lavish splendour, was marred by several unfortunate incidents. The King himself, 'in full robes of great size and richness' and wearing a brown wig, the thick curls of which fell over his forehead and over the nape of his neck, appeared 'distressed, almost to fainting' as he made his way up the aisle with uneven steps and evident difficulty. During the ceremony, which lasted for five hours on a particularly hot day in July 1821, he was several times 'at the last gasp', Lady Cowper noticed, 'and looked more like the victim than the hero of the fête'. But, revived by sal volatile, he behaved on occasions in a highly improper fashion, according to the Duke of Wellington, 'even in the most important and solemn' parts of the ceremony – looking amorously at his mistress, Lady Conyngham and other lady friends with 'soft eyes, kisses on rings which everyone observed'. Fortunately these 'follies' and '*oëillades*' – which were also remarked upon by Lady Cowper who, 'being in the line of fire, had a full view' – were abandoned during the sternly admonitory sermon of the Archbishop of York who, with evident doubt of the King's willingness to perform them, referred to a sovereign's duties to 'encourage morality and religion', to preserve the morals of the people from 'the contagion of vice' and from a general depravity which was 'the last calamity' that could befall a state. When the exhausting ceremony was at last over and the King withdrew, the peers and peeresses, the foreign ministers and their wives rushed out of Westminster Abbey as though it had been on fire. Meanwhile the King's deranged wife, whom he had expressly forbidden to attend the ceremony, had been marching up to demand admission at the various doors which were shut in her face and guarded by hefty prize-fighters.

The coronation of George IV's brother, William IV, an infinitely less extravagant and less imaginative man, had been a much more modest affair. It would, indeed, not have taken place at all, had King William had his own way; for he considered it, as his biographer, Philip Ziegler, has said 'a pointless piece of flummery, a compound of superstition and sentimental antiquarianism which attempted to veil in mystery the perfectly straightforward relationship between a sovereign and his people'. He proposed that he should merely take the coronation oath in the presence of the assembled Lords and Commons. Persuaded that this would be unacceptable, he eventually agreed to go through with the tiresome routine, provided expenses were kept to a minimum. So – at a cost of about £30,000 – the coronation was held. It was much shorter as well as cheaper than the ceremony of 1821. But even so, though it was conducted without too many mishaps, there were times when the congregation seemed on the verge of laughter. The King, with his red-thatched face looking like a frog's head carved on a coconut, was 'very infirm in his walk ... and looked oppressed with the immense weight of his robes and crown'. The Queen had to avert her eyes for fear of bursting into laughter at the sight of Lord Brougham, the Lord Chancellor, whose 'ugly features', twitching nose, and wig hanging down 'on each side of his face, surmounted by his coronet, made him resemble the lion in the royal arms'.

The coronations of both George IV and William IV were, however, models of decorum compared with the ceremony that took place in Westminster Abbey on 28 June 1838 when their niece was crowned as Queen Victoria at a cost of £200,000. On that occasion peers, generals and maids-of-honour scrambled on the floor for coronation medals tossed about by the Treasurer of the Household. The Queen's ladies, who chattered together throughout the service, could not manage their trains, which so impeded them when carrying the Queen's that they often pulled her to a stop and had to be scolded by the Duchess of Sutherland, the Mistress of the Robes. The Queen's mother burst into tears. During the Homage, the frail and extremely aged Lord Rolle tripped up on the skirt of his robes and tumbled to the bottom of the steps to the throne. As he picked himself up and shakily but manfully began to climb them again, the Abbey reverberated with loud cheers which grew even more vociferous when the Queen, anxious that he might roll over again, whispered: 'May I not get up and meet him?' and then rose from her throne and held out her hand to assist him.

Although there were times when she looked as though she wanted 'to creep under the Archbishop's wing', the Queen 'performed her part with great grace and completeness', Disraeli told his sister. But this, he continued, could not be said of the other performers:

They were always in doubt as to what came next, and you saw the want of rehearsal. The Duke [of Wellington] was loudly cheered when he made his homage. Melbourne [the Prime Minister] looked very awkward and uncouth, with his coronet cocked over his nose, his robes under his feet, and holding the great sword of state like a butcher ... The Duchess of Sutherland walked, or rather stalked, up the Abbey like Juno; she was full of her situation. Lady Jersey and Lady Londonderry blazed among the peeresses ... Lyndhurst ... committed the *faux pas* of not backing from the presence ... I saw Lord Ward after the ceremony ... drinking champagne out of a pewter pot, his coronet cocked aside, his robes disordered, and his arms akimbo, the very picture of Rochester.

The bishops were quite as awkward and almost as unfamiliar with the order of the service as the laity. The Bishop of Durham lost his place in the prayer book, and at the wrong moment thrust forward the orb which was so unexpectedly heavy the Queen nearly dropped it. Then the Archbishop of Canterbury came forward to hand her the orb, saw that she had it already, looked round for the Bishop of Durham who had 'disappeared', and was '(as usual)', so the Queen recorded, '*so* confused and puzzled' that he too 'went away'. Later, she suffered agonies as the Archbishop forced the ruby ring which had been made to fit her little finger on to her fourth where it became lodged so firmly that it could be removed only after the finger had been bathed in iced water. Finally the Bishop of Bath and Wells, the learned but absent-minded brother of Lord Ellenborough, turned over two pages at once and, oblivious of the error at the time, had to call Her Majesty back later from St Edward's Chapel where she had retired to find 'what was *called* an *Altar* covered with sandwiches, bottles of wine, etc. etc.'

The coronation of the Queen's son, King Edward VII, was marred by quite as many disasters. The ancient Archbishop of Canterbury lost his place in the order of service, almost fell over as he returned from the altar with the crown which he would have placed on the King's head the wrong way round had he not been prevented, later found such difficulty in rising to his feet after making homage to the King on behalf of the Church that His Majesty, assisted by three bishops, had to help him up, and then loudly and crossly replied to the solicitous enquiry of the Bishop of Winchester as to whether he needed any further help, 'go away!' The Queen had some of the sacred oil dropped on her nose; a duchess tripped up and fell down at the feet of a cabinet minister; a baronet had a fit; and a peeress temporarily lost her coronet down a lavatory.

The coronation of King George VI was not characterized by nearly so many mistakes and misfortunes as were those of his predecessors, although there were times before the appointed day when it seemed that it would be. The Queen – who with her husband, had collapsed in helpless, almost hysterical laughter when the photographer disappeared beneath his black cloth to take pictures of them in their robes – completely lost her nerve on one occasion, according to Sir Edward Marsh, and cried out, 'I can't go through with it, I can't be crowned!'

Then the precious orb was lost until the six-year-old Princess Margaret was discovered, rolling it about on the floor.

At least one of the rehearsals in the Abbey was chaotic. Tom Driberg, who attended this rehearsal on behalf of the readers of the *Daily Express*, recalled in his memoirs how the Lord Chamberlain, whose duty it was to expose His Majesty's chest so that a few drops of the anointing oil could be poured upon it, fumbled helplessly with the button of the 'gigantic guardee, who was standing in for the King'; and how the Archbishop of Canterbury, Cosmo Gordon Lang, 'white-haired, exquisitely groomed, like a delicate old lady', wandered about the Abbey, wringing his hands and crying, 'Where is the Lord of the Manor of Worksop? Where *is* the Lord of the Manor of Worksop?' 'This improbable title', Driberg explained, 'was that of one of the feudal functionaries – persons of the utmost unimportance – who had a traditional right to appear for a few seconds at a coronation, to hand the new monarch a rose or a peppercorn or whatever; in this case an embroidered glove.'*

While the actual ceremony passed off more smoothly than those who attended this rehearsal can have expected, for a man as shy and meticulous as King George VI, it was both an ordeal and an irritant; and for long periods, so he afterwards told Ramsay MacDonald, 'he was unaware of what was happening'. He had been most anxious to ensure that the crown should be placed on his head the right way round. It was accordingly arranged that a small thin line of red cotton should be inserted under one of the principal jewels on the front. But someone, believing the thread had got caught there by accident, removed it. The consequences were recorded in the King's own account of the ceremony:

The hours of waiting before leaving for Westminster Abbey were the most nerve racking. At last the time came & we drove in the State Coach to the Abbey in our Robes. On our arrival our pages & train bearers met us to carry our robes to our retiring rooms. Elizabeth's procession started first but a halt was soon called, as it was discovered that one of the Presbyterian chaplains had fainted & there was no place to which he could be taken ... I was kept waiting, it seems for hours, due to this accident, but at last all was ready for my progress into the Abbey ... I had two Bishops, Durham, & Bath & Wells, one on either side to support me & hold the form of service for me to follow. When the great moment came neither Bishop could find the words, so the

* The Duke of Newcastle was then Lord of the Manor of Worksop. By the time of the Coronation of Queen Elizabeth II, however, the Manor had become part of a limited company which the Duke had established to look after his estates; and the Court of Claims decided that for the purpose of the glove ceremony the possession of the Manor was no longer effective. The office of handing the glove to the Queen was therefore entrusted to the Chancellor of the Duchy of Lancaster. (Earl of Woolton, *Memoirs*, p. 383.)

Archbishop held the book down for me to read, but horror of horrors his thumb covered the words of the Oath.

My Lord Great Chamberlain was supposed to dress me but I found his hands fumbled so I had to fix the belt of the sword myself. As it was he nearly put the hilt of the sword under my chin trying to attach it to the belt ... The supreme moment came when the Archbishop [his hands trembling, so Tom Driberg noticed, and his pince-nez, secured by broad black tape, slipping down his nose] placed the St Edward's Crown on my head. I had taken every precaution as I thought to see that the Crown was put on the right way round, but the Dean and the Archbishop had been juggling with it so much [looking for the missing line of red cotton] that I never did know whether it was right or not ... As I turned after leaving the Coronation Chair I was brought up all standing, owing to one of the bishops treading on my robe. I had to tell him to get off it pretty sharply as I nearly fell down.*

By the time of their coronation the King and Queen had left 145, Piccadilly, but they kept on the Royal Lodge as well as Sandringham and Balmoral after they had taken over Buckingham Palace and Windsor Castle. In March 1937 they gave a large party at Buckingham Palace which satisfied much curiosity about the new style of the Court. In knee-breeches and silk stockings, one of these guests, Harold Nicolson, arrived punctually at twenty past eight to find Lord David Cecil and Stanley Baldwin talking to each other as they waited for their respective wives. 'I then go upstairs,' Nicolson wrote in his diary, 'a little alarmed by the fact that upon each fourth step stands a footman

* The coronation of Queen Elizabeth II was a marvellously dignified and well-ordered ceremony, thanks largely to the many rehearsals, calm competence of the Archbishop of Canterbury, Geoffrey Fisher, and the organizational skills of the Earl Marshal, the sixteenth Duke of Norfolk, a much abler man than either his tortoise-like appearance or drawling, plummy voice suggested. These two principal dignitaries, as the Archbishop said, 'trusted each other completely, and worked together in complete harmony'. (William Purcell, *Fisher of Lambeth*, p. 239.) Neither of them was responsible for the few mishaps that occurred, as for instance, in the manipulation of the long velvet trains of the royal ladies. 'Princess Marie Louise, agonizingly old, but still athletic, is obviously very angry with her fatuous lady-in-waiting for making such a balls-up with her train,' one observer noted. 'The Gloucester boys, too, give their mother a moment or two of anxiety as they tug and mishandle her train. Likewise the attendant of Princess Alexandra is at fault.' (Cecil Beaton, *The Strenuous Years*, p. 143.)

Richard Dimbleby, the commentator for the BBC – which had with great difficulty managed to overcome the deep suspicions of the Household and to gain permission for the coronation to be televised – was horrified by the litter left by the peers when he returned to the Abbey after the ceremony. 'Tiers and tiers of stalls on which the peers had been sitting', Dimbleby recorded, 'were covered with sandwich wrappings, sandwiches, morning newspapers, fruit peel, sweets and even empty miniature bottles.' (Jonathan Dimbleby, *Richard Dimbleby*, p. 240–1.)

The Household's reluctance to allow television cameras into the Abbey was not shared by the Duke of Norfolk, who had not the least objection to his directorial talents being given the widest possible display. It was, however, the personal decision of the Queen that the BBC should be given the facilities they sought. (Earl of Woolton, *Memoirs*, p. 393.) Although it was far less usual for families to have television sets then than it is today, it was estimated by BBC audience research that 56% of the adult population, that is to say 20,400,000 people, watched the programme and a further 32%, 11,700,000 listened to the radio broadcasts. (Philip Ziegler, *Crown and People*, p. 114).

dressed in scarlet and gold epaulettes and powdered about the hair.' In the first drawing-room he found a group of Equerries, Ladies-in-Waiting and various other guests including Lloyd George, the Dukes and Duchesses of Rutland and Buccleuch, Montagu Norman, Governor of the Bank of England and Oliver Stanley, President of the Board of Education.

After that we are all arranged in another drawing-room, and at about 8.45 the King and Queen enter silently and immediately start shaking hands all round. When they have completed this procession ... they start to [walk] towards the dining-room, but the unfortunate thing is that whereas the King knows that the dining-room is due east, Mr Baldwin imagines that it is due west. For one moment they start processing in opposite directions [until] the intervention of the Lord-in-Waiting. We then file in behind ... As we approach the dining-room, the band of the Grenadier Guards, which is in the room beyond, plays 'God Save the King', and there is a moment's uncertainty among the company whether they should continue their slow progress through the drawing-room or should stand at attention.

The dining-room table was 'one mass of gold candelabra and scarlet tulips'; and behind the chairs 'the whole of the Windsor plate' was massed in tiers. The dinner was 'unwisely selected', consisting of soup, fish, quail, ham, chicken, ice and savoury. The wine, 'on the other hand', was 'excellent and the port superb'.

After the meal, the King rose and everyone returned to one of the drawing-rooms where the equerries told the men to leave the ladies and to proceed to a drawing-room beyond for brandy and cigars. Here the King spoke to Lloyd George and Baldwin, while Nicolson discussed with Lord David Cecil the reasons why they had been asked. Cecil said that he had been asked 'as a young member of the British aristocracy'. And Nicolson supposed he had been asked as a rising politician, an explanation by which Cecil was not as convinced as Nicolson 'might have wished'.

Having finished their brandy, the men passed on to the Picture Gallery where they were joined by the ladies. Lady Maureen Stanley 'is at once summoned by the King and occupies most of his attention', Nicolson continued his account:

The Queen then goes the rounds. She wears upon her face a faint smile indicative of how she would have liked her dinner-party were it not for the fact that she was Queen of England. Nothing could exceed the charm or dignity which she displays, and I cannot help feeling what a mess poor Mrs Simpson would have made of such an occasion. It demonstrated to us more than anything else how wholly impossible that marriage would have been. The Queen teases me very charmingly about my pink face and my pink views.

117

Thereafter the Queen drops us a deep curtsey which is answered by all the ladies present. We then go away.

A fortnight or so after this Duff Cooper, and his wife Lady Diana, were invited to a rather less grand dinner at Windsor Castle. On this occasion the men were allowed to wear trousers rather than knee-breeches; but otherwise the arrangements were much the same: dinner was at 8.30 after which the men went through to one drawing-room, the ladies to another. At 10.15 the men reappeared in the ladies' drawing-room and 'soon afterwards the King and Queen ... such a sweet little couple and so fond of one another ... said goodnight to the cringing company and the party broke up'.

I waited for my husband to escort me to bed [Lady Diana told a friend] and waited in vain, and behaved as I behave only on race-courses, tearing round to one and all saying: 'Where's Duff? Have you seen Duff?' and asking in vain. At last I'm down to a butler who replies with an inscrutable face: 'He is with the Queen.' I had the humiliation of being taken to my rooms through the mazes of the Castle by a red-liveried man. I'm pleased of course ... but I cannot bear to be missing anything ... 12.15 Duff's not back yet. It will be high treason and the block. Through dinner they had what I thought was an inferior make of loud gramophone playing airs from 'Our Miss Gibbs' and 'The Bing Boys', but from seeing a red-uniformed band playing after dinner I suppose it was them muffled.

I'm to be down with the staff at 9 to-morrow, and then to make the Castle tour with Dick Molyneux. My admiration and love for the Queen did not stop me talking ... Still Duff is in the Queen's bower ... He came back at 12.30. One hour so-called drinking tea with the Queen. She put her feet on a sofa and talked of Kingship and the 'intolerable honour' ... Shan't write any more. Too tired. Duff so happy, me rather piqued.

Shortly after the coronation, Stanley Baldwin retired from the office of Prime Minister as he had told the King he wished to do. The King was very sorry to see him go; but his relations with his successor, Neville Chamberlain, were always extremely friendly. Chamberlain was a man of integrity and principle, self-confident, obstinate and vain. One of his most passionate admirers, 'Chips' Channon, thought him 'the shrewd-est Prime Minister of modern times'. He was 'nuts about him', 'in love with him', Channon confessed. He was 'the Man of our Age'. Other estimates were less flattering. When Harold Nicolson was asked if Chamberlain's mind had broadened recently, he replied, 'Yes, in the same way that a darning-needle is broader than a sewing-needle.' But of Chamberlain's great talents and administrative gifts there could be no doubt. Although he was forty-nine before he entered the House of Commons as Conservative Member for the Ladywood division of Birmingham – a city in whose government he had greatly distinguished

22 The Throne Room at Buckingham Palace *c.* 1914.

23 King George V with his Private Secretary, Lord Stamfordham, at work in the garden of Buckingham Palace during World War I.

24 The King and the Prince of Wales with Lloyd George at Victoria Station, 1919.

25 King George v and his Equerry taking an early morning ride in Hyde Park, 1934.

26 George v and Queen Mary leaving Westminster Abbey after the distribution of Maundy money on 24 March 1932. This was the first time for more than two hundred years that a King of England had personally distributed the money.

27 The Prince of Wales on the bridge of the ss *Empress of Australia*, 1927. Mr and Mrs Baldwin are standing on his right.

28 King Edward VIII on a visit to Pentrebach Training Centre on his tour of the distressed areas in South Wales, 1936.

29 King Edward VIII and Mrs Simpson, drawn by Etienne Drian.

30 Sir Alexander Hardinge, Private Secretary to George V, Edward VIII and George VI, and Extra Equerry to Elizabeth II until 1960.

31 Sir Henry 'Chips' Channon.

32 The Coronation of King George VI in Westminster Abbey, 12 May 1937.

33 King George VI and Queen Elizabeth leaving St George's Chapel, Windsor, after the Order of the Garter service, 1937.

34 King George VI holds an investiture in the desert during his visit to the Desert Air Forces. Air Marshal Francis Linnell is being knighted.

35 King George VI meets Churchill on his return from his North African tour, June 1943.

36 King George VI and Queen Elizabeth chatting to workmen demolishing bombed buildings.

37 'I'm glad we've been bombed, too,' was Queen Elizabeth's comment when Buckingham Palace had a direct hit, 'I can now look the East End in the face.'

38 King George VI and Queen Elizabeth on their silver wedding anniversary, 1948.

39 King George VI at his desk with Princess Elizabeth.

40 King George VI with his corgi dog, shortly before his death.

himself – Chamberlain was immediately recognized as a man of outstanding ability. He was soon given office; and within five years was appointed Chancellor of the Exchequer. When Baldwin resigned there was no one on his side of the House who could rival his claim to the premiership.

The King found him congenial, always ready to discuss his problems with him and most punctilious in keeping him informed of the Government's business and intentions. When, however, Anthony Eden was about to resign as Foreign Secretary in protest against the Cabinet's policy of appeasement towards Fascist Italy, it was in a newspaper rather than in an official communication that the King first read the news. He, therefore, instructed Major Hardinge – who had been confirmed in his appointment as Private Secretary and knighted – to make a strong protest.

His Majesty feels, with, in my humble opinion much justification [Sir Alexander Hardinge accordingly wrote to Sir Maurice Hankey, Secretary of the Cabinet], that he should not have been left to learn from an unreliable Press of the difficult situation in which his Government was placed as the result of the Cabinet Meeting on Saturday night. I feel sure you will agree that some arrangement should be devised to enable the King to receive immediate intimation of any serious development of this nature, and I would welcome the opportunity of discussing the matter with you.

After the consultations which then took place it was agreed that in the future the Secretary of the Cabinet should be responsible for reminding the Prime Minister that it was his duty to inform the King of any threatening crisis; and, if, for any reason, the Prime Minister could not get into touch with the King immediately, the Secretary of the Cabinet should be free to communicate with the King's Private Secretary on his behalf. It was further arranged, at the King's own instigation, that a draft copy of the Cabinet minutes should be sent to him at the same time as it was sent to the Prime Minister so that His Majesty would always be enabled to fulfil his constitutional duty with full and up to date knowledge of his Government's dilemmas.

The King had never found Eden easy to talk to, and was not really sorry to see him go. Eden claimed in his memoirs that when he went to deliver up his seals of office at Buckingham Palace, in accordance with custom he first went into the Private Secretary's room where Hardinge said to him, 'As part of my duty I have read every telegram and all the minutes in connection with this difference between you and the Prime Minister and I should like to tell you that in my judgement you are right at all points.' Eden confessed to having been 'astonished and gratified' by these remarks.

He then went for his audience with the King who, so Eden said, expressed 'sympathy with my point of view' and added that he did not think 'it would be long before he saw me again'. But whatever he may have said to Eden, the King was certainly very pleased that his place was being taken by Lord Halifax with whom he felt far more at ease and whose views on foreign policy, akin to those of Chamberlain, he shared.

The King strongly supported the 'courage and wisdom' of Chamberlain's decision to fly to Germany in September in 1938 in an effort to avoid war by an interview with Hitler at Berchtesgaden. And on the morning of Chamberlain's departure he asked Lord Halifax if he thought a personal letter from himself to Hitler, as from 'one ex-serviceman to another', would help the Government to keep the peace. Halifax was not enthusiastic, but promised to refer the matter to the Prime Minister on his return. Chamberlain, however, was no more taken with the idea than Halifax had been; and, though the King repeated his offer more than once, he was finally dissuaded from writing when the Prime Minister suggested that he would probably receive an insulting reply. And by the time of Chamberlain's return from his second visit to Germany such a letter was in any case no longer necessary as peace seemed assured. The King sent for Chamberlain to come to Buckingham Palace so that he could express personally his 'most heartfelt congratulations' on the success of his visit to Munich 'to one who by his patience and determination [had] earned the lasting gratitude of his fellow countrymen throughout the Empire'.

Convinced that Chamberlain's policy was right, the King felt wholly out of sympathy with those who protested that peace had been bought at too high a price and that Czechoslovakia had been forced to make unfair sacrifices for the sake of the rest of Europe. When Duff Cooper felt compelled to resign as First Lord of the Admiralty the King was 'frank and charming', but said that, while he 'respected those who had the courage of their convictions', he could not agree with him.

He continued to be a warm advocate of Chamberlain's policy and upon learning that the Prime Minister was preparing to leave with Halifax for an interview in Rome with Mussolini, he suggested writing the kind of letter to King Victor Emmanuel that he had proposed writing to Hitler. Again, however, he was advised against such a course; and although he later returned to the idea and wrote a letter, it was decided that it would be unwise to send it.

The letter was written after war had been declared on Germany, at the time of the disastrous campaign in Norway where the small British force which was landed to help the Norwegians was ignominiously re-embarked within three weeks. This, the first major setback of the Second World War, led to renewed and violent attacks on Chamberlain's Government, not only by the Opposition, but also by various members of his own Conservative Party, including Leopold Amery whose dramatic use of Cromwell's words to the Long Parliament rang round the House: 'You have sat here too long for any good you have been doing. Depart, I say, and let us have done with you. In the name of God, go!'

The King was deeply shocked by these attacks. And when Chamberlain came to see him and – with that characteristic stubbornness which even his most faithful admirers found it difficult now to regard as determination – assured the King that he did not intend to resign, His Majesty encouraged him not to do so. He told him that he 'did not like the way in which, with all the worries & responsibilities he had to bear in the conduct of the war, he was always subject to a stab in the back from both the H[ouse] of C[ommons] and the Press'. 'It is most unfair on Chamberlain to be treated like this after all his good work,' the King wrote later. 'The Conservative rebels like Duff Cooper ought to be ashamed of themselves for deserting him at this moment.' He offered to speak to Clement Attlee, the Leader of the Labour Party, and to urge him to 'realize that they must pull their weight and join' a national coalition government.

A coalition government with himself as leader is what Chamberlain wanted and endeavoured to bring into existence. But the Labour Party would not entertain the idea; and when on 10 May 1940 the German army attacked the Low Countries and France, those few Conservatives who up till then had supported him in his resolve to remain in office no longer felt able to do so. So, in the late afternoon of 10 May the Prime Minister went to Buckingham Palace to offer his resignation.

The King accepted it with the utmost regret, told him 'how grossly unfairly' he thought he had been treated and that he was 'terribly sorry that all this controversy had happened'. Turning to the subject of Chamberlain's successor, he said that 'of course' he would like Lord Halifax. So would have many Conservatives; so, indeed, would have several Labour Party leaders, although others preferred Amery. But as Chamberlain said, while Halifax would have been his choice, too, there were strong objections to having a Prime Minister in the House of Lords. The King proposed that his peerage could be 'placed in abeyance for the time being'. But this was not a proposition that recommended itself either to Chamberlain or to other members of his Party; and upon the King's asking him whom then should he send for, the Prime Minister replied that Winston Churchill was the man.

It was not a name that appealed to the King who associated Churchill with the opposition both to Baldwin at the time of the abdication crisis and to Chamberlain over the policy of appeasement. He sent for him with evident reluctance.

It was a reluctance, however, which he was too tactful to display and which, in any case, Churchill in the excitement of his triumph would not perhaps have noticed. 'His Majesty received me most graciously and bade me sit down,' Churchill recorded in his history of the war. 'He looked at me searchingly and quizzically for some moments, and then said, "I suppose you don't know why I have sent for you?" Adopting this mood, I replied, "Sir, I simply cannot imagine why." He laughed and said, "I want to ask you to form a Government." I said I would certainly do so.' Churchill was, the King commented, 'full of fire and determination to carry out his duties'.

Despite his evident friendliness, the King was not for the moment reconciled to the prospect of the new premiership. 'I cannot yet think of Winston as P.M.,' he wrote in his diary the next day. 'I met Halifax . . . I told him I was sorry not to have him as P.M.'

The King's attitude to Churchill soon changed, however. The Prime Minister's emotional regard for the crown, and the flattering attention which he always paid to His Majesty's opinions, won the King over. The distrust which he had previously felt for him was transformed into a deep respect; and the power of Churchill's personality which the King had once found rather overwhelming no longer intimidated him. Within a few months the formal weekly audiences at five o'clock were replaced by intimate lunches at which they would help themselves from dishes on a side-table. At the end of the year the King was convinced that he could not have had a better Prime Minister. And when, at the time of the fall of Singapore, Churchill was harshly criticized for the fatal mistakes that had been made, the King was as resentful of the attacks as he had ever been of those upon Chamberlain. 'I do wish people would get on with the job', he wrote, 'and not criticize all the time, but in a free country this has to be put up with.' He was not blind to Churchill's faults. He recognized that he liked getting 'his own way with no interference from anybody'. Yet the King was infinitely appreciative of Churchill's gifts and unfailingly grateful for the way in which the great man took him into his confidence at those weekly lunches which, as he told him, he enjoyed immensely and to which he looked forward 'so much', paying him 'the singular compliment', so one of the King's equerries said, 'of himself coming to the door and waiting at the top of a short flight of stairs to receive him'. 'Ever since he became my Prime Minister', the King wrote to his mother at the beginning of 1943, 'I have studied the way in which his brain works. He tells me, more than people imagine, of his future plans & ideas & only airs them when the time is ripe to his colleagues & the Chiefs of Staff.'

The respect and affection which he felt for Churchill, the Prime Minister felt also for the King. He wrote:

122

During the four and a half years that our Tuesday lunches continued I became aware of the extraordinary diligence with which the King read all the telegrams and public documents submitted to him. Under the British constitutional system the Sovereign has a right to be made acquainted with everything for which his Ministers are responsible, and has an unlimited right of giving counsel to his Government. I was most careful that everything should be laid before the King, and at our weekly meetings he frequently showed that he had mastered papers which I had not yet dealt with. It was a great help to Britain to have so good a King and Queen in those fearful years, and as a convinced upholder of constitutional monarchy I valued as a signal honour the gracious intimacy with which I, as first Minister, was treated, for which I suppose there has been no precedent since the days of Queen Anne and Marlborough during his years of power.

Happy as was his relationship with Churchill, the King was only too conscious of the fact that, in comparison with the Prime Minister, he could do but little to help in the waging of war. Occasionally, as head of state, he could write an inspiring or cautionary letter or grant what it was hoped would be a flattering and memorable audience. He wrote, for instance, a 'personal note' to his 'brother Sovereign' King Boris of Bulgaria, a monarch whom he knew and liked, sympathizing with him and the 'brave people' over whom he ruled in their 'particularly difficult and delicate position' and encouraging him to stand firm in his neutrality. It was a letter which, followed by another similar communication a year later, was believed to have had some influence over the Bulgarian King who was certainly much moved by it.

King George wrote also to President Lebrun, appealing to him not to allow his government to send the French fleet to North African ports where it would be in danger of falling into hostile hands. He addressed an equally fruitless message of goodwill to Marshal Pétain after the fall of France, declaring that the inevitable British victory over Germany would carry with it the restoration of the freedom and greatness of the Marshal's country and expressing the confidence that there would be no dishonourable collaboration with the Nazis. And after consultation with his Ministers, he wrote long, personal letters to Prince Paul of Yugoslavia and to King George of Greece.

If these letters achieved little or nothing, it was generally agreed that an audience granted to the Turkish General Mehmet Kazim Orbay was of far more significance. Orbay had come to London after the initialling of a treaty of alliance which provided for his country being supplied with various armaments by Britain. But the sorry stock of supplies for Britain's own forces had made it impossible for the General to be offered much more than some generous hospitality, 'in fact,' as it was said, 'cutlets instead of cannon'. He was naturally much displeased and seemed about to go home in a huff when he was summoned to an audience with the King. He had expected this, as he said himself, to be a brief formality. Instead he stayed for nearly half an hour while the King, understanding and sympathetic, gave him a full explanation of why, since the British themselves needed nearly all the guns and aircraft that were available, the commitment to Turkey could not at the moment be fulfilled. This private audience with the King created 'a tremendous impression' on the General, Hardinge was assured by General Ismay, Chief of Staff to the Ministry of Defence. The treaty with Turkey was signed eight days later.

It was with the President and Ambassador of the United States of America, however, that the King's usefulness as a diplomatist was most appreciated. The King and Queen had met President and Mrs Roosevelt on a visit to America before the war when they had been to dinner in the President's country house in Hyde Park, New York. They had spent the day in New York City where they had received a tumultuous reception; and they arrived at Hyde Park in the late afternoon to be greeted by the President with a tray of cocktails. 'My mother', he said, 'thinks you should have a cup of tea. She doesn't approve of cocktails.' 'Neither does my mother,' replied the King, thankfully helping himself.

The dinner party did not proceed as smoothly and pleasantly as these opening exchanges. The prospect of witnessing the King and Queen being waited upon by the President's black servants from the White House had so horrified Sara Roosevelt's English butler that he had chosen to go off on holiday. During the meal there was a thunderous crash as a side-table collapsed, scattering plates and dishes on the floor; and after that there was another fearful clatter as a black butler tripped on the steps leading down into the library and came skidding into the room on his bottom, scattering bottles, decanters, jugs, glasses and ice-cubes all over the floor.

Afterwards, though, when the men were alone, there were no further interruptions; and the President and the King had a long and friendly talk. The King was captivated by Roosevelt's charm. 'He is so easy to get to know, & never makes one shy,' he wrote later. He was 'as good a listener as a talker', and made the King feel 'exactly as though a father' were giving him 'his most careful and wise advice'. 'He had never met a person with whom he felt freer in talking and whom he enjoyed more.'

The King could not say the same for the American Ambassador, Joseph Kennedy, whose defeatism, when war came, both distressed and irritated him. After one meeting with Kennedy during which the Ambassador spoke dismally of ultimate disaster, the King, after consulting the Prime Minister, took it upon himself to send him a rather sharp letter, written, so he said, 'in a very friendly spirit' as he had 'a tremendous admiration' for America and President Roosevelt, but making it quite plain that the Ambassador's gloomy prognostications were unreasonable and unhelpful. The King was accordingly much relieved when he heard that Kennedy – convinced that Britain was doomed and America's only hope lay in isolationism – had resigned, and that he was to be succeeded as Ambassador at the Court of St James's by John G. Winant.

Within a few months of Kennedy's resignation, the British Ambassador to the United States, Lord Lothian, a Christian Scientist who declined medical help, died in Washington of uraemia. Churchill wished to appoint Lloyd George, Britain's 'foremost citizen', his successor; but Lloyd George felt that at seventy-seven he 'ought not to undertake so exacting a task'. So Churchill turned to Lord Halifax instead. Halifax also was reluctant to go; and the King's help had to be enlisted in order to persuade him. His Majesty urged Halifax to believe that the post of 'Ambassador in the USA was more important than the post of Foreign Secretary' in London. Halifax was not convinced that he was the right man for the appointment; but in the face of pressure from the Prime Minister and the King he submitted. He crossed the Atlantic in the battleship *King George V* and in January 1941 arrived in Chesapeake Bay where the President welcomed him in person. The King 'deeply appreciated' this gesture, he told Roosevelt; and when, a fortnight later, Winant came by train from London to Windsor, the King returned the compliment by going to the station to meet him, 'the first time in the history of Great Britain', so Winant recorded, 'that a King had gone to meet an Ambassador'.

Soon afterwards 'Chips' Channon, his fellow-American, asked Winant to dinner and found him fascinating. 'With his ebony locks,' Channon wrote in his diary, 'his farouche charm, his Abraham Lincoln ways and inarticulate sincerity, he completely seduced us all . . . He had a curious elegance of his own . . . and his fine, sad eyes bewitched people.' Harold Nicolson also found him 'one of the most charming men' he had ever met. He had 'emphatic eyes and an unemphatic voice'. But he was embarrassingly shy, given to twisting his hands together and making 'a series of coy platitudes'. 'Yet somehow the superb character of the man' pierced 'through his ungainly charm, and made one realize that he was a real if inarticulate force'.

The King naturally found this inarticulacy which, according to Channon, 'only a lot of whisky' could conquer, rather unnerving. Both Winant and his wife really were 'very silent people'. Nevertheless, the King assured Roosevelt that he had 'some good talks' with him, that he and 'his charming wife' had made 'first rate contacts', and that everyone was delighted with the President's choice.

Throughout the war the King maintained a friendly and informal correspondence with the President, discussing with him methods of meeting the problems which would inevitably face the world when the war came to a close – a subject about which he felt very strongly – and backing Churchill's appeals for American aid.

Thank you so much for your personal letter of May 1st [runs one characteristic message, written before America had entered the war]. The Queen and I often think of the delightful days which we spent with you and Mrs Roosevelt ... Since you wrote your letter, the British Empire has had to face a series of disasters for which it has been little to blame. But the spirit here is magnificent, and the people of these islands ... are inspired by the thought that it is their own soil which they now have to defend against an invader. Their resolution and their confidence are supreme.

As you know, we are in urgent need of some of your old destroyers to tide us over the next few months. I well understand your difficulties, and I am certain that you will do your best to procure them for us before it is too late. Now that we have been deprived of the assistance of the French fleet ... the need is becoming greater every day if we are to carry on our solitary fight for freedom to a successful conclusion.

Although he appreciated the President's replies to his letters, the King was rather annoyed that he had to wait so long for them. Victor Cazalet, granted an audience with the King on his return from America in the summer of 1941, reported to Lord Halifax the gist of their conversation:

I told him how much you had said the President enjoyed getting his letter to which the King answered in a loud voice, 'Oh, so he's got it, has he?' I then said you had told me about it and that the President was full of it, etc., laying it on perhaps a little thick but you know how it is with royalty! To which he said, 'Oh, it is about five weeks since I wrote it and I have had no acknowledgement yet.' The Queen chipped in here and said, 'I also wrote to Mrs R[oosevelt] and I have never had an answer.' The King then said the last letter I wrote to him got lost somehow in the diplomatic bag and never reached him at all! ... I felt so sorry for them sitting down and writing long letters to the President and Mrs R. and never even getting them acknowledged – I do think it is quite funny.

In 1942 Eleanor Roosevelt came to England. 'I wish much that I could accompany her,' the President wrote to the King, 'for there are a thousand things I want to tell you and talk with you about. I want you and the Queen to tell Eleanor everything in regard to problems of our troops in England which she might not get from the Government or military authorities.'

Mrs Roosevelt stayed at Buckingham Palace which she found extremely uncomfortable. She was given the Queen's own bedroom,

the window panes of which had been replaced by small wooden case-
ments with mica panels. It was a huge room whose single small electric
heater was no match for the cold and chilly air. The food served on the
gold and silver plates was the kind of frugal fare to which English people
had by then grown accustomed and which, as the Minister of Food,
Lord Woolton, observed, would have deeply shocked the King's grandfather. Nor was the company in which she dined on her first night very
lively. Both the King and Queen were about to catch colds; and the
Prime Minister was silent and withdrawn, waiting anxiously for news
from North Africa where the 8th Army had opened their attack on the
German lines at El Alamein that morning. After watching Noël
Coward's resolute performance as captain of a doomed destroyer in the
film *In Which We Serve*, which was shown after dinner, Churchill could
bear the suspense no longer and went to telephone 10 Downing Street
for news of the battle. He came back lustily singing 'Roll Out the
Barrel'.

The King had long wanted to go out to see the troops in North Africa
himself. But since the beginning of the war his Ministers had considered
it one of his principal duties to move about his own country as much as
he could, visiting servicemen and encouraging the people, doing his
best to show them that he shared their dangers and that, as he assured
them in the broadcasts which he found it such an ordeal to make each
Christmas, he had an unwavering confidence in ultimate victory.

Indefatigably he travelled to bombed cities as soon after the air raids
as could be arranged. He went all over London; he went to Birmingham
and Bristol, Southampton and Coventry. 'I was horrified at the sight [of
Coventry],' he wrote in his diary. 'I talked to members of the emergency
committee who were quite dazed by what they had been through ... I
walked among the devastation ... The people in the streets wondered
where they were, nothing could be recognized ... I talked to many
people. I think they liked my coming to see them in their adversity.'
Although some did not know he had been and others were openly
indifferent to his coming, these visits were well worthwhile.

Lord Dudley, Regional Commissioner for Civil Defence for the Midlands, was quite convinced that the people were deeply grateful that the
King had been to see their devastated city and to commiserate with the
survivors. 'His visit has had a wonderful effect,' Dudley told Hardinge.
'It fired the imagination & determination of the people to an unbeliev-
able extent. It was certainly very moving to see their faces light up as
they recognized him & we are all more grateful than we can say for his
coming down there.'

'I feel that this kind of visit does do good at such a moment,' the King
recorded in his diary after a visit to another bombed city. 'And it is one

of my main jobs in life to help others when I can be useful to them.' Churchill agreed with him. 'This war', he assured the King, 'has drawn the Throne and the people more closely together than was ever before recorded, and Your Majesties are more beloved by all classes than any of the princes of the past.'

Often the Queen also went to cities which had suffered in air raids. In January 1941 she went to Sheffield where she was taken round the city by Lord Harlech, the North-Eastern Regional Commissioner for Civil Defence, who afterwards told Harold Nicolson:

When the car stops, the Queen nips out into the snow and goes straight into the middle of the crowd and starts talking to them. For a moment or two they just gaze and gape in astonishment. But then they all start talking at once. 'Hi! Your Majesty! Look here!' She has that quality of making everyone feel that they and they alone are being spoken to ... a truly miraculous faculty of making each [person] feel that it is him whom she has greeted and to him that was devoted that lovely smile ... It is, I think, because she has very large eyes which she opens very wide and turns straight upon one. Billy Harlech says these visits do incalculable good.

It had been suggested at the beginning of the war that their two daughters should be sent to Canada for their safety. But their mother had explained why that was quite impossible: 'The children won't leave without me; I won't leave without the King; and the King will never leave.' 'I should die if I had to leave,' she told Harold Nicolson, whom she met at a luncheon given by Mrs Arthur James. 'She also told me', Nicolson reported to his wife, 'that she is being instructed every morning how to fire a revolver. I expressed surprise. "Yes," she said. "I shall not go down like the others." I cannot tell you how superb she was. I anticipated her charm. What astonished me is how the King is changed. He is now like his brother. He was so gay and she so calm. They did me all the good in the world ... *We shall win*. I know that.'*

Early one morning a bomb which had fallen the night before on the north side of Buckingham Palace exploded beneath the King's study, shattering the windows. And three days later, while the King was talking to Hardinge in his sitting-room, six more bombs fell on the palace, two in the forecourt, two in the quadrangle, one on the chapel and the other in the garden. Hearing the resounding crashes, the King and Hardinge looked at each other and 'were out into the passage as fast as [they] could get there'. The King recalled:

* While the Queen learned how to fire a revolver, the King practised rifle shooting in the grounds of Buckingham Palace. Lord Halifax, who, while still at the Foreign Office, had been given permission to walk there from his house in Eaton Square through the palace grounds, wished he knew the times when this practice took place! (Earl Birkenhead, *Halifax*, p. 216.)

We all wondered why we weren't dead. Two great craters had appeared in the courtyard ... The fire hydrant had burst and water was pouring through the broken windows in the passage ... The Chapel is wrecked ... E[lizabeth] and I went all round the basement talking to the servants who were all safe, & quite calm through it all ... There is no doubt it was a direct attack on Buckingham Palace ... It was a ghastly experience & I don't want it to be repeated. It certainly teaches one to 'take cover' on all future occasions, but one must be careful not to become 'dugout minded'.

Although, as his father had once confided in Lady Airlie, the King had 'more guts than the rest of his brothers put together', he was badly shaken. But he was not sorry that the attack had been made. It had helped him, so he thought, to find a new bond with the people now that his own home had been bombed like theirs, for he was quite aware that up till then many survivors of the raids were resentful that he had a grand palace to be driven away to while their own circumstances were so very different. The Queen was emphatic. 'I'm glad we've been bombed,' she said. 'It makes me feel I can look the East End in the face.'

The King's long-held ambition to extend his visits to the troops overseas seemed likely at last to be realized when, on 31 March 1943, the War Cabinet, with whom he dined that evening, approved his suggestion that he should go out to North Africa. For months he had been following events there with the closest attention. The year before, when Harold Macmillan had been appointed Minister Resident at Allied Headquarters in North West Africa, the King had received him before his departure. Macmillan wrote of this interview:

Although I had some acquaintance with the King, it was the first time I had been received as a Minister. In the last day or two I had done my best to find out something about the situation in Algiers and had enjoyed the advantage of an hour's talk with the Deputy Head of the Foreign Office, Sir Orme Sargent, and had read through a large file of telegrams. But when I talked with the King I had my first experience of the extraordinary diligence and accuracy with which successive occupants of the throne make it their task to study all the details of the manifold problems which it is their duty to master.

Travelling incognito as 'General Lyon', the King left for the Mediterranean by air – though he still hated flying – on 11 June accompanied by Hardinge; the Honourable Sir Piers Legh, one of his equerries and Master of the Household; and Wing Commander Edward Fielden, Captain of the King's Flight, an organization created by King Edward VIII.

It had been intended that the aircraft should land on the way in Malta. But thick fog prevented this; and when the Queen heard that the landing had not been possible and the aeroplane was flying straight on to Algiers, she paced up and down her room, 'staring at the telephone' and imagining 'every sort of horror' until news arrived that the aircraft had at last touched down. She subsequently learned that the King had been driven away to a house taken over from a French wine merchant in which – as in all French houses, so he maintained – 'the plumbing was defective & erratic'.

During the next fortnight, manfully enduring an attack of enteritis as well as badly sunburned knees and arms, the King discussed the military situation with Generals Alexander, Montgomery and Wilson. He talked to General Eisenhower with whom, Macmillan noted, he was 'very good'; had luncheon with Generals Giraud and de Gaulle; and drove past thousands upon thousands of soldiers, a group of whom crowded round him, singing 'For he's a jolly good fellow'. He was evidently much more confident and much more at his ease than he had been during his visit to the British Expeditionary Force in 1939 when Victor Cazalet had written, 'he is hard to talk to and there were long periods of silence'. At his own insistence the King sailed home by way of Malta, to which, in commemoration of the Maltese people's brave endurance of heavy bombing and the threat of starvation, he had awarded the George Cross, the decoration he had himself devised as an award for outstanding bravery available to civilians as well as servicemen. And as he sailed up the Grand Harbour in Valetta, standing at the salute in his white naval uniform with the sun streaming down on the deck of the cruiser *Aurora* which had brought him there through a rough sea, he confessed to feeling proud and moved almost to tears. 'I had made up my mind that I would take a risk to get to Malta & I had got there by sea,' he wrote. 'Mussolini had called the Mediterranean sea his Italian Lake a short time ago ... Every bastion & every view point [was] lined with people who cheered as we entered.'

Admiral Cunningham, Commander-in-Chief Mediterranean, who was also aboard the *Aurora*, had never heard such cheering. He had witnessed 'many memorable spectacles, but this was the most impressive of them all ... Men, women and children were wild with enthusiasm ... and all the bells in the many churches started ringing when [the King] landed.' Macmillan was equally moved and impressed. 'As we steamed into the Grand Harbour, a slow passage lasting at least three quarters of an hour,' he wrote, 'all the cliffs and forts, filled with troops, sailors, airmen and civilians, thundered out a tremendous welcome. It was really a most moving ... a memorable sight.'

As the King drove through the city and the inland villages, the cheering never ceased. People threw flowers into his car, covering his uniform with pollen and dust. 'You have made the people of Malta very happy today, Sir,' the Lieutenant-Governor told him. He replied that the happiest person on the island that day was himself.

The success of his visit to the Mediterranean encouraged the King to suggest that he should go abroad again as soon as the invasion of Western Europe began. He had not been in favour of this operation. After discussions in October 1943 with the persuasive General Smuts, Prime Minister of South Africa, he was convinced that the planned invasion of France, already known as 'Operation Overlord', was a potentially disastrous mistake and that Churchill's original strategy of striking at 'the under belly of the Axis' ought to be reconsidered. 'We are now in Italy,' he wrote. 'Italy has surrendered to us ... We are masters of the Mediterranean ... S[muts] feels we must ... land in Greece & in Yugoslavia across the Adriatic, thus liberating those 2 countries, which in turn may make Roumania and even Hungary give in. Turkey may come in on our side as well ... I agree with S[muts] about all this ... Why start another front across the Channel? ... The Russians do not want us in the Balkans. They would like to see us fighting in France, so as to have a free hand in the east of Europe.'

For the first time in the war the King felt that he must exercise his constitutional prerogative to warn the Prime Minister on a matter of supreme strategic importance. He accordingly wrote to Churchill to say he was so impressed by what Smuts had said 'that he would like them both to join him for dinner so that they could talk these things over undisturbed'. Churchill accepted the invitation; but he had long since decided that 'Operation Overlord' must go on and was likely to be successful. Having made his protest, the King, as pliable in Churchill's hands as he had been impressionable when confronted by the equally powerful personality of Smuts, concurred; and he was soon making plans to accompany the invasion force himself. He told the Queen about this 'idea & she was wonderful as always & encouraged [him] to do it'. He also told Churchill when he came to the palace for one of his weekly luncheons. Churchill, who had himself 'hoped to see the initial attack from one of the bombarding ships', 'reacted well'. But Sir Alan Lascelles, who had been the King's Private Secretary since July 1943 when Hardinge was obliged to retire due to ill health, was horrified by the suggestion.

He asked the King to consider what an appalling responsibility he would be imposing upon the captain of the ship in which he sailed, and if he had considered the necessity of advising Princess Elizabeth on the choice of a Prime Minister in the event of both her father and Mr Churchill being killed. The King was persuaded that Lascelles was right. He wrote to Churchill to tell him that he had 'come to the conclusion that it would not be right for [either of them] to be where [they had] planned on D Day'. 'We should both I know love to be there,' he added, 'but in all seriousness I would ask you to reconsider your plan ... The right thing to do is what normally falls to those at the top on such occasions, namely, to remain at home and wait. I hope very much that you will see it in this light too. The anxiety of these coming days would be very greatly increased for me if I thought that, in addition to everything else, there was a risk, however remote, of my losing your help and guidance.'

But this letter had no effect on the Prime Minister's determination to sail with one of the bombarding cruisers. Nor had the arguments of Admiral Ramsay, the Naval Commander-in-Chief, with whom Churchill and the King, accompanied by Lascelles, discussed the plan the next afternoon. As the Prime Minister repeated that he had quite made up his mind to be there, Lascelles's normally impassive features betrayed irritation and concern.

'Your face is getting longer and longer,' the King said to him.

'I was thinking, Sir,' he replied, 'that it is not going to make things easier for you if you have to find a new Prime Minister in the middle of "Overlord".'

'Oh, that's all arranged for,' Churchill interposed. 'And, anyway, I don't think the risk is 100–1.' He added that he had already flown to America, the Middle East, Moscow and Teheran and had crossed the Atlantic by sea. The King then protested that these visits were necessary for the future strategy of the war, while this proposal of his was more in the nature of a 'joy ride' and a quite unnecessary risk for one holding his important position. But Churchill remained adamant; and the King returned to the palace 'very worried over the P.M.'s seemingly selfish way of looking at the matter'.

General Ismay, who was equally concerned, asked the King to write another letter imploring the Prime Minister not to go. The King immediately did so, urging Churchill 'most earnestly to consider the whole question again' and not to let his personal wishes, which were entirely understandable, lead him to depart from his own high standard of duty to the State. 'Please consider my own position,' the King urged him. 'I am a younger man than you, I am a sailor, & as King I am the head of all three services. There is nothing I would like better than to go to sea but I have agreed to stop at home; is it fair that you should then do exactly what I should have liked to do myself?'

To this letter there was no immediate reply. And when the King heard that the Prime Minister had left for General Eisenhower's headquarters near Portsmouth he telephoned Lascelles to tell him that he intended to follow Churchill by car so as personally to prevent him carrying out his hazardous intention. Lascelles in turn telephoned the train in which the Prime Minister had travelled to Portsmouth, and was infinitely relieved to be told that, as Churchill subsequently wrote, he 'felt obliged to defer to his Majesty's wishes & indeed commands'. 'It is a great comfort to me to know', the Prime Minister's letter, which began rather haughtily, concluded, 'that [these commands] arise from Your Majesty's desire to continue me in your service. Though I regret that I cannot go, I am deeply grateful to Your Majesty for the motives which have guided Your Majesty in respect of Your Majesty's humble and devoted Servant and Subject, Winston Churchill.'

After the war the King was quite confident that Churchill would win the general election. So the Labour Party's victory came, as he himself admitted, as 'a great surprise to him'. It also surprised the Party's leader, Clement Attlee, who received his summons to the palace while having tea with his family at the Great Western Hotel in Paddington.

At first the King and Attlee did not get on very well together. It was not that the King made it obvious to the new Prime Minister that the defeat of Churchill had come as a shock and disappointment to him; on the contrary he was as determined to get on as well with his Labour Ministers as his father had got on with those in MacDonald's Government. But both he and Attlee were innately shy and they found communication difficult. The early audiences were marked by long silences.

Gradually, however, this constraint was overcome and the two men began to have what the King described as 'long talks' together. 'You will find that your position will be greatly strengthened,' his cousin, Lord Mountbatten, had told the King soon after the result of the general election was known, 'since you are now the old experienced campaigner on whom a new and partly inexperienced Government will lean for advice and guidance.' This proved to be the case; and during the coming months there were to be several occasions upon which the King exercised his constitutional right to advise and warn his Ministers about their proposed socialist policies, of many of which he disapproved. As his biographer, Sir John Wheeler-Bennett, has said, he was aware that in his talks with them 'he was not infrequently successful in presenting arguments which caused them to reconsider decisions at which they had already arrived'.

At Attlee's first audience, so the King recorded, 'I asked him whom he would make Foreign Secy. & he suggested Dr Hugh Dalton. I disagreed with him & said that Foreign Affairs was the most important subject at the moment & I hoped he would make Mr Bevin take it. He said he would . . .'

Attlee, in his 'somewhat preoccupied state of mind', afterwards said that he did not remember this part of his conversation with the King and that after his audience he still thought it best to send Dalton to the Foreign Office and Bevin, who wanted himself to be Chancellor rather than Foreign Secretary, to the Treasury. Indeed, on returning from the palace, he told Dalton that this was 'almost certainly' what he intended to do. Later on that day, however, he changed his mind, partly because he thought it best not to have Bevin and Herbert Morrison, who was to be Lord President of the Council, and who did not get on with Bevin, 'together on the home front', and partly because he considered that the Russians could be better dealt with by 'a heavy tank rather than a sniper'.

The King liked Bevin. He was also on good terms with Morrison who said to Harold Nicolson in 1949, 'I am a monarchist. Your old boy [George V] was a good King, and so is this one. We may consider ourselves damned lucky.' The King also, to his surprise, found Aneurin Bevan quite congenial and 'easy to talk to', despite his tiresome refusal to wear proper clothes. But there were others whom the King found 'rather difficult' to communicate with. And this combined with the tensions and exertions of being a scrupulously conscientious monarch, determined to keep a watchful eye on all the departments of Government as well as on those of his own Household, had already worn him out by the time Churchill returned to power in 1951.*

The King did not then have long to live. He had recovered so well from an operation performed at Buckingham Palace in 1949 that in Ascot Week the following year, when 'Chips' Channon saw him at a cocktail party at Coppins, the Duchess of Kent's country house, both he and the Queen were in sparkling mood:

The Queen was still in her Ascot frock of white with pearls and rubies, but the King had changed into a blue suit ... She was round-faced and smiled her world-famous smile and smelt, to use her favourite word, 'delicious' ... The King in a rollicking mood – after several glasses of champagne – put his finger to my cheek – and asked how I managed to look so young at my age ... I was full of admiration for their easy informality ... Ascot this year was highly enjoyable, and obviously the King, who now dotes on society and parties, adored it. He looks much younger than the Duke of Windsor.

Less than two years later, however, the King was obliged to undergo another operation, this time for the removal of his left lung; and

* The King might have found his duties less exhausting had he felt able to entrust his Private Secretaries with keeping a written record of his audiences with his Ministers. His father always sent for Lord Stamfordham 'after he had seen a Minister and told him exactly what had happened', Sir Alan Lascelles told Sir Harold Nicolson. 'Stamfordham then went off and wrote it down & sent his memo to the King for his approval. The present King just says to Tommy, "Oh, he was optimistic as usual" or "he was worried about the coal situation" and never goes into any detail.' He took it upon himself to keep the written record in his own hand. (Harold Nicolson, *Diaries*, 1945–62, p. 204.)

although only fifty-five, he thereafter looked old and drawn and tired. His increasingly scrupulous, not to say obsessive, regard for detail and for the particularities of life continued to make his work far more exhausting than it need have been, and often caused him to fly into a rage at some trifling annoyance. His anger, like his father's, soon cooled, but his servants dreaded arousing it and having to be confronted by the highly-strung King, his voice raised in anger and the muscles twitching in his cheek.

His entourage and relations learned to be as careful as his grand-father's had had to be in the wearing of dress and decorations, for his eye was quite as sharp and his knowledge quite as profound as King Edward VII's. Nothing escaped him: once when attending a gillies' ball at Balmoral he sent for the pipe-major immediately on entering the room. Could he not see anything wrong with the kilt of one of the pipers? the King asked him. The pipe-major could not. 'Why the pleats are pressed the wrong way round,' said the King. 'I noticed it as soon as I came into the ballroom.'

Sharp on occasions with his servants, he was often caustic, too, with guests to whom he did not take or with 'clever-sticks' who, he felt, were putting on airs, a failing he found difficult to tolerate. His comments to such people were likely to take the form of a sort of disdainful, sarcastic cantankerousness. For his enduring belief in his own inferiority never completely left him; and his continuing nervousness in the presence of strangers now tended sometimes to be masked by an almost aggressively domineering manner wholly alien to his true nature. 'His natural shyness and an inferiority complex ... made him on the defensive,' 'Chips' Channon, who claimed to 'know him fairly well at different times', wrote in a rather waspish characterization. 'He had no wit, no learning, no humour, except of a rather schoolboy brand. He was nervous, ill at ease, though slightly better after some champagne.* He had no vices and few interests other than shooting. He had few friends and was almost entirely dependent on the Queen whom he adored: she was his will-power, his all. He was an affectionate father and a loyal friend to the few people he liked.'

Lord Halifax, who knew him better, paid the King a less grudging tribute: 'Few people were endowed with judgement more wise or more

* The King's penchant for champagne was well known. When he was Duke of York, Lady Astor invited him and the Duchess to dinner in St James's Square. She told her friend, James Stuart, who sometimes acted as host when her husband could not be there, that she intended to serve no alcoholic drinks. Stuart, who had formerly been aide-de-camp to the Duke, was one of the few people who ever stood up to the formidable Christian Scientist teetotaller. 'In his languid, low voice he replied in some such words as these: "Well, if I'm to act as host, I only do so on one condition that there's champagne for the Duchess – and me – at my end of the table, and I strongly advise you to have some at your end for the Duke. That is, if you ever want to have them again."' Champagne was served at the dinner. (Christopher Sykes, *Nancy: The Life of Lady Astor*, p. 286.)

penetrating than his, rooted in simple and assured standards and frequently salted with humour uninhibited and robust.'

The illnesses of the King's later years and his worry over the political and economic crisis of the country were made much easier for him to bear, not only by the lasting devotion of his wife, but also by the knowledge that he would be succeeded by a daughter who, he knew, would not betray her trust and who had found a husband he liked and admired to help her in her work.

Neither he nor her mother had at first encouraged the marriage. 'We both think she is too young for that now, as she had never met any young men of her own age,' he told Queen Mary. 'I like Philip. He is intelligent, has a good sense of humour & thinks about things in the right way ... [But] we are going to [say] that P. had better not think any more about it for the moment.' When it became clear, however, that Princess Elizabeth's love for Prince Philip was far from a passing fancy for the first attractive and eligible young man she had ever been able to meet, the King gave his consent.

On her honeymoon he sent her a loving letter which touched her to the heart:

I was so proud of you & thrilled at having you so close to me on our long walk in Westminster Abbey, but when I handed your hand to the Archbishop I felt that I had lost something very precious. You were so calm & composed during the Service & said your words with such conviction, that I knew everything was all right.

I am so glad that you wrote & told Mummy that you think the long wait before your engagement & the long time before the wedding was for the best. I was rather afraid that you had thought I was being hard hearted about it. Our family, us four, the 'Royal Family' must remain together with additions of course at suitable moments!! I have watched you grow up all these years with pride under the skilful direction of Mummy, who as you know is the most marvellous person in the world in my eyes, & I can, I know, always count on you, & now Philip, to help us in our work. Your leaving us has left a great blank in our lives but do remember that your old home is still yours & do come back to it as much & as often as possible. I can see that you are sublimely happy with Philip which is right but don't forget us is the wish of

Your ever loving & devoted

Papa

Part 2

Queen
Elizabeth II

7 The Queen and her Ministers

On learning that King George VI had died in his sleep at Sandringham, Winston Churchill, a man much given to weeping, sat up in bed gazing at the wall of his room, tears in his eyes, scarcely able to speak. 'I really did love him,' he said.* He was also distressed by the prospect of having to deal with the new Queen, a girl of twenty-five. He did not know her very well; he doubted that he would be able to establish the same kind of relationship he had enjoyed with her father. 'His advice was so good', he said, 'and I could always count on [it] in times of difficulty. She is only a child.' When telephoning the Foreign Secretary to break the news of the King's death, he began the conversation by saying to Eden, 'Imagine what is the worst thing that could happen to us.'

He asked Eden, as well as Lord Woolton, Lord President of the Council, and the Leader of the Opposition, Clement Attlee, to go to the airport with him to meet the Queen on her return from Africa. And Eden recalled years later how moved he had been by 'the sight of that young figure in black coming through the door of the aircraft, standing there poised for a second before descending the gangway to the duties which lay before her'.

Churchill's own deeply romantic attachment to the monarchy led him to treat the new Queen with an almost extravagant devotion and respect. It was some time before he felt at ease with her, before he realized how much trouble she took to keep herself well informed and to make it possible for him to talk to her not only about racing and other interests they shared in common, but also about politics and affairs of state. The weekly audiences, for which he always donned a frock-coat, were short at first but grew more lengthy and unconstrained. He set great store by them, returning from her presence 'overflowing with her praises'. 'What have the British people done to deserve her?' he once asked Lord Chandos who thought he was 'completely captivated' by

* Clement Attlee, Churchill's successor as King George VI's Prime Minister, at this time Leader of the Opposition, was equally distressed. 'Only once did I ever see Attlee emotionally affected in public,' Michael Foot has written. When aroused from sleep in San Francisco in May 1945 to be told that the war with Germany was over, Attlee 'just got back into bed. He was cool even when he spoke of Ernest Bevin whom he clearly loved. But when he spoke of George VI's death tears were in his eyes and voice.' (Michael Foot, *Aneurin Bevan: A Biography*, II, p. 349.)

her. He delighted in the letters she wrote to him. 'All in her own hand,' he would say with that profound satisfaction and in the same proud tones in which he had announced the receipt of holograph letters from her father. Frequently he looked at the photograph of her he kept in his bedroom and at other photographs which caught his eye in the newspapers; and he would exclaim: 'Lovely, inspiring. All the film people in the world, if they had scoured the globe, could not have found anyone so suited to the part . . . Lovely! She's a pet. I fear they may ask her to do too much. She is doing so well . . . The country is so lucky.' Once having seen a photograph of her receiving some Italian film actresses, he pronounced proudly: 'She knocks 'em all sideways. Lovely she is!'* The pleasure Churchill took in being her Prime Minister was, as he himself admitted, yet another reason why, though he often talked of retirement, he did not want to resign.

By the early 1950s however, it was obvious that he could not possibly carry on much longer. He had had a stroke while staying with Lord Beaverbrook in 1948, and had subsequently suffered from two arterial spasms. Both his doctors and his Cabinet colleagues were aware that for most of the time he was quite incapable of carrying out the arduous duties expected of a Prime Minister. His physician, Lord Moran, went to see Lord Salisbury, Lord President of the Council and Leader of the House of Lords, to ask if his patient's tasks might be lightened. But Lord Salisbury said bluntly, 'A Prime Minister cannot shed his responsibilities.' It was then suggested that Churchill might, while remaining Prime Minister, be persuaded to go to the House of Lords where he would find life much easier than in the Commons. But there was only one person who could persuade him to do this, Moran thought, and that was the Queen. Churchill's Joint Principal Private Secretary, John Colville, who was devoted to his master and who had been called into

* The other Ministers in Churchill's Cabinet were almost as taken with the young Queen and as ready to praise her as was the Prime Minister himself. 'A few people fulfil their responsibilities with success,' wrote Lord Chandos, then Colonial Secretary, 'it is not obsequious to say that the Queen discharges hers as nearly to perfection as a mortal can.' (Viscount Chandos, *Memoirs*, p. 425.) Lord Kilmuir, Home Secretary at the beginning of the Queen's reign, later Lord Chancellor, wrote glowingly of her receptions of the Privileged Bodies – the representatives of various institutions such as the Corporation of the City of London, the Bank of England, and Oxford and Cambridge Universities – who have a traditional right to be received separately at the beginning of each reign, but whom Edward VIII carelessly and deeply offended by receiving together and addressing one reply to them all. The Queen, in characteristic contrast, received all twenty delegations on their own: and 'there was something breathtaking,' Lord Kilmuir thought, 'in seeing the young figure of Her Majesty greet the successive waves of mostly aged men. More affecting even than the public function was an episode when I arrived [as Minister in Attendance] a quarter of an hour before it started. Lord Clarendon, who was then Lord Chamberlain, beckoned me to a window overlooking the garden of Buckingham Palace. There was the Queen in yellow shirt and jodhpurs, kneeling on the grass and calling a dog to come to her. Within a quarter of an hour she had changed and was a sovereign receiving her subjects.' (Earl of Kilmuir, *Political Adventure*, p. 200.)

these discussions, said that there was just one person he would like to consult before any definite overtures were made – the Queen's Private Secretary, Sir Alan Lascelles.

'Yes,' Salisbury agreed, 'he might help, and he's as close as the grave.'

When Moran and Colville went to the palace, however, Lascelles did not think that anything would come of an approach by the Queen. 'If she said her part,' he predicted, '[Churchill] would say charmingly, "It's very good of you, Ma'am, to think of it" – and then he would very politely brush it aside. The King might have done it,' he added thoughtfully, 'but he is gone.'

So nothing was done at that time; and Churchill carried on as Prime Minister in the House of Commons. His condition deteriorated, though; and he agreed to resign in April 1955, making way at last for the man who had been recognized as his successor for more than a decade, Anthony Eden. Had Churchill died at the time of his second arterial spasm in June 1953, as Lord Moran had considered probable, it would have been necessary to appoint a temporary Prime Minister, since Eden was also ill. Fortunately in 1955 the Queen was spared this unwelcome duty, for Eden was by then fit enough to take over immediately. No two men, as Churchill himself remarked, have ever changed guard more smoothly. At his final audience he did not, however, mention Eden's name to the Queen as his successor. He was not asked for his advice and was careful, therefore, not to offer any. Before leaving office he caused this to be recorded, together with his opinion that no outgoing Prime Minister had a right to volunteer advice unless the sovereign asked for it.

Naturally Churchill wanted to go out of office in fine style. He was offered a dukedom by the Queen who said to him in an amusingly offhand way: 'Would you like a dukedom – or anything like that?' He felt inclined to accept the offer and had already considered being created Duke of London before he was dissuaded from going to the House of Lords with so grandiose a title by his son, Randolph, who would have inherited it. But he did become the first Prime Minister ever to act as host to a reigning monarch at a dinner at 10 Downing Street where he greeted her wearing Court dress with knee-breeches and the riband of the Order of the Garter at a decidedly irregular angle.*
After the dinner, 'in defiance of all precedent', Churchill made a speech proposing the health of the Queen; and the Queen in her 'charming' reply, said that she wished to do something which few of

* Churchill's example of inviting the Queen to dinner at 10 Downing Street was followed by Harold Wilson on the eve of his resignation in March 1976. On this occasion the Prime Minister wore a black tie and the Queen arrived in evening clothes without tiara or decorations.

her predecessors had had an opportunity of doing, and that was to propose the health of her Prime Minister. The next day Eden was summoned to the palace and asked to take over.

When Eden himself was forced to resign less than two years later – after the Anglo-French intervention in Egypt which followed upon Colonel Nasser's seizure of the Suez Canal – the succession was far less smoothly organized. For, at this time, there was no universally recognized successor. While Eden was vainly endeavouring to recuperate his health in Jamaica, R. A. Butler, the Lord Privy Seal and Leader of the House of Commons, acted as his deputy. But Butler's less than enthusiastic support of the Suez operation had aroused much resentment in the Conservative Party; and when Eden came home to eventual resignation, there was a strong feeling in Tory circles, particularly on the right, that a more worthy and more decisive successor would be the Chancellor of the Exchequer, Harold Macmillan, a man eight years older than Butler and one who had, apparently, supported Eden's action against Nasser from the beginning.

Rather than offer the Queen direct advice as to his successor – for which, Macmillan gathered, perhaps mistakenly, that Eden had not been asked – Eden suggested that she should ask Lord Salisbury to consult informally the members of the Cabinet. These were, accordingly, summoned in turn to Salisbury's room in the Privy Council offices where they found him, in the company of Lord Kilmuir, now Lord Chancellor, waiting for their verdict. According to Kilmuir 'practically each one began by saying, "This is like coming to the Headmaster's study." To each Bobbity [Salisbury, who found difficulty in pronouncing his rs] said, "Well, which is it, Wab or Hawold?"'

Most answered Harold. Preference for Macmillan was also expressed not only by the Chairman of the Party and the Chairman of the 1922 Committee, representing most of the Conservative Members in the House of Commons, but also by a majority of those consulted by the Chief Whip. Faced with what Kilmuir described as this 'overwhelming' support for Macmillan, the Queen's advisers were satisfied that she must now send for him. Before doing so, however, she additionally consulted Lord Waverley, Lord Chandos, and Winston Churchill who arrived at the palace in morning dress and a rather shabby top hat. Churchill, as he subsequently told Butler, 'went for the older man', Macmillan. So did Waverley and Chandos.

The subsequent summons to Macmillan, delivered on the telephone by the Queen's Private Secretary, Sir Alan Lascelles's successor, Sir Michael Adeane, found him in the downstairs sitting-room at the Chancellor of the Exchequer's residence, 11 Downing Street, where he had spent the morning re-reading *Pride and Prejudice*. When informed of this fateful summons, his wife, Lady Dorothy Macmillan, her mind preoccupied with the thoughts of one of their grandchildren who was ill, asked rather impatiently, 'What do *they* want?'

The Queen had done all that was constitutionally required of her. But it had not been seen to be done; and the Press, which had almost unanimously supposed that Butler would be the next Prime Minister, were critical of what was mistakenly supposed to be the narrow range of consultations which had led to the choice of Macmillan, the old Etonian son-in-law of a ninth duke, as successor to Eden, the old Etonian son of a seventh baronet. But if this sort of criticism was widespread, it was not nearly so harsh and damaging as when, in 1963, Macmillan was, in turn, succeeded by the old Etonian son of a thirteenth earl.

On this occasion, the outgoing Prime Minister was prepared to offer his advice although, as he later claimed, he would have preferred not to do so. He remembered that Bonar Law had pleaded that he was too ill to be consulted in 1923, and Macmillan 'seriously thought' of following Law's example. On reflection, however, and after it had been intimated 'quite clearly from the Palace that the Queen would ask for advice', he decided that it would be 'a mean evasion' not to give it.

The Queen had been aware for some time that a change was inevitable. The Prime Minister's maladroit handling of a scandal involving a member of his Cabinet, a call-girl, and an official of the Russian Embassy had been followed by an illness which made his resignation not merely advisable but inevitable. As in 1957 there was no obvious successor. Indeed, there were several claimants. The leading candidate was seen by many to be, once more, R. A. Butler who was considered to be – and termed himself – Deputy Prime Minister, though the Queen rightly pointed out that there was no such official post. Butler's principal rival in the House of Commons was Reginald Maudling, whom Macmillan had recently appointed Chancellor of the Exchequer. But it was unfortunate for Maudling that the Prime Minister's resignation coincided with the annual conference of the Conservative Party at Blackpool. For here Maudling made a sadly lack-lustre speech which dispirited his supporters as much as it encouraged his rivals. A far more lively speech was made by the Leader of the House, Iain Macleod, who was always at his best on such occasions, and who, excited by the standing ovation which the delegates had accorded him, brashly said to his friend, Randolph Churchill, 'Keep your eye on the back of the field.'

'You mean looking for a dark horse.'

'That's it.'

'Would the dark horse be called Macleod?'

'That's about it.'

In fact, Macleod, whose term in office as Colonial Secretary had dismayed the right wing of the Party, had little chance of winning sufficient support. In the House of Lords, though, there was a strong candidate in Lord Hailsham, Lord Salisbury's successor as Lord President of the Council, who had proved a brilliant Chairman of the Party and had many influential supporters, including at least four members of the Cabinet, amongst them Macmillan himself. But Hailsham, an impressionable and excitable as well as a highly gifted man, was quite carried away by the wild enthusiasm of his uninhibited champions at Blackpool, and ruined his chances by his susceptibility to their flattery, his evident lack of judgement and discretion. Butler's supporters were, in particular, appalled by his behaviour and were now as violently opposed to his selection as were Hailsham's champions to Butler's.

So, gradually, attention turned to another member of the House of Lords, the Foreign Secretary, the Earl of Home. It was Home, who had first suggested to Macmillan that perhaps the moment had come for the Prime Minister to resign. Macmillan at that time had decided to stay on; but since then he had been forced to change his mind: he had become aware of a strong feeling in the Party, shared by *The Times*, that a change was advisable; also, he believed himself to be more seriously ill than he actually was. Before undergoing his operation he had summoned Home to the hospital where he had pressed him to consider himself as a candidate for the succession. Home had dismissed the idea out of hand; and it was then that Macmillan had seemed to consider Lord Hailsham as the most suitable alternative. So, for the moment, had Home.

Hailsham's undignified antics at Blackpool had, however, transformed the situation. And, one after the other, important members of the Party came to see Home at his hotel and endeavoured to persuade him to offer himself as a candidate. They would not have Hailsham, they all told him. Nor would they have Butler. If Home himself would agree to run for the leadership, he would be rendering a great service to the Party by preventing a feud from which only their opponents could benefit. Home remained reluctant and unconvinced; but he did agree to see his doctor to make sure he was fit enough to undertake the responsibility of the premiership should it be forced upon him. 'The doctor,' so Home put it himself, 'unfortunately said I was fit.'

In the meantime, Macmillan, known to be implacably opposed to Butler's succession, had given instructions for enquiries to be made within the Party so that a firm recommendation could be made to the Queen. Aware that his own choice as Eden's successor, being made by the Cabinet alone, had come in for a good deal of criticism, he decided that the Party as a whole should be consulted. The Cabinet would be asked for their views by the Lord Chancellor; the Conservative Members of the Commons would be consulted by the Chief Whip, Martin Redmayne; the Tory peers by the Chief Whip in the Lords; the Party in the country as a whole by the leaders of the National Union through agents, prospective candidates and Young Conservatives. This was accordingly done.

It was done, though, in a rather tendentious way. According to Macleod, the Whips, as well as several senior back-benchers, worked hard to influence a decision in favour of Home. Many Members who had initially put Home on their lists, but not at or even very near the top, 'were asked if their order of preference would be different if they knew for certain that he would be prepared to renounce his peerage and was a firm candidate who alone could unite the party', a leading question which induced a number of them to alter their list.

So far as the Cabinet were concerned, eleven of the twenty members were, again according to Macleod, in favour of candidates other than Lord Home. But when the Chancellor reported his findings to Macmillan, he said that there was an 'overwhelming' preference in the Party for Home: Lord St Aldwyn reported the same feelings amongst the Tory peers. The results for the country at large, where it was not known for sure that Home was a candidate, showed about sixty per cent in favour of Hailsham and forty per cent for Butler. Macmillan was assured, though, that once it became known that Home was prepared to stand, most people would rally round him. The Prime Minister felt convinced that these various findings were sufficient for his purpose: he was ready to advise the Queen.

In fact, the opposition to Home was far deeper and more widespread than Macmillan liked to suppose. On the evening of Thursday 17 October the telephone at the Foreign Secretary's official residence in Carlton Gardens rang repeatedly. One of the callers was Lord Hailsham who said that he would not be prepared to serve in a government under Home. Macleod and Enoch Powell, the Minister of Health, also declared their unwillingness to accept him as Prime Minister and implied that Maudling and F. J. Erroll, President of the Board of Trade, were also of their opinion.

After their telephone calls to Carlton Gardens, Macleod and Powell, together with Maudling, Erroll and Lord Aldington, the Deputy-Chairman of the Conservative Party Organization, all met at Powell's house in South Eaton Place. It was agreed between them that Butler ought to be Prime Minister. They telephoned Redmayne, the Chief Whip, to tell him so and to assure him that Hailsham supported them.

Informed by Redmayne of what had taken place at Powell's house, Macmillan decided to act immediately. On the morning of Friday 18

October he sent his private secretary to Buckingham Palace with his resignation and telephoned Carlton Gardens to tell Home that he had done so and that he was going to advise the Queen to ask him to form a government. He had heard all about the previous evening's events, he said, and brushed them aside. 'Go ahead,' he added when Home seemed hesitant. 'Get on with it ... Look, we can't change our view now. All the troops are on the starting line. Everything is arranged. It will just cause ghastly confusion if we delay.'

Later that morning the Queen was told that the Prime Minister was ready to see her. She left to consult him at the King Edward VII Hospital for Officers where he had been moved to the boardroom on the ground floor so that she should not be put to the indignity of having to go up in the slow and rickety lift.

A high chair was put ready for her on my right [Macmillan recorded] ... At 11 am ... she came in alone, with a firm step, and those brightly shining eyes which are her chief beauty. She seemed moved; so was I. She referred to the very long time I had served her – nearly seven years – and how sorry she had been to get my letter of resignation. She then asked for my advice as to what she should do. I asked leave to read her a memorandum which I had written yesterday, and brought up to date this morning, after hearing of the so-called 'revolt' of certain Ministers. I said I was not strong enough to trust myself to speak without a text, and I also wanted my written memorandum in the Queen's archives, to be there as a full justification of any action she might take on my advice.

She expressed her gratitude, and said that ... she did not intend to seek any other advice but mine. I then read the memorandum. She agreed that Lord Home was the most likely choice to get ... support, as well as really the best and strongest character. Then what of the revolt? ... I said that I thought speed was important and hoped that she would send for Lord Home immediately – as soon as she got back to the Palace ... She agreed. Before leaving she thanked me again most generously for my thoughtfulness for her over this ... She gave me her hand and left, carrying the memorandum – in an immense envelope – which I could see (as the door opened) she gave to Adeane – which [he being so short a man] made him look ... like the Frog Footman [in Alice in Wonderland].

'One thing I should record,' Macmillan added. 'I advised the Queen, both verbally, and in the second part of the written memorandum, not to appoint Home as Prime Minister at his first audience, but to use the older formula and entrust him with the task of forming an administration. He could then take his soundings and report to her.'

Having returned to the palace, the Queen, acting quite properly, as Macleod himself afterwards admitted, lost no time in sending for Lord Home in accordance with Macmillan's advice. He was a close friend of her mother's family and she felt sure she would be able to get on well with him, as indeed she did: he later compared the audiences he was to have with her as those a friendly headmaster might grant in his study to one of his senior prefects.

Home arrived soon after noon and was asked to form a government. As yet unsure that he could do so, he replied that he would try; and, after lunch, in the Cabinet room at 10 Downing Street, he began a series of interviews with his colleagues. At first Butler, Hailsham and Maudling, as well as Macleod and Powell, all declined to serve under him. But they were unable to agree on a common policy of opposition; and their stand against him soon crumbled. Hailsham, accepting the impossibility of a united opposition, decided that he must accept office under Home for fear lest his refusal was seen as the selfishness of a defeated candidate. Butler followed Hailsham's example the next morning.* Then Maudling gave way, too. Macleod, his own ambitions disappointed and annoyed that, as Chairman of the Party and Leader of the House of Commons, he had not been more closely consulted, stood firm in his refusal, maintaining that Lord Home's upper-class background would be damaging to the Party at the next election and that it was a grave mistake to allow it to be led, for the first time for forty years, from the right of centre. Enoch Powell also remained aloof, telling Home, as Macleod also did, that his social background would make it difficult if not impossible for the Conservative Party to win a general election in the second half of the twentieth century.

Lord Home was, of course, able to form a government without them; and he drove to the palace during the morning of Saturday 19 October to assure the Queen that he was now in a position to take up her commission. But he was uneasily aware that their refusal to join him seriously weakened the Party and he afterwards felt sure that it was responsible for the Conservatives' loss of the election the following year.

The victor in that election, Harold Wilson, arrived at the palace on the afternoon of 16 October 1964 with his wife whom he had asked to go with him, followed by his father and sister in another car. He had been told that he would have to wear a morning coat and striped trousers. But he asked a friend who had driven him about during the election to call at his house in Hampstead Garden Suburb to fetch him a short black coat instead; and in this he appeared. 'It turned out', as he put it, 'that no constitutional issue was raised. Strangely to me and contrary to all I had understood about the procedures,' he added, 'there was no

---

* In a letter to *The Times* Butler subsequently explained his decision, which caused dismay to various of Home's opponents, as being dictated by a fear that had Home failed to form a government the Queen would have had no alternative but to send for Labour. 'I am sure', Sir Harold Wilson has commented, 'this view was ill-founded. The Conservatives still had an overall majority of around ninety and an alternative Conservative leader would almost certainly have been invited to accept the Queen's commission.' (Harold Wilson, *The Governance of Britain*, p. 26.)

formal kissing of hands such as occurs with the appointment of all other senior Ministers. It was taken as read . . . [The Queen] simply asked me if I could form an administration.'* He said he could and did so.

From the first Wilson was impressed by the Queen's firm grasp of affairs, of the contents of the papers that were sent to her, and by her evident determination to ensure that the Prime Minister recognized that she knew what she was talking about, and was, therefore, worth talking to. As others had already found, she was prepared to listen closely to what was said to her. She then asked sensible and sometimes penetrating questions. She obviously enjoyed discussing politics, and was intrigued by the personalities and foibles of individual politicians, the waxing and waning of their reputations and fortunes. She was also, surprisingly it seemed, fascinated by money and the cost of things: many of her questions were directed towards rising prices and inflation.

When Wilson became Prime Minister for the first time she was thirty-eight years old. She had been Queen for nearly thirteen of them. Her confidence had enormously increased. In the past she had sometimes appeared rather unsure of herself with her Prime Ministers, at a loss as how to deal with the ageing Churchill, who was at first inclined to treat her as a granddaughter to be indulged and venerated rather than consulted, or with Eden whose tense evasiveness grew ever more marked as his problems overwhelmed him. Even with Macmillan, who was more anxious to take her into his confidence and, being at his best with young people, was in turn regarded with both affection and respect, there were occasions in the early months when their relationship seemed a little uneasy and strained although, as he says, he was always invited to sit down – which Queen Victoria's Prime Ministers, other than Melbourne and Disraeli, rarely were – and this made conversation easier. In time the slight unease disappeared, and was replaced by an atmosphere of continuous trust and understanding. In the various volumes of his memoirs Macmillan has paid tribute both to the Queen's industriousness and to her sympathetic understanding of her Prime Minister's problems and responsibilities. 'The Queen received me with the greatest kindness and consideration,' he wrote,

---

* It is the senior Ministers who have seals who literally kiss the Queen's hand on appointment, that is to say the Lord High Chancellor, the Chancellor of the Exchequer, the various Secretaries of State, the Lord President of the Council, the Lord Privy Seal and the Chancellor of the Duchy of Lancaster. They, and Privy Councillors who also kiss the Queen's hand when sworn, are told that, as they kneel on the footstool provided, 'the Queen proffers her right hand, palm downwards, with fingers lightly closed, to the person who is to kiss hands. He will extend his right hand, palm upwards, and take the Queen's hand lightly in his and kiss it. His lips should no more than just touch Her Majesty's hand.'

The term 'kissing hands' is, however, also used to denote other audiences with the Queen when the actual ceremony is no longer performed, such as that of a Prime Minister on his appointment and those of Ambassadors, Governors-General and Governors.

recalling his first audience as Prime Minister. 'I remember warning her, half in joke, half in earnest, that I could not answer for the new government lasting more than six weeks.'

'She is astonishingly well informed on every detail,' he recorded in his diary after having submitted the names of his Cabinet Ministers for her approval. 'She particularly liked the decision about the Foreign Office,' where Selwyn Lloyd, who had loyally supported Eden during the Suez crisis, was to remain.

'One of the more agreeable aspects of my new job is the weekly audience,' Macmillan decided a few months later. 'This is usually on Tuesday evenings. The Queen is not only very charming but incredibly well informed. Less agreeable, are visits and letters from the Archbishop of Canterbury [Geoffrey Fisher]. I try to talk to him about religion. But he ... reverts all the time to politics.'

Of the Queen, Macmillan continued to write in the same affectionate and complimentary vein throughout his years as Prime Minister:

The Queen was very sympathetic ... She listened with her usual sympathy and knowledge ... The Queen was very gracious ... Once again when I had my audience on 4 April I was astonished at Her Majesty's grasp of all the details sent over in various messages and telegrams ... I was fortunate in receiving from the Queen the most complete co-operation and confidence, and I look back with gratitude to the many kindnesses which I enjoyed at her hand.

Macmillan's successor, Lord Home, has also written of the pleasure he took in these weekly audiences and of the Queen's understanding and sympathy:

There is one recurring engagement of which it is safe to say that every Prime Minister has the happiest recollections. It is the weekly audience during the Parliamentary session. The Queen, after twenty-five years of her reign, knows almost every Head of State and Leader of Government in foreign countries; while as Head of the Commonwealth she has an intimate knowledge of the leading political personalities and of their ways. Her experience is readily put at the disposal of the Prime Minister and is invaluable to him ... The Queen, as I and my predecessors and successors can readily testify, is always up to date and fully versed in the niceties of every national and international problem.

The matters discussed during these audiences are naturally confidential; and it will be many years before historians can learn anything like as much about the Queen's relations with her Prime Ministers as we know of Queen Victoria's. It is at least clear from Richard Crossman's memoirs that when talking to certain other Ministers she is very sensibly reluctant to express views which might be misinterpreted or indulge in confidences which might be betrayed. 'Over lunch I started

149

to discuss the Philby story, which had dominated all the Sunday papers, and asked whether she had read it,' Crossman wrote of one conversation which she brought to an abrupt halt. 'She said, "No, she didn't read that sort of thing." I was suddenly aware that this was not a subject which we ought to discuss.'

'I saw her wrapping her fingers round each other,' Crossman wrote of another occasion when they were together watching Harold Wilson making his television broadcast about the devaluation of the pound, 'and I too felt more and more uncomfortable because I realized that any comment she made would be political and might itself be a political criticism. Sure enough when it stopped there was a long, long silence and then she said *sotto voce*, "Of course it's extraordinarily difficult to make that kind of speech."'

With her Prime Ministers she can afford to be less guarded. But it is to be doubted that, even with them, she is outspoken or demanding, though it is widely believed that in the winter of 1975 her anxiety lest the United Kingdom might be broken up persuaded the Prime Minister to abandon legislation, proposed for that session, which would have established separate assemblies for Scotland and Wales. As Sir John Colville, who was her Private Secretary before her accession, has written: 'The Queen has had seven Prime Ministers in the United Kingdom alone, and although we may be denied, perhaps for many decades, the knowledge of the extent to which they have been guided by her occasional advice – for it must be doubted if she makes a habit of offering it except when her experience or feminine intuition imperatively prompt her to do so – it is still more doubtful whether any of the seven would doubt that she is wise.' In the penultimate volume of his memoirs Macmillan concluded:

Although as centuries and governments have passed the effective power of the monarch has been considerably reduced, in many ways the royal influence has grown. Apart from the example that the Head of the Royal Family gives to her people, the Queen has a right as well as a duty to be fully informed of all the affairs not only of the United Kingdom but also of all the countries of the Commonwealth, as well as of foreign countries. This duty was always conscientiously performed. All Cabinet papers, all foreign telegrams are sent to her, and carefully studied by her. All the Cabinet's decisions, which under the Cabinet secretarial system are rapidly and accurately circulated, are available to her immediately. All great appointments under the Crown must never be a matter for formal approval ... We are fortunate that these duties, which are always so important, and may well in a critical situation become vital, are scrupulously performed. Moreover, as the years pass, the Queen will necessarily accumulate more political experience and knowledge than most of her advisers. I shall have occasion to recount later in this volume the incident of the Queen's visit to Ghana in 1961 which showed her to be at once courageous and determined.

The visit to Ghana was undertaken at a time when there was violent unrest there occasioned by the authoritarian rule of the President, Kwame Nkrumah. The country was disrupted by strikes and demonstrations and threats had been made against Nkrumah's life. Many of the Queen's advisers and several elder statesmen, including both Churchill and Eden, thought that the visit ought to be cancelled or postponed. 'I have discussed [the problem] with her Majesty,' Macmillan told President Kennedy. 'She is of course a person of great courage and is determined to carry out the visit and to complete the programme unless she is specifically advised by the government that she should not do so.' Her attitude then – like her attitude in 1964 when she was equally determined to go to Canada where extreme French separatists had made threats of assassination – was that it was her duty to go; that danger, as she put it, was 'part of the job'; that if the visit were to be cancelled now, 'Nkrumah might invite Khrushchev instead and they wouldn't like that, would they?'

Macmillan recorded in his diary, after Duncan Sandys, the Commonwealth Secretary, had travelled over the proposed route 'with stately deliberation' in the company of President Nkrumah and it had been decided to go ahead with the tour:

The Queen has been absolutely determined all through. She is grateful for MPs' and Press concern for her safety, but she is impatient of the attitude towards her to treat her as a *woman*, and a film star or mascot. She has indeed 'the heart and stomach of a man'.* She has great faith in the work she can do especially in the Commonwealth.† If she were pressed too hard and if the government and people here are determined to restrict her activities (including taking reasonably acceptable risks) I think she might be tempted to throw in her hand. She does *not* enjoy society. She likes her horses. But she loves her duty and means to be a Queen and not a puppet.

The tour turned out in fact to be a continuous triumph.

After their first wary exchanges the Queen and her fifth Prime Minister, Harold Wilson, also came to like and trust each other. 'He's devoted to the Queen', Crossman recorded in December 1966, 'and is very proud that she likes his visits to her.' Such a rapport proved more difficult to establish with the Queen's sixth Prime Minister, the edgy, reserved and less ingratiating Edward Heath, whose lack of her own

---

* It was Queen Elizabeth I who said to the troops at Tilbury on the approach of the Armada, 'I know I have the body of a weak and feeble woman, but I have the heart and stomach of a king, and of a king of England, too.'

† The Commonwealth now comprises thirty-six sovereign independent states of which nineteen are republics but in all of which she is recognized as the symbolic head.

passionate interest in the Commonwealth more than once distressed her.

Deeply concerned with social problems, as some others of her family are not, less ready to make the assumptions rightly supposed to be common amongst the rich, and well aware how important it is for the monarchy to appear to be above politics, the Queen has proved quite as capable of earning the respect of her Labour Ministers as were her father and grandfather. And in some ways she has been able to help them in their policies. In his account of his years in office from 1964 to 1970, Harold Wilson provided one example of this. It occurred at the time of Winston Churchill's funeral in 1965. Ian Smith, the Prime Minister of Rhodesia, was in London at the time, but was not entitled to an invitation to the reception for world leaders which the Queen planned to hold at Buckingham Palace, as he was not representing a sovereign government. Wilson, anxious to have informal talks with Smith, whose regime was unilaterally to declare itself independent of the United Kingdom later on that year, asked the Queen if he might be invited all the same. An invitation was accordingly issued to Smith; but it elicited no reply. 'After the reception had continued for over an hour,' Wilson recorded, '– by this time it was nearly two o'clock – the Queen commented on the absence of Mr Smith. I could not answer for his whereabouts and she ordered an equerry to seek him out. He was found eating a steak in the restaurant [of the Hyde Park Hotel]. He informed the equerry that he had never received the invitation. I was told later by the High Commission that it was, in fact, in his pocket all the time.' The equerry then conducted Smith to the palace where the Queen received him politely and Wilson was able to have the talk with him he had planned.

It is only in such small ways that the Queen is able to be of practical help to her Ministers. For the monarch in Britain has virtually no effective political power, except in extraordinary circumstances. As Walter Bagehot wrote in 1867 in his famous *The English Constitution*, which King George VI was required to study closely as a young man: 'The sovereign has under a constitutional monarchy such as ours – the right to be consulted, the right to encourage, the right to warn.' In effect, he has the right to give advice, but no right to insist that his advice is followed. Britain, in fact, is, as Bagehot put it, a 'disguised republic' in which the monarchy provides a convenient façade behind which the real business of government can be conducted. Theoretically, the Queen could disband the Army, sell all the Navy's ships and dismiss all the officers of both these services as well as those of the Royal Air Force. She could sacrifice the Isle of Wight or Cornwall as the price of peace, go to war to recapture Calais, pardon every criminal, make every citizen in the United Kingdom (male or female) a peer, and every parish a university. In a word, according to Bagehot, 'the Monarch could by prerogative, upset all the action of civil government, could disgrace the nation by a bad war or peace, and, could, by disbanding our forces, leave us defenceless against foreign nations'. But, in fact, the only occasions when the monarch is now called upon to exercise any authority in political life are in the appointment of Prime Ministers and the dissolution of Parliament. And in both these cases the choices open to her are severely limited. For a long time the leader of the Labour Party has been chosen by election within the Party; and now the Conservatives, too, chastened by the events of October 1963, have also ensured that their leader is elected in a similar way.

Of course, circumstances may arise in which the monarch might be called upon to make a choice irrespective of these internal Party elections. It might, for instance, happen that a Prime Minister finds himself in a minority in the Cabinet. He might, therefore, be forced to resign at a time when a general election was impossible or inadvisable. If this were to happen the monarch could either call upon the leader of the next largest party in the House of Commons; or he could ask the Prime Minister to remain until another Leader had been elected who could then be appointed his successor; or he could select that successor himself; or he could endeavour to bring into existence a coalition. None of these courses would be unconstitutional.

It is generally accepted, however, that once a Prime Minister has been appointed, the monarch would be acting unconstitutionally in dismissing him, except for some such reason as his going mad. Certainly, no Prime Minister has ever been dismissed by his sovereign since Melbourne was required to resign by William IV in 1834. It is also generally accepted that, while the monarch has the right to dissolve Parliament, this right cannot be exercised against the expressed wishes of the Prime Minister. On the other hand, the monarch is not bound to grant a Prime Minister's request for a dissolution.

This right of refusal assumed a more than academic interest in 1974. In the general election of that year, the Labour Party won 301 seats; the Conservatives won 296 seats; the Liberals fourteen; and other parties twenty-four. Although Labour were, therefore, the largest Party in the House of Commons, Edward Heath was still Prime Minister and was constitutionally entitled to remain so until defeated in the House of Commons on a vote on his intended policies as outlined in the Queen's Speech. He could only hope to do so with the help of the minor parties; and since such a coalition proved impossible to arrange, he was obliged to resign. Harold Wilson thus became Prime Minister for the second time. Many of his supporters hoped that he would ask the Queen for a dissolution, sensing that an early second election that year would result in an increased majority. He was careful and skilful enough to give the impression that he was quite confident that he would be granted a dissolution if he asked for one. But the Queen was certainly not bound to give way to him. Politicians were thus made aware that the Crown did enjoy some residual power after all; and there were – and still are – imaginable circumstances in which that power might yet be used for the benefit of the nation as a whole.

It has been said that the true authority of the Crown lies not in its own power but in the power it denies to everyone else. And it is not entirely fanciful to suppose that the day might come when it would be necessary for the Queen, who is the official head of the civil service as well as commander-in-chief of the armed forces, to act in her role as guardian of constitutional legitimacy. A government of the future might conceivably, for instance, as Lord Blake has suggested, repeal the Parliament Act, which provides for the dissolution of every Parliament within five years of its election, thus perpetuating its power. The House of Lords would be entitled to exercise an absolute veto in these circumstances, the only ones in which it can do so. But the government might then demand the creation of sufficient peers to carry its measure. Should such a situation arise the powers of the monarchy would have to be invoked if the resultant constitutional calamity were to be avoided. The Queen could refuse to create the peers; or, if the House of Lords proved submissive to the government, she could revive the royal veto, which has not been used since the reign of Queen Anne, and refuse her assent to the government's Bill; or she could dismiss the Prime Minister, enforce a dissolution of Parliament and bring about a general election. She would have it in her power, in fact, to save the country from totalitarian dictatorship.

8 The Queen at Work

The Queen's daily routine is now well enough established. At about eight o'clock she wakes up in her bedroom on the northern side of Buckingham Palace overlooking Constitution Hill and beyond that Piccadilly. A footman brings up her morning tea which is taken into her bedroom – outside which a uniformed police sergeant has been on duty all night – by her dresser, Margaret MacDonald, known as Bobo, a devoted servant, friend and confidante. The daughter of a Scottish gardener who became a railway worker, Miss MacDonald is an outspoken, forthright and down-to-earth woman who was the Queen's nurserymaid and used always to refer to her proprietorially as 'my little lady'. She is now a highly privileged member of the staff with her own suite at Buckingham Palace where she exercises considerable influence over an often intimidated administration.

The morning's delivery of letters are also brought into the Queen's room, together with a selection of newspapers, including *Sporting Life*, the *Daily Telegraph* – whose main crossword she often attempts and usually finishes – and *The Times*, if that is available, which, when this book was written, it was not. Copies of these and other newspapers are also read in the Palace Press Office where items of particular interest are marked for the attention of the Queen and her Private Secretaries. She reads them carefully, yet as rapidly as she reads everything else; and, according to the late Dermot Morrah, one of the monarchy's most learned, well-informed and skilful apologists, she used to take 'a rather mischievous pleasure in catching out her staff on matters relating to the day's news'. She still is quick to point out any ambiguities or inconsistencies in all the other documents she has to read which offend her sound common sense.

As well as reading the newspapers she listens to the news on the wireless while she is having breakfast, a meal for which Prince Philip joins her when he can, coming in from his own bedroom and providing occasional and characteristically caustic comments on the newsreader's announcements. Breakfast is concluded to the sound of bagpipes which, in continuance of a tradition established in the days of Queen Victoria, are played for a quarter of an hour outside the dining-room windows by the Royal Pipe Major.

After breakfast, the Queen goes to her desk which is decorated with flowers and covered with photographs. Her Private Secretary or the Deputy or Assistant Private Secretary, summoned by dictograph, comes into her room with those letters and documents which are considered to require or merit her personal consideration, having dealt with the immense numbers of others that arrive at the palace every day, invitations, enquiries, compliments, insults, pleas for help, assurances of loyalty, all of which are answered, except those from manifest lunatics, some by the Ladies-in-Waiting, others by the Government department to which they are passed by one of the Secretaries. Occasionally a personal reply is sent on behalf of the Queen rather than by the Government department to which the letter eliciting it would usually be referred. In 1978, for instance, her Private Secretary replied direct to a letter from a woman, the mother of three children, who had sought refuge from a violent husband in a home established for such wives in Chiswick. The mother, who had pleaded that her fellow-refugees and their children living in the overcrowded home should not be evicted as had been threatened, was assured that no evictions would take place, that the Queen was 'most concerned about the plight of battered women' and deplored the dispute between the organizers of the home and the local council. But such letters are not written without previous discussions with the department concerned.*

At the beginning of her reign her Private Secretary, Sir Alan Lascelles, described his appointment as 'not by any means beer and skittles'. Nor is it now, though members of the Royal Household are more generously treated than they were then, their salaries and leave having been placed on a par with those they might expect in the Civil Service.

Sir Alan – who has crossed swords not only with King Edward VIII but also with Princess Margaret's friend, Peter Townsend – was succeeded in 1953 by Lieutenant-Colonel Sir Michael Adeane, a grandson

---

* The Queen does not, however, deny herself the right to make spontaneous and public comments on certain issues when these comments will not embarrass a government department. When a foreign film maker announced his intention of making in England a film about the sex life of Christ, for instance, she let it be known that she found the proposal 'obnoxious'. But such comments by members of the Royal Family may have unwelcome and unexpected repercussions. In the summer of 1978, for example, Prince Charles, in a speech at a Salvation Army Congress, made some incidental and seemingly unexceptionable remarks which received the widest publicity. On the day of the speech his cousin, Prince Michael of Kent, was married in Vienna Town Hall to Baroness von Reibnitz, a Roman Catholic whose previous marriage had been dissolved. Since the Baroness had not undertaken to do her best to ensure that any children of the marriage would be brought up in the Roman Catholic faith, the Pope had refused to grant a dispensation for the church wedding which she and her husband had both wanted. Prince Charles's comments about 'needless distress' being caused by Christians arguing about doctrinal matters were taken by some to be a criticism of the Pope and were strongly condemned as such by the Roman Catholic Archbishop of Glasgow, who spoke of the 'annoyance and anger' caused to 'millions of the Queen's loyal subjects'. The matter became front-page news in the following Sunday's newspapers and the next week filled column after column in the correspondence page of *The Times*.

of Lord Stamfordham. Adeane, whose father was killed in action with the Coldstream Guards in 1914, also served with the Coldstream Guards after gaining a first in history at Cambridge where he had gone from Eton. In 1942 he was appointed to the Joint Staff Mission in Washington and later fought with his regiment in North-Western Europe where he was wounded and mentioned in despatches. An excellent shot and keen fisherman, he is also a talented artist in watercolours. Small, urbane, neat and amusing, he proved himself an ideal Private Secretary, at once reticent, courteous and sociable.

Sir Michael, who became Lord Adeane of Stamfordham on his retirement in 1972, was succeeded by the Honourable Sir Martin Charteris (now Lord Charteris and Provost of Eton) his assistant for the previous twenty years. Three years younger than Adeane, Charteris comes from very much the same kind of background and has the same sort of charm and quiet humour. He also had the same skill in the composition of the Queen's speeches, the occasional jokes and asides in which he would listen to when they were delivered with a kind of disarming satisfaction, smiling or laughing tactfully as though they were Her Majesty's own.

A younger son of Lord Elcho, who, like Adeane's father, was killed in the First World War, and a grandson of the ninth Earl of Wemyss, Charteris, too, was at Eton and reached the rank of Lieutenant-Colonel (in the King's Royal Rifle Corps) in the Second World War. He is married to a daughter of Lord Margesson, a grandson of the sixth Earl of Buckinghamshire, who was a Conservative Chief Whip and Minister of War for a time under Churchill. He is also a good shot and a talented artist, a sculptor. While, during his time as Private Secretary, Lord Adeane belonged to the Guards' Club, Brooks's and the Beefsteak, Charteris was a member of White's and the Travellers', thus making it possible to have between them a wide acquaintanceship with the kinds of people with whom they might be expected to have to deal.

Sir Philip Moore, who succeeded Lord Charteris in 1977, comes from a different kind of family than that '"tweedy" sort' which, so Lord Altrincham had complained twenty years before in the *National and English Review*, had been in the past traditionally called upon to supply the members of the monarch's entourage. Sir Philip, whose father was in the Indian Civil Service, went to Cheltenham and then, as a Classical Exhibitioner, to Brasenose College, Oxford. In 1940, at the age of nineteen, he joined the Royal Air Force and served in Bomber Command, before being taken prisoner in 1942. Returning to Oxford after the war he obtained blues in both rugger and hockey, and played rugger for England six years later. He has also played cricket for Oxfordshire. Before joining the Royal Household he had a distinguished career in the

Civil Service. Principal Private Secretary to the First Lord of the Admiralty from 1957 to 1958, he was British Deputy High Commissioner in Singapore from 1963 to 1965 and Chief of Public Relations at the Ministry of Defence until 1966. He belongs to no clubs other than the Marylebone Cricket Club.

The Deputy Private Secretary is W. F. P. Heseltine, formerly the Queen's Press Secretary, a sturdy, friendly and unassuming Australian, the son of a schoolmaster. He went to Christ Church Grammar School, Claremont, Western Australia and then to the University of Western Australia where he obtained a first in history. For four years he was Private Secretary to the Prime Minister of Australia before becoming the Acting Official Secretary to the Governor-General in 1962. His successor as Press Secretary was Ronald Allison, once a football reporter as well as court correspondent, who was, in 1978 in turn succeeded in the appointment by Michael Shea, a former Deputy Director General of British Information Services in New York, a post in which he helped with the arrangements for the visit of the Queen and the Duke of Edinburgh to New York in 1976 and with the Prince of Wales's tour of the United States in October 1977. Forty years old, the author of political thrillers under the name of Michael Sinclair, he was educated at Gordonstoun, has a Norwegian wife and two daughters.

The Press Secretary has two assistants. One of these is Mrs Michael Wall, an admiral's daughter, who has held the appointment for twenty years; the other is John Dauth, an Australian who is expected to stay until 1980 and then be succeeded by someone else from the Commonwealth, having himself been preceded by two Canadians and two New Zealanders.

The Assistant Private Secretary is Robert Fellowes, son of Sir William Fellowes, the agent at Sandringham for nearly thirty years. In 1977, Robert Fellowes, who was then thirty-six, married Lady Jane Spencer, the twenty-one-year-old daughter of Earl Spencer whose other daughter, Lady Sarah Spencer, had that year been on a ski-ing holiday in the Prince of Wales's party at Klosters.

So, it is either Fellowes or Heseltine or Sir Philip Moore who brings in the Queen's morning work, bowing slightly as they come through the door. She makes such decisions as are required of her, and tells the Secretary how she would like him to reply, leaving the actual wording to him. Letters to friends she writes in her own hand, addressing the envelopes herself and initialling them E R in the corner. These are then delivered by messenger or sent by registered post to avoid giving temptation to an acquisitive Post Office worker.

As well as her correspondence the Queen has to attend to the papers which come to the palace each day from the Ministries in Whitehall.

These arrive in despatch cases covered in red, green or black morocco leather with brass handles at one side, a lock on the other, and the name of the ministry or department of their origin stamped on the front. For security reasons they are no longer transported through the streets in the small horse-drawn maroon carriage which was in use until quite recently, but in Government vans. When Parliament is sitting the Queen also reads *Hansard*, the official verbatim account of proceedings in Parliament, which is supplemented by a report of the previous day's business.

This report used to be prepared by the Leader of the House of Commons, or, in some administrations, by the Prime Minister. But it is now written by the Vice-Chamberlain, a member of the Household who is also a member of the Government and appointed to the post by the Prime Minister. The present Vice-Chamberlain is Anthony Berry, member for Southgate. He prepares his report, about six hundred words long, every evening in the House of Commons library, then it is delivered by messenger to Buckingham Palace or, if the Queen is at Balmoral or Sandringham, transmitted by Telex.

On some mornings the Queen is required to give her royal assent to various Bills which have passed all their stages through both Houses of Parliament. A Commission listing the names of the Bills, and appointing Commissioners who will give the assent in the Queen's name, is prepared by an official known as the Clerk of the Crown in the Lord Chancellor's Office in the House of Lords. When signed by the Queen and sealed in the Lord Chancellor's Office with the Great Seal, it empowers the Commissioners, who are both peers and Privy Councillors, to make known to the Houses of Parliament that the royal assent has been given to the Bills named in it.

Occasionally also there are Privy Council meetings to attend when Orders in Council require the Queen's approval. These Orders in Council, the more important of which have to be laid in draft before Parliament which has the power to annul them, are more flexible and more speedy than Acts of Parliament. They cover a wide variety of matters from grants of independence to former colonies and changes in the constitution of overseas territories to the giving of consent to the marriage of British subjects who are in the direct line of succession to the throne, from legislation connected with diplomatic privilege to the appointment of High Sheriffs.

The names of the High Sheriffs nominated for each county are presented to the Queen by the Clerk of the Privy Council on a long vellum roll wound round a wooden roller and tied with green ribbons. The Clerk unwinds the roll and the Queen pierces the appropriate names with the spike of a brass bodkin, shaped like a doorknob and engraved with the Privy Council Arms, a custom believed to date from the time of Queen Elizabeth I who was presented with the Sheriff's Roll for her approval one day when she was sewing in the garden and, having no pen with which to make the usual dots against the chosen names, pricked them with her needle.

Most of the meetings of the Privy Council take place at Buckingham Palace; but they can be held anywhere the Queen happens to be, not only at Windsor, Balmoral or Sandringham but at a country house, such as Goodwood House or Arundel Castle, where she might be staying, or even on board the royal yacht *Britannia*. The travelling which this entailed much annoyed Richard Crossman who was appointed Minister of Housing in 1964. Crossman was also exasperated by what he considered the 'idiotic flummery' and absurdly archaic manner in which the meetings were conducted, particularly when new Privy Councillors have to be sworn and kiss hands. After he himself had been sworn he came to the conclusion that nothing 'more dull, pretentious, or plain silly [had] ever been invented'. For over an hour he and the other new Ministers were rehearsed in the Privy Council offices, told how to kneel on one knee, how to stand up, 'how to raise the hand with the Bible in it, how to advance three paces towards the Queen, how to take the hand and kiss it, how to move back ten paces without falling over the stools – which had been carefully arranged so that you did fall over them'. During the actual ceremony at Buckingham Palace fortunately no one did fall over. The new Ministers, sixteen of them, 'entered a great drawing-room'. 'At the other end,' Crossman continued, 'there was this little woman with a beautiful waist, and she had to stand with her hand on the table for forty minutes while we went through this rigmarole. We were uneasy, she was uneasy. Then at the end informality broke out and she said, "You all moved backwards very nicely," and we all laughed. And then she pressed a bell and we all left her.'

Although there were no mishaps on this occasion, Sir Godfrey Agnew, the Clerk of the Council, told Crossman of a previous meeting in the time of Sir Edward Bridges which went 'fantastically wrong'. Somehow the Privy Councillors 'got themselves kneeling on the wrong side of the room, facing Sir Edward. He waved them away and they crawled across the room on their hands and knees.' While they were doing so one of them knocked off the table a book which had to be rescued by the Queen 'who looked blackly furious'. After the Councillors had all gone, 'Sir Edward crept back into the room and she said something very pleasant to him. He said how terribly sorry he was and she said, "You know I nearly laughed." Then he realized that when she'd looked terribly angry it was merely because she was trying to stop herself laughing.'

In the case of Jews and Quakers the ceremony which Crossman described has to be modified. When the first Lord Samuel, who became Chancellor of the Duchy of Lancaster in 1909, was sworn in he not only took his oath on the Pentateuch but carried his hat into the King's presence with him and held it over his head as he kissed the book. Joseph Pease, later Lord Gainford, who was appointed Chief Whip by Asquith and sworn of the Privy Council at the same time as Samuel, declined, as a Quaker, to take the usual oath but made affirmation which he read for himself.

When there is no swearing of new Ministers to be done, the meetings of the Privy Council are much simpler. The present practice is for the Queen to receive the Lord President before the Council meets for a few minutes' conversation. The other Privy Councillors, usually three, then join them followed by the Clerk of the Council, Neville Leigh. The meeting generally takes place in the white and gold silk-lined room on the ground floor of Buckingham Palace overlooking the garden beneath the State Apartments, the 1844 Room as it has been called since it was redecorated for the Czar Nicholas I who stayed there in that year. Beneath a portrait of the Czar, the Queen stands beside a small round table. On her right are the Lord President and the other Councillors; on her left the Clerk. The meetings are more relaxed and unstrained than they were in the earlier years of her reign. New Ministers find her perfectly easy and agreeable, all the more so as they get to know her better. Even Richard Crossman was won over in the end, though he found his first conversation with her rather heavy going.

In our ten minutes she talked, [Crossman recorded] as I am told she always does, about her corgis. (Two fat corgis, roughly the same colour as the carpet, were lying at her feet.) She remarked how often people fell over the dogs. I asked what good they were and she said they were Welsh dogs used for rounding up cattle by biting their legs. So we talked about whether cattle stepped on them and I said our Suki, a poodle, was much quicker than a corgi at evading the cows. Then the Queen got on to talking about cows and said how terribly pleased she was when she had entered for the Dairy Show for the first time and won the championship for Jersey cows. Then she talked about Charles at Gordonstoun and whether it was a good school, and remarked that Charles had taken his O-levels young for his age. It was a fairly forced performance.

Not long after this conversation and shortly before Crossman took up his appointment as Lord President of the Council, he dined with Lord Porchester and 'got into one of [his] furious intellectual rows ... about monarchy', dilating 'on the snobbery of the people who love the monarch and the dreary role both of the monarchy and the court'. Thinking about it afterwards he decided that it was not very polite to his host as he knew quite well that Porchester was one of the Queen's most intimate friends – 'maybe the food and drink were too good'. Anyway, growing more heated, he thanked God he was Minister of Housing and did not have to mix with the court. Lord Porchester said: 'The Queen is one of my greatest personal friends, and I am a tremendous admirer.' 'In a way,' Crossman commented, 'that put me in my place but I said, "Well, may be! But she finds me boring and I find her boring and I think it is a great relief I don't have to see her."'

As Lord President of the Council he did have to see her far more often; and on the first occasion upon which he met her in that office, in August 1966, she began the conversation by saying: 'Ah, Lord Porchester was telling me about you.' It was 'very clever of her to mention it straight away,' Crossman had to admit, 'and let it be known Lord Porchester had passed on my remarks – and I found it was perfectly simple and straightforward to get on with her. Indeed, she puts one at ease immediately and we were able to chat about other things fairly happily. George Brown [then Foreign Secretary] took over and was as familiar and cosy with her – "My dear" and such nonsense – as anyone could possibly be.'

At a subsequent Council meeting held at Balmoral, Crossman once again remarked how 'extremely good' the Queen was at 'keeping things going' when the Councillors went for a drink in the drawing-room. He also noticed, 'this time even more than last' how – despite this growing social accomplishment – how shy she could still suddenly become:

I was carrying my papers and she was carrying hers. I put mine down on a side table and she held hers tight in her hand. Somebody tried to take them off her and she said, 'No, I must go and get rid of them.' But she stood there for three minutes without a drink, with the papers in her hand and with nothing to say. If one waits for her to begin a conversation nothing happens. One has to start to talk and then suddenly the conversation falters because both are feeling, 'Oh dear, are we boring each other?' She has a lovely laugh. She laughs with her whole face and she just can't assume a mere smile because she's really a very spontaneous person.

Four months later, after a Privy Council meeting at Sandringham, Crossman left for London feeling that 'it had been a great deal easier'. He supposed 'the truth is that she really likes people she knows and every time you see her she tends to like you better simply because she's got more used to you'.

Crossman was still annoyed, all the same, by the amount of travelling which Ministers were required to undertake in order to attend Privy Council meetings. 'It's striking', he recorded, 'that when the government is at work in London and the Privy Council is called, she doesn't come down from Balmoral to the Palace but the Ministers have to go up to her private home in the north of Scotland.' And once at least, according to Crossman, when 'with great difficulty' he had gathered four Ministers prepared to travel to Balmoral for a Privy Council meeting, he was suddenly told that the Queen had said, 'I'm so sorry. I have a private engagement. It just can't be done.' 'Surely there must be a limit to which busy Ministers are compelled to sacrifice their time to suit private engagements,' Crossman commented. 'This I think is unchivalrous. It's only fair to add, however, that I am pretty certain the Queen herself knows nothing about all this and it's all a matter between endless courtiers.'

Describing a typical meeting which had taken place earlier at Balmoral, Crossman wrote:

As Lord President I had to go and see the Queen first with the papers for the meeting. We chatted for a few minutes, then the others came in and lined up beside me and I read aloud the fifty or sixty titles of the Orders in Council, pausing after every half a dozen for the Queen to say 'Agreed'. When I'd finished in just two and a half minutes, I concluded with the words, 'So the business of the Council is concluded.' The Privy Council is the best example of pure mumbo jumbo you can find. It's interesting to reflect that four Ministers, busy men, all had to take a night and a day off and go up there with Godfrey Agnew to stand for two and a half minutes while the list of titles was read out. It would have been far simpler for the Queen to come down to Buckingham Palace but it's *lèse majesté* to suggest it.

In fact, the Queen was perfectly prepared to revise the procedure for calling a Privy Council meeting; and Sir Michael Adeane later assured Crossman that she wanted 'to use these occasions for getting to know her Ministers' rather than having them, as Crossman said, withdrawing 'after two minutes' strained conversation'.

Crossman thought that there ought to be about six meetings a year 'at which she actually had a discussion with people, with lunch at least', and that all the other meetings should be cut down 'to the merest formality', with the attending members selected from a pool of long-standing Privy Councillors so that busy Ministers need not be bothered unnecessarily. When he put these proposals to the Queen she 'listened very attentively', and he 'became convinced' that 'he could have gone much further'. At the first of these 'new-style Privy Councils' the Queen was 'in tremendous form'. After the formalities were over, Crossman and the four other Ministers present withdrew to the Caernarvon Room where drinks were served. She described a television programme of a wrestling match she had seen the day before:

An all-in wrestler had been thrown out over the ropes, landed on his feet, and after writhing in agony had suddenly shot back into the ring, seized his opponent and forced him to resign. She said what tremendous fun that kind of all-in wrestling was, 'Do you want a Royal Charter for them?' I asked, and she said, 'No, not yet.' It was interesting to hear what a vivid description she gave of the whole scene, writhing herself, twisting and turning, completely relaxed. It was quite an eye-opener to see how she enjoyed it. Afterwards each of the Ministers had a good long talk with her alone before we all slipped off.

When Crossman relinquished the Lord Presidency of the Council on his appointment as Secretary, Department of Health and Social Security, he had 'a little talk with the Queen and she asked where [his office] was going to be'. He said, 'The Elephant and Castle'. 'Oh,' she said, 'what a with-it address.' 'A funny remark, showing how completely out of touch she is,' Crossman observed, 'because of all the places that are not exactly with-it that dreary part of London is the worst, brand new and yet unpopular and unmodish. However perhaps she meant to be nice to me.'* Undoubtedly she made an effort to be nice to Crossman when he came to say goodbye to her after the defeat of the Labour Government in 1970. She thanked him and was 'perfectly decent'. Crossman asked her whether she minded elections. Some time before he had asked Sir Godfrey Agnew 'whether she preferred the Tories to us because they were our social superiors'. And Agnew had said, 'I don't think so. The Queen doesn't make fine distinctions between politicians of different parties. They all roughly belong to the same social category in her view.' Now the Queen herself replied to Crossman's enquiry as to whether she minded elections: 'Yes, it means knowing a lot of new people.' 'I suppose that's it,' Crossman concluded. 'She doesn't make all that difference between Labour and Conservative and, for her, all this simply means that, just when she has begun to know us, she has to meet another terrible lot of politicians.'

Either before or after a Privy Council meeting, the Queen may grant an audience to those various people whom it has been arranged for her to

---

* Perhaps she did. Certainly she was being ironic and making a joke which Crossman failed to understand. It was not a very good joke, as Dame Rebecca West has commented, but it was 'seaworthy'. Crossman's was 'really a double boner', Dame Rebecca continued, 'for he should have known that the Crown owns some interesting property near the Elephant and Castle, and in her administrative capacity the Queen must have had to consider its character'.

Dame Rebecca West knew Crossman quite well. He was at Oxford with her husband and was for some time a neighbour of theirs in the Chilterns. 'We both found him a charming companion and a virtuoso conversationalist and not a selfish one,' she has written. 'He was a wonderful hand at conducting a general conversation and could bring out the best in the shy and the alien. But he had his handicaps. The chief of these was his failure to tell the truth ... It was an idiosyncrasy which raised the problem by what mechanism do we distinguish between our memories and our fantasies? ... He also had no sense of humour.' (*Spectator*, 19 November 1977.)

Not so reliable a witness as Dame Rebecca, the former Privy Councillor and Minister, John Stonehouse, who was sentenced to imprisonment for theft and false pretences in 1976, also considered Crossman incapable of telling the truth. 'He is a shameless liar,' he told Cecil King, 'and when President of the Council he habitually arrived five minutes late for the Council meetings to keep the Queen waiting.' (*The Cecil King Diary, 1970–74*, pp. 89–90.)

see. When the visitor is a representative of a foreign state, the Queen has with her the Foreign Secretary or, more usually, a Minister of State, Parliamentary Under-Secretary of State, or Foreign and Commonwealth Office official; but she sees members of the Commonwealth and British visitors on her own. Sometimes there are as many as seven people to see and to talk to in one day; but usually there are no more than three. They vary from the highly distinguished to the relatively obscure. Some of them, during the audience, may have some honour bestowed upon them. On his reception by the Queen at Buckingham Palace on 16 March 1978 Jack Jones, the trade union leader (Mr James Jones as he was styled in the Court Circular), was 'invested with the Insignia of a Member of the Order of the Companions of Honour'. Sometimes a man is knighted at a private audience. On these occasions he drops to one knee on the investiture stool which has been placed ready in the room, is tapped lightly with a sword as at a public investiture, but is never commanded, 'Rise Sir . . .' After the new knight has risen to his feet the Queen shakes hands with him.

When a High Commissioner or an Ambassador is to receive an audience in order to present his Letters of Credence, Lord Michael Fitzalan Howard, Marshal of the Diplomatic Corps, goes to fetch him in a State landau. Extra landaus, seating four people each, are also despatched from the Royal Mews for senior members of his staff. The Ambassador, wearing diplomatic uniform or evening dress, is taken to the Grand Entrance of Buckingham Palace where he alights to be greeted by the Vice-Marshal of the Diplomatic Corps and the Equerry-in-Waiting.

He walks up the steps and is introduced to the Comptroller of the Lord Chancellor's Office and to the Permanent Under-Secretary at the Foreign and Commonwealth Office. From the Bow Room he is conducted next door into the 1844 Room with the Marshal of the Diplomatic Corps on one side and the Comptroller on the other. The Queen is waiting there for them. They take one pace forward, bow, take another step and bow again. The Marshal of the Diplomatic Corps then announces the Ambassador before withdrawing with the Comptroller.

The Ambassador walks towards the Queen, bows once more, shakes hands and gives Her Majesty his Letters of Credence and the Letters of Recall of his predecessor. After talking to him for a time, usually in English, sometimes in French, the Queen asks him to present his staff, who come into the room one by one, and to introduce his wife who is brought into the room by the Marshal of the Diplomatic Corps and who either curtsys to the Queen or makes some national gesture of salutation. There is a little further conversation; then the Ambassador and his wife walk back to the door where they turn round; he bows and she curtsys or repeats her salutation before leaving.

From time to time the Queen also receives a new bishop of the Church of England who comes to make his homage to her after his consecration. For the Queen is styled supreme Governor of the Church of England and appointments of bishops, like appointments of Lords-Lieutenant of the Counties, are Crown appointments made by the Queen on the recommendation of the Prime Minister. There are members of the Church who feel, as the former Archbishop of Canterbury, Lord Ramsay, did, that it should have firmer control over diocesan appointments.* Yet, if this were so it is possible that certain controversial bishops like Dr Mervyn Stockwood, the Socialist author of *The Cross and the Sickle*, who became Bishop of Southwark in 1959, would not be appointed. 'Chaps like you for instance,' the Duke of Edinburgh said, when discussing this point with Dr Stockwood, 'would never become a bishop.' Besides, nominations to the episcopal bench are often nominations to Parliament, for the Archbishops of Canterbury and York, the Bishops of London, Durham and Winchester, as well as a further twenty-one bishops, who take their place on the basis of seniority of their sees, automatically become members of the House of Lords.

In the Queen's grandfather's time, in accordance with a section of the Bill of Rights of 1689, a monarch was required, before delivering his Speech at the first Opening of Parliament of his reign, to declare himself a Protestant, to repudiate the doctrine of transubstantiation and to proclaim that 'the invocation or adoration of the Virgin Mary, or any other saint, and the Sacrifice of the Mass, as they are now used in the Church of Rome, are superstitious and idolatrous'.

King Edward VII protested at having to use such 'crude language' which he considered an insult to his Roman Catholic subjects. With the approval of the Cabinet he asked that the law should be changed immediately. But it was felt that such a change might lead to unwelcome 'No Popery' agitations; so nothing was done, much to the annoyance of the King who accused the Lord Chancellor, Lord

---

* In an Answer given to Parliament by the Prime Minister in June 1976 it was acknowledged that there was 'some disquiet' in the Church about the system of appointing archbishops and diocesan bishops. In the Prime Minister's view there were 'cogent reasons' why the State could not 'divest itself from a concern with these appointments of the established Church; but he believed there was a case for making some changes in the present arrangements so that the Church should have, and be seen to have, a greater say in the process of choosing its leaders'. It was therefore suggested that a standing committee should be set up by the Church to assess candidates for vacancies. The names of recommended candidates would be submitted by the committee to the Prime Minister who would have the right to ask for further names if he disapproved of those proposed. This committee has been in operation since 1977. In the case of suffragan bishops, the diocesan bishop submits two names to the Prime Minister for recommendation to the Sovereign, one of whom is presented by letters patent for consecration by the archbishop. In practice the first name submitted is always chosen.

Halsbury, of 'bungling incompetence'. And when King George v came to the throne the offensive declaration was still required of him. He refused, however, to open Parliament until a less insulting form of words had been substituted. An Act was therefore passed modifying the language of the declaration so that the Queen at her accession was merely required to 'profess, testify and declare that' she was 'a faithful Protestant' and that she would, 'according to the true intent of the enactments which secure the Protestant succession to the Throne of [her] Realm, uphold and maintain the said enactment to the best of [her] powers according to the law'.*

A new bishop who comes to make his Homage is announced to the Queen by the Master of the Household. He approaches her in his robes, accompanied by the Clerk of the Closet, the Bishop who is head of her Ecclesiastical Household, at present the Bishop of Sheffield. The new bishop kneels before the Queen who is sitting in a chair with the Home Secretary at her side. He places the palms of his hands together as though in prayer. The Queen takes them between her own. The bishop then repeats, after the Home Secretary, the words of the Homage: 'I acknowledge that I hold the said bishopric, as well the spiritualities as the temporalities thereof only of Your Majesty and for these temporalities I presently give my homage to Your Majesty.' Having completed his Homage he kisses the Bible, and then has a conversation with the Queen.

In addition to bishops, the deans of cathedrals, various canons and the incumbents of certain livings are also appointed by the Crown.† For the higher appointments the Queen relies upon the advice given to her by the Prime Minister whose appointments secretary consults the Archbishop of Canterbury and, for appointments in the Northern Province, the Archbishop of York as well. The Prime Minister himself, of course, may very well not be a member of the Church of England or even a Christian. Campbell-Bannerman's parents were Presbyterian; Asquith's father was also a nonconformist; Chamberlain was brought up as a Unitarian, Sir Harold Wilson as a Baptist.

Whatever their faith, Prime Ministers have usually found the

---

* The Queen's consort is not allowed to be a Roman Catholic, but he is not required to be a member of the Church of England. Before his marriage, however, Prince Philip left the Greek Orthodox Church and was received into the Church of England.

† In bestowing Crown livings the Queen is advised by the First Lord of the Treasury who in this century has always been the Prime Minister but need not necessarily be so: Lord Salisbury, in his first and third administrations, was Prime Minister and Foreign Secretary and appointed another member of his Cabinet First Lord of the Treasury. For Crown livings within the Duchy of Lancaster, the Chancellor of the Duchy is responsible for the patronage; for those in the Channel Islands and the Isle of Man, the Home Secretary; for those in the Duchy of Cornwall, the Duke of Cornwall. Although Sandringham is a Crown living and its incumbent is a domestic chaplain to the Queen, it is a parish church not a Chapel Royal.

selection of bishops a tiresome business. When her husband was Prime Minister, Lady Salisbury told Sir Henry Ponsonby: 'I always find that anything to do with the appointing of Bishops has a special power of worrying and tiring him.' And Lord Melbourne declared, 'I believe the Bishops die to vex me.'

Once the selection has been made, however, the process of appointment is quite simple. The Queen, on the advice given to her by the Prime Minister, nominates a candidate whose name, incorporated in a licence known as a *congé d'élire*, is sent to the Dean and Chapter of the Cathedral concerned. The Dean and Chapter then automatically elect him. They are bound to do so for a *congé d'élire* is, in effect, a binding instruction. When someone argued in Samuel Johnson's presence that it had not the force of a command, but may be considered only as a strong recommendation, 'Sir,' replied Johnson, 'it is such a recommendation, as if I should throw you out of a two-pair-of-stairs window, and recommend to you to fall soft.'

In selecting the bishop to be appointed head of the Ecclesiastical Household as Clerk of the Closet, special regard is naturally paid to the monarch's own wishes. The present Clerk, the Right Reverend William Gordon Fallows, was one of the Queen's chaplains from 1953 to 1968. He and his Deputy Clerk have charge of thirty-six chaplains to the Queen and three extra chaplains. Their duties are largely honorary, though they are frequently invited to preach in the Chapels Royal. These chapels have developed from the priests and choirs, their vestments and chalices, which used to accompany the peripatetic households of the early mediaeval kings. When the king's court became more settled they were established as oratories in his palaces. Although commonly referred to as such, not all royal chapels are Chapels Royal. There are Chapels Royal at Hampton Court Palace, at St James's Palace and in the Tower of London, where the Chapel of St John is one of the finest examples of Early Norman architecture in England and the Chapel of St Peter ad Vincula was described by Macaulay as the 'saddest place on earth'. There are other royal chapels at Leeds Castle which was acquired by Queen Eleanor, wife of Edward I, in 1278 and whose chapel was re-hallowed by the Archbishop of Canterbury seven hundred years later; at Buckingham Palace; at Windsor Castle; in Windsor Great Park; and in the Strand. This last, the Queen's Chapel of the Savoy, is the only part to survive of the hospital which Henry VII built on the site of the Savoy Palace, the palace of John of Gaunt, Duke of Lancaster, whose estates were attached to the Crown when his son came to the throne as Henry IV. The Queen claims to hold it as Duke of Lancaster; and the choir sing the National Anthem with the words:

God Save our Gracious Queen,
Long live our Noble Duke,
God Save the Queen.*

On days when other more pressing engagements allow, the Queen may sit for a portrait for an embassy, a high commissioner's office, a service headquarters or some charitable institution under royal patronage. The requests for these portraits are not so numerous as they were, since so many have been supplied over the past twenty-seven years; but they are still received almost as often as are requests for fresh photographs of the Queen, and a painter is often to be seen working at the palace on a new canvas. He is usually given the Yellow Drawing Room or the Balcony Room as a studio where the Queen poses for him with patient co-operation, rarely asking to see the canvas before work on it is finished. Sometimes she seems preoccupied and non-committal but more often she talks easily and always remembers to wear the same jewellery and the same clothes which, with her approval, the artist has usually himself chosen from a selection laid out for him in the Queen's private wardrobe rooms by Miss MacDonald.

'The Yellow Drawing Room is on the extreme left of the palace,' says the painter, Michael Noakes, 'and usually the public cannot see in, but as the Queen had to stand on a dais for the painting [I had been commissioned to do of her] she could look down on the pavement. She kept up a very funny running commentary on people's reactions to seeing her. Mostly they looked up in amazement, decided it was her, then that it couldn't possibly be and ended up not quite sure whether it was or not.'

Terence Cuneo, who has painted her more than twenty times, confirms: She is very vivacious and most amusing. But it can be a bit of a nightmare if you are

---

* It is doubtful that the Queen is, in fact, Duke of Lancaster, although the Court Circular has been known to style her thus. King Edward VII, whose mother had been content to travel incognito as the Countess of Lancaster, used the title of Duke when staying at the Hotel Bristol in Paris, though the then Chancellor of the Duchy of Lancaster, Lord James of Hereford, thought that he had no right to it. In September 1905 a controversy arose in the pages of the *Westminster Gazette* on the subject, and Lord James prepared a letter, a copy of which he sent to the King's Private Secretary. This letter put forward the view that the title properly belonged to the descendants of John of Gaunt and did not go with the Duchy whose lands were vested in the sovereign. On this letter the King scrawled the comment: 'I have always imagined that I was Duke of Lancaster, as the Sovereign of England always is. Queen Victoria considered herself so, just as the heir to the throne is Duke of Cornwall, and I have no wish to give up my rights.' Lord James was prevailed upon to suppress the letter. (Sidney Lee, *Edward VII*, II, pp. 298–9.)

The controversy was renewed in the next reign when King George V asked for his health to be drunk in Lancashire as Duke of Lancaster. Charles Hobhouse, the then Chancellor of the Duchy, consulted the Duchy's Attorney who expressed the view that it was 'extremely unlikely' that His Majesty was also Duke of Lancaster. Hobhouse reported this opinion to the King who gave him 'a *very* cold bow indeed' the next time he saw him. (Edward David, *Inside Asquith's Cabinet: From the Diaries of Charles Hobhouse*, p. 144.)

trying to work. You are longing to pay close attention to what she is saying and all the time you are working against time as you never have as long as you would like ... I don't know how she can be so relaxed. She is also extremely kind. One day I took along a print of my painting of the coronation and asked if she would be kind enough to autograph it for me. I handed her my pen and would this damn pen work! Not on your life. She gave me a smile and said, 'I think I had better get my pen', and she walked to her apartments at the other end of the Palace and came back with a pen to sign it for me.

Other artists who have painted the Queen have also emphasized her humour and naturalness.

She is an extremely amusing person [says Norman Hepple]. Once I was talking about the portraits that had been painted of her and saying that she had not been very lucky with her likenesses. She said, 'One day when I was driving out of the Palace the car stopped just outside the gate and an old lady came up and peered in at me and said' – and she mimicked a cockney voice beautifully – 'She ain't very like her pictures is she.' It amused me that she put it that way round instead of complaining that 'my portraits are not really like me.' ... I was painting her standing in very heavy robes, which is enormously tiring. After she had stood for an hour I said to her, 'Ma'am, wouldn't you like to sit down?' She said, 'No, I am used to standing. I have been standing all my life.' No one else would have put up with it.

'It is obvious she relaxes with painters and talks easily,' Ken Howard observed. He gave this account of a sitting at Buckingham Palace:

She said, 'I love to see the horses coming down the Mall in the afternoon.' I, like a fool, replied, 'Have you many horses, Ma'am?' and she said, 'Yes, Mr Howard. I have quite a few horses – some people would say I had too many horses.' She asked me where I lived and I told her I was converting an old Victorian school on Dartmoor ... She told me she was 'also doing a small conversion'. I asked where and she said, 'Sandringham.' I told her I was adding a couple of bedrooms and she said she was taking ten rooms away.* It was such a homely conversation ... She was so natural it was incredible. We were left completely undisturbed for an hour with no sign of any security.†

---

* He evidently misheard the Queen or has been misquoted. The demolition at Sandringham involved the removal of ninety-one rooms.

† All these artists seemed to have managed better with the Queen than did Augustus John with her mother. John's name had tentatively been suggested as a royal portrait painter for George v in 1925. But Lord Stamfordham, well aware of his reputation, had been horrified by the idea: 'No!' Stamfordham had exclaimed, 'HM wouldn't look at AJ!!' Some years later, however, in 1937, John was asked to paint the new Queen whom he was invited to meet before starting work. But, he was sternly warned, he must arrive at the Palace dead sober. 'For a moment he looked murderous, then, his face clearing, he enquired: "Must I be dead sober when I leave?"'

When the portrait was at last begun 'it struggled on', as John's biographer has written, 'from one crisis to the next', bedevilled by the artist's 'paralysing shyness'. Before the preliminary interview John felt very odd and fancied that he was suffering from influenza, an explanation which appeared in his letter of apology for not arriving at the palace on the appointed day as suffering from the 'influence'. Then there were troubles over the background, the clothes, the

Sitting for portraits, like visits from hairdressers and dressmakers, may not be too demanding, may sometimes be relaxing and pleasurable; but on a busy day it can be irksome. For often the Queen has to return to her desk to attend to some unfinished business. As Sir Michael Adeane testified before a parliamentary committee in 1971:

Nobody who does not carry such a burden of responsibility is in a position to appreciate the strain it imposes. The Queen is never absolutely free to do as she likes in the way that ordinary men and women are, or to take a complete holiday. Her job is continuous and she cannot, like other hard worked people, look forward to a period of retirement at the end of her life ... Every day ... whatever her public or private engagements, the Queen may spend up to two or three hours in reading State papers in order that, as Head of State, she can have a general knowledge of all current problems ... And always at the end of the day there are papers to sign and read and the Queen is never too tired to deal with them.

A member of the committee, Douglas Houghton, a former Chancellor of the Duchy of Lancaster, questioned Adeane on this last point, contending that Ministers were often too tired to deal with their papers at the end of the day and asking whether or not the committee were intended to take this literally. Were there not times when the Queen felt that she had 'to leave work aside'?

'If she does not do [her papers] on Monday she has to do them on Tuesday,' Adeane replied. 'I think it is probably very much the same in the life of a Minister. If there is anything outstanding at the end of the day it goes into a red box and it goes upstairs and in nine cases out of ten when I come in the following morning the box has been done and is sitting on my table. If it is not sitting on my table I know that the Queen will do it after breakfast.'

easel, and the light in the room chosen for the sittings. It was thought that John might be more relaxed if sherry were to be provided for him. So a bottle was brought up, while brandy was placed in the cupboard reserved for his equipment, and the Griller quartet ('unnervingly misheard by John as the Gorilla quartet') was wheeled into the ante-room to soothe him. But, although, as he said, the Queen was 'absolutely angelic in posing so often and with such cheerfulness', he could not get her looking real upon his canvas. And everyone was relieved when Buckingham Palace was bombed in the war and the sitting came to an end. After the war, during which John shut the portrait away, allowing no one to see it, the Queen wrote to ask him if he would consider painting Princess Margaret. 'I could easily bring her to your studio,' she told him, 'and I promise that I won't bring an orchestra with me.' Nothing came of this; but in 1961 the portrait of the Queen Mother, which John had improved with the help of photographs, but which was still unfinished, was bought by a shipping company and presented to her. 'I want to tell you what a tremendous pleasure it gives me to see it once again,' she wrote to him. 'It looks so lovely in my drawing-room, and has cheered it up no end!' (Michael Holroyd, *Augustus John*, II, pp. 101–3.)

9 The Royal Household

Towards the end of the reign of King Henry VIII an Act was passed listing 'the Great Officers of the Realm'. They were the Lord Chancellor, the Lord President of the Council, the Lord Privy Seal, the Lord Great Chamberlain, the Earl Marshal, the Lord High Constable, the Lord Steward of the Household, the Lord Chamberlain and the Master of the Horse. All these officers, whose titles were already ancient in the sixteenth century, still survive today. The first three are now members of the government, the others, with the exception of the Lord Chamberlain, have little other than ceremonial duties to perform. In fact, the Lord High Constable of England, who used to be commander-in-chief of the Army when the King himself was not in the field, holds an office which is now revived only for ceremonial occasions and which exists for only one day. It was last revived for the Queen's coronation when Field Marshal Lord Alanbroke was appointed to the office, and may not be revived again until the next coronation.

The offices of both Earl Marshal and Lord Great Chamberlain – not to be confused with the Lord Chamberlain – are hereditary. The Earl Marshal, formerly the deputy of the Lord High Constable in the armies of the mediaeval kings, is at present the seventeenth Duke of Norfolk, the premier earl and duke of England. His ancestor, the fourth Earl of Norfolk who died in 1270, inherited the office of Marshal from the family of his mother, Matilda Marshal, the daughter of William Marshal, Earl of Pembroke. King Richard confirmed the family's right to the office in 1385 by appointing Thomas Mowbray, the first Duke of Norfolk as Earl Marshal when his army marched against the Scots. A century later in 1483, King Richard III fixed the salary of the Earl Marshal at £20 a year in perpetuity. In 1672, Henry Howard, who succeeded his brother as sixth Duke of Norfolk, was confirmed in office as hereditary Earl Marshal, and his descendants have held the office ever since. On ceremonial occasions, the Earl Marshal always carries a staff with the royal arms in gold at one end and the Duke's arms at the other.

The office of Lord Great Chamberlain was vested in the de Vere Earls of Oxford whose direct male line died out in 1626. The office continued in the female line but was perpetually in dispute, there being at one time five squabbling sisters with apparently equally valid rights to appoint their husbands as their deputies. The wrangling continued until 1902 when the Court of Claims decreed that the office of Lord Great Chamberlain was vested, in alternate reigns, in the family of the Marquess of Cholmondeley. In those reigns when the office was not held by this family it was to be held by the families of the Earl of Ancaster and the Marquess of Lincolnshire. The Marquess of Lincolnshire was Lord Great Chamberlain in the reign of King George v, the fifth Marquess of Cholmondeley in that of King Edward viii, the second and third Earl of Ancaster in that of King George vi, and the sixth Marquess of Cholmondeley therefore holds the office today. In the next reign the Lord Great Chamberlain will be Lord Carrington, descendant of the younger brother of the Marquess of Lincolnshire, whose only son died of wounds in 1915.

The office of Lord Steward of the Household is also now largely a ceremonial one. Theoretically the royal palaces are still under the control of the present Lord Steward, the tenth Duke of Northumberland, descendant of the brilliant soldier and skilful, avaricious administrator, John Dudley, the first Duke, who made his family's fortunes during the reigns of Henry viii and Edward vi. But although the Lord Steward continues to supervise the arrangements for State banquets and various other important ceremonial occasions, in practice the palaces are run by the Master of the Household, Vice-Admiral Sir Peter Ashmore, once Chief of Allied Staff at nato Naval Headquarters, and his Deputy, Lieutenant-Colonel B. A. Stewart-Wilson. The many duties of their department, whose offices are in Buckingham Palace, include responsibility for the Court Post Office, the palace police, security passes and the Court Circular – that daily record of the royal family's public activities which is printed every day in the *Daily Telegraph* – and the administration of the Board of Green Cloth, an ancient institution whose jurisdiction is now confined to the licensing of certain premises within what was known as the Verge of the Court.* The Master of the Household is also responsible for assisting the Lord Chamberlain in organizing official entertainments, for issuing invitations in the Queen's name to most functions at Buckingham Palace –

* The Verge of the Court originally denoted the area comprised within a radius of twelve miles around the sovereign's palaces. It was later limited to the area within twelve miles of Whitehall Palace only. All taverns within the verge of the Palace were subject to the Lord Steward's licence since it was unseemly 'that any brawling, duelling, drunkenness, thieving and so on, should take place in the immediate neighbourhood of The King's person'. The premises still licensed by the Board include three public houses – the Silver Cross, the Old Shades and the Clarence – Crockford's Club, the National Gallery, the Royal Society and Whitehall Court which houses the Authors' Club, the Junior Army and Navy as well as eight other clubs.

except for those to garden parties and the evening receptions of the Diplomatic Corps which are the responsibility of the Lord Chamberlain – as well as for the general supervision of the royal dining-room.

Under his control are the palace steward, the senior member of the domestic staff; the yeoman of the wine cellars; the pages of the backstairs and of the presence; and the chef who prepares alternative menus each day for the approval of the Queen who, not being a devoted gourmet, usually chooses the simpler ones, though occasionally she suggests a dish for a special occasion or crosses out one which she thinks her guests will not enjoy. From time to time she sees the chef to discuss an important meal with him.

From time to time, also, she sees the housekeeper to talk about the possible renewal of linen or upholstery. In fact, the upholstery in the palace – many of whose rooms are far more shabby than those few normally seen by visitors – is renewed infrequently, not only because the Queen does not like to see money spent unnecessarily but also because she finds it both difficult and irksome to spare the time to choose the appropriate materials. The painter, Michael Noakes, has related that, when he was engaged upon a portrait of the Queen in the Yellow Drawing Room at Buckingham Palace one day, almost the first thing she said to him was that 'she really must do something about the curtains'. 'The next time I came', Noakes continued, 'there were a few samples of curtain material lying around. But four years later, when I went back to paint her again, the samples were still there. She had been so busy she hadn't had time to do anything about them.'

The Queen's financial affairs, her expenses in running her palaces and estates are in the hands of the Keeper of the Privy Purse who is also Treasurer to the Queen and who works in close collaboration with her solicitors, Messrs Farrer, her bankers, Messrs Coutts & Co, the Crown Estate Commissioners and with officials both of the Department of the Environment, over works at Buckingham Palace, Windsor Castle and St James's Palace, and of the Duchy of Lancaster. In addition to his other duties he is Receiver-General of the Duchy, the chancellor of which is now Mr Norman St John-Stevas. The Keeper of the Privy Purse is also officially responsible for the financial affairs of the Queen's racing stables and the Ascot Office, for the pages of honour and Military Knights of Windsor, and for the supervision of the Queen's extremely valuable stamp collection. He is, in addition, Secretary of the Royal Victorian Order. The office is at present held by Major Sir Rennie Maudslay, an old Harrovian former officer in the King's Royal Rifle Corps who was five times mentioned in despatches in the war and afterwards went into business before joining the Lord Chamberlain's office in 1952.

The Lord Chamberlain is the senior officer of the Royal Household. Upon his appointment he receives a wand, the symbol of his office, which is broken at the end of the monarch's funeral service. Until 1971 the Lord Chamberlain was the first Lord Cobbold who was appointed to the post in 1963 and is now Permanent Lord in Waiting. Educated at Eton and King's College, Cambridge, scion of an old family of Suffolk brewers, he had formerly been Governor of the Bank of England for twelve years and was a director of British Petroleum, Guardian Royal Exchange Assurance and the Hudson's Bay Company. His wife is a daughter of the second Earl of Lytton. His successor is Lord Maclean. The inheritor of a baronetcy created in 1631 and the twenty-seventh Chief of Clan Maclean, he was educated at Canford School, Wimborne and served during the war in the Scots Guards from which he retired as a Major. He was once Chief Scout of the Commonwealth and is a Lieutenant in the Royal Company of Archers (the Queen's Bodyguard for Scotland). He has a house in St James's Palace and a home in Scotland, Duart Castle, Isle of Mull.

Lord Maclean's principal assistant, the Comptroller of the Lord Chamberlain's Office, is Lieutenant-Colonel Sir Eric Penn. Like Lord Cobbold he was at Eton and Cambridge, and like Lord Maclean he served in a Guards regiment during the war, the Grenadiers, with whom he won the Military Cross in 1944. The Assistant Comptroller, Lieutenant-Colonel J. F. D. Johnston, also won the Military Cross with the Grenadier Guards. He is married to the daughter of the late Private Secretary to King George v, Edward viii and George vi, Lord Hardinge of Penshurst.

The Lord Chamberlain does not see the Queen every day as one or other of her Private Secretaries does, but there are nevertheless frequent occasions on which he does consult her as he is not only nominally responsible for all departments of the household – which are to all intents and purposes autonomous – but he is actually responsible for the organization of State Visits by foreign Heads of State, for garden parties, and for Court ceremonies such as royal weddings and funerals, except the funerals of the sovereign which are supervised by the Earl Marshal. The Lord Chamberlain is further responsible for most appointments to the Household, including the Ecclesiastical and Medical Households, the Marshal of the Diplomatic Corps, and the Gentlemen and Extra Gentlemen Ushers who, without pay, help to organize such occasions as investitures and garden parties. Under the Lord Chamberlain's authority also come the Gentleman Usher to the Sword of State and the Gentleman Usher of the Black Rod – the chief parliamentary officer of the House of Lords who carries an ebony rod, surmounted by a golden lion rampant, when he goes to summon the

House of Commons to the Lords at the Opening of Parliament – as well as the Honourable Corps of Gentlemen at Arms, the Queen's Bodyguard of the Yeomen of the Guard and the Queen's Bodyguard for Scotland.*

In addition, the Constable and Governor of Windsor Castle, the Superintendent of the State Apartments at St James's Palace and the Keeper of the Jewel House, Tower of London, come under the authority of the Lord Chamberlain, as do those in whose care are the sovereign's immensely valuable collection of pictures, drawings, prints and other works of art, books and manuscripts. Also responsible to him are the Master of the Queen's Music, Malcolm Williamson; the Poet Laureate, Sir John Betjeman; the Queen's Bargemaster who attends her with some of the Watermen when she attends any functions connected with the Thames; and the Keeper of the Swans who is responsible for rounding up all the new season's cygnets on the river between London Bridge and Henley, marking those that belong to the two City livery companies, the Dyers and Vintners, and counting the few hundred that still belong to the Queen. The Master of the Queen's Music receives a purely nominal salary. The Poet Laureate's equally modest remuneration which has remained unchanged since the time when Ben Jonson was Poet Laureate in the reign of James I, was augmented by Charles I who awarded him an annual terce (42 gallons) of Canary wine.† The Queen's Bargemaster and his Watermen, who are

* Including the Captain (who is Chief Whip in the House of Lords), the Lieutenant, the Standard Bearer, the Clerk of the Cheque and Adjutant, and the Harbinger there are thirty-two members of the Honourable Corps of Gentlemen-at-Arms which was founded by King Henry VIII. On ceremonial occasions they wear scarlet coats, blue trousers and gilt metal helmets crowned by white swans' feathers. Their Captain in the last Labour government was a woman, Baroness Llewelyn-Davies of Hastoe. She was mercifully permitted to wear a badge rather than the uniform of her gentlemen.

The Queen's Bodyguard of the Yeomen of the Guard is a more numerous corps, there being five officers under their captain, Lord Strabolgi, and some eighty men. It was founded in 1485 for the coronation of King Henry VII and is not only the oldest royal bodyguard but the oldest military corps in the world. Its distinctive Tudor uniform of scarlet knee-length tunics, white ruffs and round black hats is distinguished from that of the Yeomen Warders of the Tower of London (the Beefeaters) by a cross belt originally designed for supporting an arquebus.

The Queen's Bodyguard for Scotland, also known as the Royal Company of Archers, is a still more numerous body having about four hundred members. Included among its thirty-three officers are the heads of several of the oldest families in Scotland. They wear a green uniform, for which they pay themselves, with black Kilmarnock bonnets in which eagles' feathers denote their rank: Lord Home is a captain; Lord Maclean a lieutenant; the Earl of Airlie an ensign. They carry bows and three arrows in their belts. Their Captain General, the Earl of Stair, is Gold Stick for Scotland, that is to say the Queen's ceremonial personal bodyguard there. The Gold Sticks for England and Wales, so called because of the gold-tipped sticks which are their symbols of office, are Field Marshal Sir Gerald Templer and Lord Mountbatten.

† When Henry James Pye was Poet Laureate in 1800, the terce of wine was commuted to £27 a year. But on Sir John Betjeman's appointment in 1972 it was suggested by the Privy Purse Office that he should receive instead the equivalent value in bottles of wine, which Sir John now does from the Queen's wine merchant. 'The Laureatship', as he has observed, 'is now officially

actively connected with the river in day-to-day employment, and the Keeper of the Swans, who is a boat builder by profession, also receive only nominal salaries. Finally, the Lord Chamberlain is responsible for issuing warrants to shops and firms that have enjoyed or still enjoy royal patronage, from Booth's gin to Garrards, the jewellers, and Pear's soap to Huntsman and Sons, the tailors.

The female counterpart of the Lord Chamberlain, by whose side she walks at State functions, is the Mistress of the Robes, formerly the Dowager Duchess of Devonshire, now the Duchess of Grafton. It is her responsibility to organize the rota of the Ladies-in-Waiting. There are eight of these Ladies. The two senior, styled Ladies of the Bedchamber, are the Marchioness of Abergavenny who is married to the brother of the Duke of Edinburgh's Private Secretary, Lord Rupert Nevill, and the Countess of Airlie, an American from Newport, Rhode Island, who is sister-in-law of Princess Alexandra of Kent. They attend the Queen when she carries out the more important of her public duties. Under them are four Women of the Bedchamber, who take turns helping the Queen with her work in the palace, or go with her whenever she fulfils an official engagement, answer some of her letters, particularly the many she has from children, and generally act as personal assistants. There are also two Extra Women of the Bedchamber. These Ladies-in-Waiting, who are paid a modest salary and reimbursed for their expenses, do not live in the palace during their turn of duty which usually lasts for a fortnight, but go home after their day's work unless there has been a late evening engagement or a very early start has to be made in the morning when they spend the night in a bedroom reserved for their use. They have their meals in the Household Dining-Room at Buckingham Palace with the fifteen or so other senior members of the Household. But when the Court moves to Windsor for Easter and Ascot week they lunch and dine with the Queen, as they do at Balmoral and Sandringham where they help to look after her guests.

The staff at Buckingham Palace, which with its six hundred rooms is the largest town house in England, forms a hierarchy in itself. There are the senior members of the Household who are served by footmen in their own dining-room; there are the officials and clerks who eat in a different dining-room; and there are the domestic servants, including about forty-five catering staff, fifty-eight housemaids, and fifty-three pages, footmen and other male staff, who have a self-service canteen. Most of the domestic staff are British and are members of the Civil

regarded not as a spur to further verse but as a reward ... for work already done.' This was unfortunately not understood by one of his predecessors, John Masefield, who felt obliged to submit verses of extremely dubious merit to *The Times* with painful regularity.

Service Union, though some of the kitchen staff are foreigners and belong to no union. Up till 1967, except on ceremonial occasions, the footmen used to wear a plain navy-blue battle dress, with the ER cypher on the breast pocket, which had been introduced in 1940. They now wear a black tailcoat and trousers, a soft white shirt with turn-down collar and black tie and a scarlet waistcoat trimmed with very narrow gold braid. The pages wear a blue coat and black trousers, white shirt and black tie, and a blue waistcoat with gilt buttons. In their off-duty hours they are entitled to wear the Royal Household Social Club tie which has navy blue, maroon and thin gold stripes, or the tie of one of the Household sports clubs to which they might belong.

As in the households of Victorian England, the most rigid class distinctions were observed by all these indoor servants until quite recently. On moving into Buckingham Palace from Clarence House, the Duke of Edinburgh's valet found the atmosphere there 'most fussy and fastidious'. The elderly housemaids, some of whom had been there for forty years, addressed him as 'Sir', and one actually bowed her way out of his presence when he came upon her cleaning his room. In the Steward's Room, where luncheon was served promptly at noon, the servants sat at the long table in strict order of precedence. Before the meal they all stood behind their chairs waiting for the Steward of the Palace to say grace. After the meal, which was served by waitresses and Steward's Room boys, no one could leave the table until the Steward had recited the closing grace which was followed by toasts, drunk in water, to their royal employers. Then the Queen's head dresser would lead the way out of the room, followed by the others, still in strict order of precedence. The Duke's valet had 'a shrewd idea it was more fun in the lower servants' hall where people were younger'. Certainly it is more fun in the servants' canteen today.

In addition to the indoor servants there are nine gardeners as well as about a hundred maintenance staff and engineers employed by the Department of the Environment, eleven chauffeurs and thirty-nine grooms and coachmen. These grooms and coachmen are technically under the control of the Master of the Horse, the Earl of Westmorland, who lives in Gloucestershire not far from Badminton, the home of his predecessor, the Duke of Beaufort, whom he succeeded in March 1978. The Master of the Horse has various ceremonial duties to perform: being responsible for the Queen's safety whenever she is mounted on a horse or riding in a carriage, he has to be in attendance on such occasions as her birthday parade, when he rides in the group immediately behind her, and the Opening of Parliament, when he is to be seen in the following carriage. Occasionally he inspects the royal stables: but, in practice, his duties, for which he is not paid, are carried out by the Crown Equerry, Lieutenant-Colonel Sir John Mansel Miller, another old Etonian Guards Officer, holder of the Distinguished Service Order and the Military Cross, who appropriately lists his recreations in *Who's Who* as hunting, polo and driving. As well as being responsible for the Queen's thirty horses (ten Greys and twenty Bays), her five coachmen, fifteen grooms (who act as postillions on ceremonial occasions) and her seventy carriages, from state coaches to phaetons, all in working order, the Crown Equerry has charge of her twenty-odd cars, including the £60,000 three-ton Phantom Six Rolls Royce which was presented to the Queen in 1978 by the Society of Motor Manufacturers as a Jubilee present. It is his duty to ensure that the Queen's transport is always in the right place at exactly the right time, and that her travelling arrangements are conducted with their apparently effortless efficiency, particularly when she has to attend one of those important ceremonies which form a large part of her responsibilities.

10 Court Ceremonies

The most spectacular Court ceremonies are those which take place at irregular intervals such as royal weddings and funerals and those connected with royal jubilees which in 1977 were so successfully combined with an innovation that characterizes the changing nature of royal appearances – the so-called 'walk-abouts'. But there are certain others which the Queen attends every year. The most important of these, and the only one during which she wears a crown and her Robe of State, is the State Opening of Parliament, a ceremony which Queen Victoria had allowed to lapse but which King Edward VII revived on his accession in 1910. It takes place in the Chamber of the House of Lords in the Palace of Westminster which is still so called because in the eleventh century, after the English kings had moved their main residence from Winchester, a royal palace stood here next to Westminster Abbey. This palace was taken over by William the Conqueror, whose arrogant and ostentatious son William Rufus built Westminster Hall, the largest Norman hall in the country, where the early Parliaments once sat. Throughout the thirteenth, fourteenth and fifteenth centuries new buildings were added to the palace and old ones restored. But in the sixteenth century King Henry VIII took over York Place, the London residence of the archbishops of York where the disgraced Cardinal Wolsey had lived in a style as grandiose as that of the royal Court itself. The King much enlarged York Place, which became known as Whitehall Palace; and thereafter the Palace of Westminster became the centre of the King's administrative rather than personal life.

Escorted by soldiers of her Household Cavalry, the Blues and Royals,* the Queen drives here in the Irish State Coach, a handsome but none too sturdy carriage which was bought by Queen Victoria from an

---

* The King's Troop, Royal Horse Artillery, is also part of the Household Division. It was established after the Second World War – when all horse artillery batteries had been mechanized – by King George VI who expressed the wish that the practice of firing salutes on state occasions (such as royal birthdays and the anniversaries of the coronation and accession) by a battery of Royal Horse Artillery, mounted and dressed in the traditional manner, should be revived. On her accession the Queen decided that the battery should continue to be known as the King's Troop in memory of her father and not be called the Queen's Troop. It shares with the Queen and her immediate family, and with no one else, the privilege of being allowed to pass under Marble Arch.

Irish coach builder in Dublin in 1852. The coach moves out of Buckingham Palace, down the Mall, into Whitehall and across Parliament Square, past lines of troops of the Household Division, and stops outside the royal entrance to Westminster Palace beneath Victoria Tower. Already the cellars below the palace have been searched by the Queen's Bodyguard of the Yeomen of the Guard, as they have been searched before the opening of Parliament ever since that November day when Guy Fawkes was discovered hiding in them ready to blow up the Parliament of King James I. The Yeomen of the Guard still carry lamps with them down into the cellars, which are brilliantly lit by electric light, but are now accompanied by officers with the more searching eyes of the Special Branch of the Metropolitan Police.

Wearing an evening dress and a diamond diadem made for George IV, the Queen steps down at the royal entrance where she is met by the Lord Chancellor, the head of the judiciary, in his gold and black robes, the Lord Great Chamberlain and the Earl Marshal.

Preceded by these officers of state, the Queen, accompanied by Prince Philip in service uniform, walks up the steps to her robing room where, beneath frescoes by William Dyce representing Hospitality, Mercy, Religion, Generosity and Courtesy in terms of Arthurian Legends, she is cloaked in her ermine-lined crimson velvet Robe of State and her diadem is replaced by the Imperial State Crown. This, the most valuable of her crowns, was made for Queen Victoria in 1837. As well as four rubies, eleven emeralds, sixteen sapphires, two hundred and seventy-three pearls and almost three thousand diamonds, it contains the huge second part of the Star of Africa cut from the celebrated Cullinan Diamond, a sapphire believed to have been set in a ring belonging to the eleventh-century King Edward the Confessor, and the great spinel ruby which was given by Don Pedro of Castille to the Black Prince in 1369 and is said to have been worn in his coronet by King Henry V at the battle of Agincourt.

When the Queen is ready four Pages of Honour come forward to lift her long and heavy train. They wear gilt swords, coats of that brilliant scarlet which has been the colour of the royal livery since the time of King Canute, white breeches and stockings and shoes with gold buckles and red heels. Followed by them, by the Mistress of the Robes, her Ladies-in-Waiting and various other members of the Royal Household, the Queen then slowly walks to the House of Lords. In front of her proceed the Lord Great Chamberlain and the Earl Marshal, walking backwards, her Heralds and Pursuivants, her Kings of Arms,*

* The three Kings of Arms, known respectively as Garter, Clarenceux and Norroy-and-Ulster, are the Earl Marshal's lieutenants and the sole authorities for granting Arms by Letters Patent under authority delegated to them by the sovereign. They are assisted by six Heralds – Windsor,

Equerries, further members of her Household, and the peers who carry the Cap of Maintenance – that ancient symbol of unknown significance which may represent the long lost duchy of Aquitaine – and the Sword of State.*

As she enters the Chamber, the lights, which have been dimmed, flare up again. They reveal the peers in their parliamentary robes of scarlet cloth and white ermine, the law lords in their more sombre robes, the bishops in their episcopal gowns, diplomats in their bemedalled and ribanded uniforms, peeresses in evening dress and tiaras.

Her left hand just touching her husband's right, the Queen passes the Gentlemen-at-Arms on duty by the doorway, walks up the three steps of the dais, turns and sits upon the gilded throne, a marvellously inventive work of art with a large canopy and metal candelabra which was designed for Queen Victoria's use by Augustus Pugin. She says: 'My Lords, pray be seated.'

Her Household group themselves on either side of her; the Lord Great Chamberlain stands on the step below her. Prince Philip used also to sit below her, outside the canopy. But in 1967 Prince Charles and Princess Anne both attended the ceremony, Princess Anne occupying the place formerly taken by her father, Prince Charles sitting outside the canopy on his mother's right. So the Prince Consort's throne, whose back is not quite so high as the sovereign's, was brought out of storage from the Lord Great Chamberlain's country house and placed next to the Queen's under the canopy. Since then Prince Philip has always occupied this place.

The official known as the Gentleman Usher of the Black Rod is then despatched to the House of Commons to fetch the Members to the bar of the Upper House. Upon their arrival the Lord Chancellor bows to the Queen, comes forward, kneels before her, takes the printed copy of the 'Most Gracious Speech from the Throne' from his embroidered

Richmond, Somerset, York, Lancaster and Chester – who were originally the sovereign's messengers and responsible for the organization of royal tournaments and jousts. The Heralds work at the College of Arms in Queen Victoria Street, for a salary fixed in the sixteenth century of £17.80 a year; but they are permitted to undertake work for private clients and for organizations that need advice on heraldry, genealogy and armorial bearings. In addition to the six Heralds there are four Pursuivants, known as Portcullis, Rouge Croix, Rouge Dragon and Bluemantle. The Scottish equivalent of the College of Arms is the Court of the Lord Lyon in Edinburgh. Lord Lyon King of Arms is assisted by three Heralds – Rothesay, Albany and Marchmont – and three Pursuivants – Unicorn, Ormond and Carrick.

* When Richard Crossman was Lord President of the Council he asked to be excused from attending the Opening of Parliament, which he felt was out of keeping with the principles of a Socialist Minister, and approached the Queen's Private Secretary on the subject. 'It will certainly occur to her,' Adeane replied adroitly, pointing out that public ceremonies could be as irksome to the Queen as to her Ministers, 'to ask herself why you should be excused when she herself has to go, since you're both officials. ... [But] all you need do is to write a letter to her asking to be excused without stating any reason why.' Crossman chose not to write the letter but to attend the ceremony instead. (Richard Crossman, *Diaries of a Cabinet Minister*, II, p. 534.)

41 Sir Winston Churchill opens the door of the royal car as Queen Elizabeth II and the Duke of Edinburgh leave No. 10 Downing Street after his farewell dinner, 1955.

42 The State Opening of Parliament, 1967.

43 Sir Michael Adeane, Private Secretary to Queen Elizabeth II from 1953 to 1972.

44 Sir Philip Moore, The Queen's Private Secretary since 1977.

45 Prince Philip in his study at Buckingham Palace.

46 The Clock Tower at St James's Palace, London.

47 The Queen receives the Prime Minister, Harold Wilson, in the Audience Room at Buckingham Palace, 1969.

48 The Queen meets the ex-Prime Minister, Sir Harold Macmillan, in Oxford.

49 The Queen at a garden party at Buckingham Palace.

50 Sandringham House, Norfolk.

51 The Royal Yacht *Britannia*.

52 Loading the *Britannia* for the Queen's Silver Jubilee voyage.

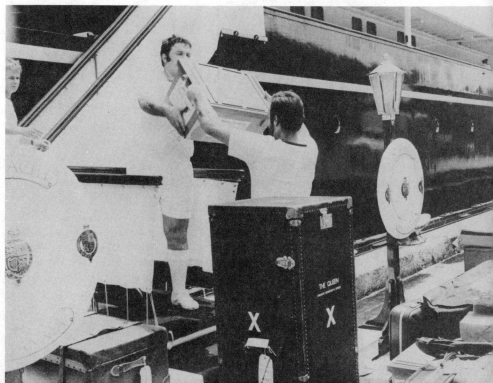

53 Prince Charles, Lord Mountbatten and Prince Philip at a polo match at Windsor, 1977.

54 The Queen presenting prizes at the Windsor Horse Show.

55 The Queen talking to President Ford during the American Bi-Centenary celebrations in 1976.

56 The Queen and Prince Philip in the State Coach halt at the Temple Bar, where the Lord Mayor of London was to offer her the Pearl Sword, during the Silver Jubilee procession, 7 June 1977.

57 The Queen and Prince Philip at the Silver Jubilee service at St Paul's.

58 The Queen at her desk at Windsor, 1977.

59 The Queen and members of the Royal Family with the leaders of seven nations at a banquet at Buckingham Palace, 1977.

purse and hands it to her. She reads it out, ending with the words: 'I pray that the blessing of Almighty God will rest upon your counsels.'

It is an exhausting process. The crown weighs nearly three pounds and is liable to give its wearer a headache. The Queen's grandfather who had the speech typed on parchment so thick that it would not be noticed how much his hands trembled, used to say that he 'knew of few worse ordeals than being obliged to deliver somebody else's speech' while at the same time balancing the crown on his head.* 'I must say', he told his mother after the first Opening of Parliament of his reign, 'that I think [it] the most terrible ordeal I have ever gone through ... The House of Lords was crammed with people and so many I knew which made it worse.' 'It was a great ordeal for us,' Queen Mary confirmed in a letter to her aunt Augusta, 'and rather nervous work but we got thro' it all right and G's speech was not so bad I think ... What I liked best was wearing Grandmama's crown and the ribbon star and badge of the Garter! I know *you* will understand what *I* felt.'

Their son, King Edward VIII, mentioned an unpleasant aspect of the ceremony which others have remarked upon since: 'Well do I recall the hush inside the House of Lords as I mounted the steps to the throne. As I looked out over the brilliant scene, my senses were suddenly assailed by an almost suffocating smell of mothballs given off by the colourful robes removed from storage for this formal airing. It was nauseating, and sitting there on the Throne I could feel the pumping of my own heart.'

He acquitted himself well, however. Harold Nicolson who had been chosen to second the Address in reply to the King's Speech told his wife: 'I woke up with a sinking feeling and at 12 went to the opening of Parliament. It is a fine sight. The King looked like a boy of eighteen and did it well. He referred to the "Amurrican Government" and ended, "And may the blessing of Almoighty God rest upon your deliberoitions."'

Because of his stammer, the Queen's father found the ceremony even more of an ordeal than either his father or his brother. 'My father always did this sort of thing so well,' he said to Lionel Logue, the specialist in speech defects who had been called in to help the King

---

* It was he, however, who had decided to revert to the custom of wearing a crown for the ceremony. His father had worn a field-marshal's cocked hat. 'The King is much exercised as to what he ought to wear on his head at the Opening of Parliament,' the acerbic Charles Hobhouse wrote in his diary on 6 March 1913. 'He wishes to revert to the Crown of the Sovereign. As none of us cares what he wears, we agreed to the crown.' (Edward David, *Inside Asquith's Cabinet: From the Diaries of Charles Hobhouse*, p. 133.) It was at one time suggested that the Queen might wear the less heavy crown with which she was crowned in Westminster Abbey. This is St Edward's Crown which was made for King Charles II in 1661 to replace the crown which, together with other regalia, was melted down and sold after the Civil War. She decided, however, to wear the Imperial State Crown as her father and grandfather had done.

overcome his stammer. Logue replied that it had taken King George v years of experience and practice before he attained his admittedly high standard. A little consoled by this, the King spent hours in his study at Buckingham Palace, the crown on his head, practising tirelessly as he read first his father's last Speech from the Throne and then the draft of his own. On 26 October 1937 he had to read the finished Speech in the House of Lords. 'Chips' Channon recorded the occasion in his diary:

It is always a splendid show; and I thought of last year when I saw King Edward perform the ceremony with his wistful smile and doomed manner.

A few moments before 12 the Royalties arrived; Kent looking ill . . . Gloucester heavier and more pompous, both their Duchesses looking lovely. At mid-day the lights were gradually lowered, and the Royal Procession very slowly and with great dignity wended its way in. The King seemed quite at ease and so did the Queen. She has become more matronly, and as she toyed with her jewels, I looked at her and thought of old days when I called her 'Elizabeth' and was even a little in love with her. The King took 10 minutes to read the speech (which he did well) and the Chamber was motionless, with an atmosphere which was almost hallowed.

When the Queen opened the first Parliament of her reign she was seen to be rather hesitant and nervous. But experience has brought confidence; and she will now even add a personal emphasis to the matter of the Queen's Speech as she did, for instance, when reading a sentence in a recent Speech about the Labour Government's intention to curb the power of the House of Lords. 'She made a little pause', Richard Crossman said, 'and read it with just a *frisson* and the whole House had just a *frisson* too.'

The Queen is also seen to be more confident at those other annual events which, provided she is in the country, she endeavours to attend – with varying degrees of pleasure – each year.* These include several sporting events such as the racing at Epsom, Royal Ascot and Goodwood, the football Cup Final at Wembley, the Test Match at Lord's and the Highland Games at Braemar; the Royal Variety Performance at the Palladium and the Royal Film Performance at the Odeon, Leicester Square; the Remembrance Day Service at the Cenotaph in Whitehall on the Sunday nearest to 11 November, Trooping the Colour on Horse Guards Parade and the distribution of the Royal Maundy on the Thursday in Holy Week.

The Maundy ceremony was instituted by King Edward i and origi-

---

* 'Most of these engagements – and several more of alike nature – are, it may be said, enjoyable; and there are many who would welcome the opportunity of attending them,' Lord Adeane has observed. 'But for the Queen who can never enjoy them with the freedom of a holidaymaker, the pleasure of attending them is bound to be tempered by the strain imposed on her as a public figure and by the knowledge that somebody is looking at her all the time and that she is being continually photographed, filmed and televised as well.' (*Report on the Select Committee on the Civil List*, p. 111.)

nally included washing the feet of the poor – to whom gifts of clothes, food and money were subsequently distributed – in commemoration of Christ's washing the feet of His disciples. By the sixteenth century the monarch had delegated the symbolic washing of feet to a series of courtiers, merely dabbing them himself with a towel soaked in scented water; and by the middle of the eighteenth century the washing had been discontinued altogether. Royal participation in the Maundy had, indeed, altogether lapsed when Queen Victoria's granddaughter, Princess Marie Louise, suggested to King George v that he should revive it. He did so in 1932, and the monarch has generally taken part in the ceremony ever since. As many poor people of each sex as the Queen is years old receive from her purses of money and specially minted silver coins. The ceremony takes place either in Westminster Abbey or in a provincial cathedral. In 1979 it was celebrated in Winchester; in 1955 in Southwark Cathedral, which was then celebrating its diocesan jubilee; and in 1957 in St Albans Cathedral whose Bishop was then High Almoner.*

While the Queen herself distributes the Maundy Money, the Monarch's personal participation in the traditional offering at the Feast of the Epiphany (6 January) lapsed in the time of George ii and has not been revived. Today the offering of gold, frankincense and myrrh, symbolic of the gifts of the Magi to the infant Jesus, is made on behalf of Her Majesty in the Chapel Royal at St James's by two Gentlemen Ushers to the Queen. The frankincense and myrrh are carried on one silver gilt salver, the gold, in the form of twenty-five sovereigns, on another. The Dean of the Chapels Royal officiates at the ceremony to dedicate the alms, the gold being returned to the Bank of England and its cash equivalent being spent on charitable purposes, the frankincense being given to an Anglican church where incense is used and the myrrh to Nashdom Abbey to be processed for a similar purpose.

Although the Queen does not personally attend the Epiphany Service in the Chapel Royal, she does take the salute at the ceremony of Trooping the Colour, which is performed on her official birthday in early June (she was, in fact, born on 21 April 1926). This is not so antique a ceremony as the Royal Maundy or the Epiphany offering, being first performed in 1755 and regularly since 1805. But it is commemorative of the ancient military practice of parading flags and

* The Royal Almonry is part of the Department of the Keeper of the Privy Purse and Treasurer to the Queen. It is responsible for the administration of the Queen's gifts to charities including her Maundy Money. The present High Almoner is the Bishop of Rochester. There is also a hereditary Grand Almoner, the Marquess of Exeter. The High Almoner and his assistants are still girded with linen towels during the Maundy ceremony and still carry the traditional nosegays of sweet herbs.

banners in front of troops so that they were made fully familiar with the colours – later emblems of regimental honour – around which they were to rally in the chaos of battle. The ceremony takes place on Horse Guards Parade; and the colours trooped are those of a battalion of one of the regiments of Foot Guards. The Queen takes the salute on horseback – in a most accomplished military manner – riding side-saddle which, since she normally rides astride, requires previous practice. 'She rides quite isolated and clearly has to know her drill-book,' wrote an observer of the 1978 Trooping the Colour, Patrick O'Donovan. 'Her horse is marvellously caparisoned. In some ways it is the most intimate of ceremonials. There she sits, dangerously exposed, closer to her people than any other ruler dares to be, yet utterly apart.'

11 Entertainments at Court

At the beginning of the century, in the reign of the Queen's great-grandfather, St James's Palace was still the scene of both morning Levees, which had been introduced by Queen Anne for the reception of gentlemen, and of afternoon Drawing-Rooms to which ladies whose husbands had attended Levees could bring their daughters or daughters-in-law for presentation to the sovereign. King Edward did not enjoy these boring functions; nor did those who attended them.

At the Levees an official was posted at the door leading into the throne room to turn away anyone who was incorrectly dressed, the King not only having a notoriously sharp eye for the niceties of costume but even believing – for he was an excessively superstitious man – that certain improprieties brought bad luck: he kept a close watch on the Master of Ceremonies to make sure he wore his jewel of office correctly 'as any displacement was of evil omen'. The official on the door, however, was not as scrupulous as the King, once letting through the absent-minded Arthur Hardinge who appeared before the horrified King with a buttoned boot on one foot and an evening shoe on the other, a blunder he weakly excused on the grounds that he was very short-sighted. 'The levee was a most wearisome performance,' Edward Marsh, then a junior clerk in the Colonial Office, wrote of one he attended in 1902, 'and I don't know whether to laugh or cry when I think of the manner in which 1,500 of the educated classes spent their morning. It took about an hour to get round, through the successive pens in which one is shut up with the same little group of people ... and when one reached "the Presence" one was rushed through with just time to make one's bow to the red, bored, stolid Sovereign.'*

The King was equally bored by the afternoon Drawing-Rooms which he eventually replaced by for the less tedious evening Courts. At

* Years later, in 1937, Edward Marsh came to Buckingham Palace to be invested as a Knight Commander of the Victorian Order and found King George vi far less intimidating than his 'red, bored, stolid' grandfather. Having both misheard Lascelles's telephone call and misread his letter, Marsh failed to arrive at the palace at the appointed time. All the same, when he did arrive, he 'had 10 minutes with King who was most charming and unshymaking'. On the way out he met the Queen in the passage. He did not expect to be recognized but, on the contrary, she was 'most gracious'. (Christopher Hassall, *Edward Marsh*, p. 597.)

these Courts he performed his duties conscientiously; but, although his grey, hooded eyes would sometimes light up as a particularly attractive girl was presented to him, the lack of any opportunity to indulge in those intimate and gossipy conversations with amusing women which he so much enjoyed was obviously irksome to him. His son, King George v, less quickly bored and with no taste for frivolities of his father's kind, was more adept at appearing unflaggingly gracious on these occasions, even when, one day in the early summer of 1914, a pretty young sympathizer with the suffragettes, instead of rising from her curtsy, spread out her arms and exclaimed, 'Your Majesty, for God's sake stop torturing women!'

In the 1920s his four annual Courts, usually held in the Ballroom at Buckingham Palace, were certainly magnificent spectacles. His Majesty would appear in the full dress uniform of either an admiral of the fleet or a field marshal accompanied by Queen Mary, dazzling with jewels, her train carried by two Pages of Honour. They would progress majestically through the State Rooms with the Lord Chamberlain and the Lord Steward, holding their white staves, walking backwards before them. As they entered the Ballroom on the stroke of half past nine the band struck up the National Anthem while they advanced to their crimson and gold thrones, the Princes and Princesses of the blood taking up their places on the dais behind them. The men were in glittering uniforms or court dress; all the women wore white feathers in their hair or tiaras.

When the King and Queen were both seated the Marshal of the Diplomatic Corps led forward the wife of the Spanish Ambassador, the doyen of the Diplomatic Corps. Holding her hand the Marshal bowed; she curtsyed: the Court was thus officially opened. Then, to the music of the stringed band in the gallery, the long procession of notabilities passed in front of their Majesties: the Prime Minister, the Archbishop of Canterbury, the Lord Chancellor, the ambassadors in their gorgeous uniforms, the long line of ladies to be presented, their names read out from the pile of cards in his hand by the Lord Chamberlain, among them now the names of certain actresses and singers not before admitted to Court. At the exit Sir Harry Stonor, the Equerry in Waiting, stood ready to guide those whom he considered sufficiently illustrious to the crimson benches from which they could watch the rest of the proceedings. The less fortunate, 'often mildly protesting at this somewhat arbitrary favouritism', were ushered round to the back of the Ballroom where they could see practically nothing.

When the ladies had curtsyed and walked away, Their Majesties stood up; the pages came forward to take up the Queen's long train; and, to the strains of the National Anthem, the royal procession slowly returned to the private apartments, while their guests enjoyed a buffet supper served by pages and footmen in state liveries with powdered hair.

The precision and timing of the whole ceremony, which lasted for about two hours, were faultless. Lady Cynthia Colville, a Woman of the Bedchamber to Queen Mary, remembered only a single mishap during all the Courts she had attended. This was when one lady stood on another's train and wrenched the dress from her shoulders. The lady thus partially denuded left the room; and, since the Lord Chamberlain was unaware of her departure, he read her name from his top card when another lady was standing beside him. Declining to be presented under a false name, this lady refused to move. The mistake was quickly rectified, however, and the procession continued as smoothly as before.

Standing behind his parents, the Prince of Wales appeared, so Lady Cynthia thought, 'always a little restless'. And, when he came to the throne as Edward VIII, the first occasion upon which he himself held a Court proved to be disastrous. Due to the six months' period of Court mourning for his father, the names of about six hundred ladies had accumulated on the Lord Chamberlain's lists. It was suggested, therefore, that the 'existing social bottle-neck', as the King called it, should be cleared by combining the presentations with two garden parties on two successive afternoons in July.

On the first afternoon the King went out into the garden of Buckingham Palace where he found the huge silken durbar canopy with hammered silver poles which his parents had brought back from India. Under it was a large gilt chair with smaller chairs behind for members of the royal family, the Diplomatic Corps and the Royal Household. A Guards' band, alternating with the pipers of a Highland regiment, played under some nearby trees. The débutantes began to parade along the red carpet in front of the King who acknowledged their curtsies with an impatient gesture, rather more than a nod but far less than a bow.

In his memoirs he acknowledged that it had 'always seemed' to him that 'women are prone to attach an excessive importance to these affairs'. Certainly he did not, on this occasion, attempt to disguise his boredom: a photograph of him, published in the newspapers the next day, revealed on his face an expression of sulky exasperation. Then the wind came up and it started to pour with rain. 'Prudently the other guests who were not being presented scampered into the protection of the tea tents. But with scarcely a waver the débutantes came on. Their costly hats and dresses, which had taken weeks to make, became progressively more bedraggled.'

The King beckoned to the Lord Chamberlain and whispered: 'We can't let this go on.' He stood up, bowed in the direction of the still unpresented young ladies, and retired into the palace. The rain soon stopped; but the King did not reappear.

'Since all the cards had been taken up,' the King disingenuously explained years later, 'it seemed to me that there was no doubt as to the social status of those débutantes who had been left, so to speak, at the far end of the red carpet. Apparently, however, there were some parents who felt that without the Sovereign's personal bow of recognition, the presentation was not quite genuine and that the social position of their daughters was in consequence left in doubt. Why, I am still at a loss to understand.'

These Courts or Presentation parties continued for a time into the present reign but – like Levees which did not survive the Second World War – they have now been abolished. They came to an end in 1958 as the number of applications on behalf of girls, not only from Britain, but also from the Commonwealth and foreign countries, were becoming so numerous that either the Queen would have had to devote far more time to them, which was thought to be impossible, or some sort of selection of débutantes would have to be introduced, which was held to be invidious. Also, it was felt that this kind of reception was an unfortunate anachronism. It was, therefore, announced by the Lord Chamberlain that additional garden parties would be held 'in order that larger numbers [could be] invited to Buckingham Palace'.

There are now normally three garden parties each summer at Buckingham Palace, as well as one in Edinburgh. They are attended by over 30,000 people in all whose invitations are dealt with – under the supervision of the Lord Chamberlain – by women employed for four months of each year in a special garden party office. Although there are about eight thousand guests at each of these parties – who are entertained at a cost of more than £1 a head – the crowds never appear excessive as there are thirty-nine acres in which they can wander; and those who wish to get as close as possible to the royal party are expertly handled by a few uniformed Yeomen of the Guard, and the more numerous Gentlemen-at-Arms and Gentlemen Ushers who wear morning dress, as many of the male guests nowadays do not, taking advantage of the dispensation on their invitations which are subscribed 'Morning Dress or Uniform or Lounge Suits'.

At four o'clock one of the military bands, which later play those light musical comedy selections that form part of the essential repertoire of military bandmasters, strikes up the National Anthem and the Queen, with Prince Philip and various members of the royal family, emerges from the garden entrance on the north side of the palace. Tenants from the Duchies of Cornwall and Lancaster are first presented to the Queen who then walks down amongst her guests. Unobtrusively and skilfully, without the use of ropes or barriers, the Gentlemen-at-Arms helped by the Yeomen of the Guard, marshal the guests who have pressed around the terrace into separate curved lanes, standing with their backs to the front row. As the Queen – the Lord Chamberlain walking beside her, a Lady-in-Waiting and an Equerry behind – moves slowly down the lane arranged for her, the Gentlemen Ushers bring forward certain guests to be presented to her. There is no list and these guests are chosen at random. The Queen speaks to them all for a moment then moves on towards her tea tent to which by their separate routes the other members of the royal family are also slowly moving, Prince Philip evidently finding no difficulty in thinking of suitable comments to make or questions to ask, provoking that loud laughter which even the mildest regal joke elicits on such occasions.

Having had tea in the royal tent, watched by those guests who have not gone to have tea in the other tents themselves, the Queen receives various distinguished Commonwealth visitors who, with their wives, talk to her for a few moments before being dismissed with a smile and a slight step backwards.

The garden parties in Edinburgh are held at the Palace of Holyrood-house, the Queen's ancient official residence in Scotland which, originally built by James iv towards the end of the fifteenth century, was rebuilt in its present form by Charles ii. Its attractive appearance is enhanced for these garden parties by the immensely tall thistles which are placed in tubs outside it and by the High Constables of Holyrood-house, those leading citizens of Edinburgh who, wearing plumed top hats and carrying batons, stroll purposefully about the grounds with the green-uniformed officers of the Royal Company of Archers, Her Majesty's ceremonial bodyguard for Scotland.

As well as these large garden parties in England and Scotland – and smaller garden, sherry or cocktail parties for special groups of people such as the staffs attending Commonwealth conferences, bishops or members of the American Bar Association – the Queen also gives an annual evening reception for the Diplomatic Corps at Buckingham Palace as well as an annual luncheon at Windsor Castle, when new Knights of the Garter are installed, and, on or near 18 June each year, a dinner to commemorate Wellington's victory over Napoleon.

This dinner is held in the Waterloo Chamber at Windsor Castle, a huge room designed for George iv by Sir Jeffry Wyatville to house the portraits by Sir Thomas Lawrence of those sovereigns, statesmen and military leaders who contributed to Napoleon's defeat. The long central table, which stands on one of the largest seamless carpets in the world and which has room for fifty-two chairs, is always decorated on the night with flowers of blue and yellow, the colours of the great Duke. His descendant, the present Duke, is guest of honour; and on the day of the dinner he is required to present to the Queen for display in the Queen's Guard Chamber a silk tricolour flag, the quit-rent for his country estate, Stratfield Saye in Hampshire. In the same way the Duke of Marlborough is required to present to her a standard bearing the arms of the Bourbon Kings of France on the anniversary of his ancestor's notable victory over them at Blenheim on 13 August 1704 as quit-rent for the royal manor of Woodstock in Oxfordshire, which was presented to the first Duke by Queen Anne and in the grounds of which was built Blenheim Palace.

Given more often than the Waterloo Dinners, and even more magnificent, are the banquets held in the Ballroom at Buckingham Palace or at Windsor Castle during a state visit. The Queen, who enters the room preceded by the Lord Chamberlain and the Lord Steward again walking backwards in front of her, sits at the centre of an enormous horseshoe table, with her guests arranged in order of precedence on either side of her.* In the place of the riband of the Order of the Garter which she wears on other ceremonial evenings in England and Wales (substituting for it the riband of the Order of the Thistle in Scotland), she normally wears the high order bestowed upon her by the head of the state in whose honour the banquet is held. She also wears some fine piece of jewellery from her collection which is one of the two or three most valuable in the world.

The senior servants wear black, gold-braided coats, with white wool cloth breeches, white stockings and black buckled shoes. The footmen, their hair no longer powdered as it was until 1960, are in their scarlet livery of gold-embroidered coats and plush breeches with pink stockings. There are two of them for every eight guests. They serve the meal – without the gloves they used to wear – on silver-gilt plates, the dessert on either Worcester porcelain made for William iv, or eighteenth-century French Sèvres, Victorian Minton or early nineteenth-century Rockingham. The wine is drunk from English cut crystal made for the Queen's coronation and bearing the cypher E II R.

Less elaborate dinners for twenty or so guests were sometimes given at the beginning of the reign; but these were abandoned in 1960 with the excuse that it was proving too difficult to find evenings on which both the Queen and Prince Philip were free. The informal luncheons which

* At other major dinner-parties, though never at State Banquets, the Queen sits at a long top table with some of her principal guests, the others sitting in groups of ten at smaller tables in front of it.

have been given since 1956 and to which people distinguished in various contrasting fields are invited, still continue, however. The number of guests at these luncheons is usually eight, or nine if another member of the royal family other than the Queen and Prince Philip is present. Unlike those invited to garden parties who are asked to return their invitations if they are unable to attend but are not otherwise expected to reply, the guests are asked two or three weeks before, whether or not they will be available, as an invitation from the Queen is in the form of a command. At a characteristic luncheon party held at Buckingham Palace at the beginning of 1978 the guests were the Head of the Home Civil Service, the Professor of Music in the University of Auckland, the Director General of the Confederation of British Industry, the Principal of Westcott House, the theological college at Cambridge, an honorary research fellow of St Thomas's Hospital Medical School, the editor of a provincial newspaper, an actor (Jack Hedley) and a novelist (Margaret Drabble).

At these luncheons, the food – of which the Queen eats very little – is good; the wines excellent; the atmosphere relaxed, though at first the conversation can be rather strained as even the most self-assured people can become tongue-tied in the Queen's presence. The embarrassment of one guest, an 'eminent man-of-letters with a modicum of aristocratic blood and a temperament of detached radicalism', has been described by Philip Ziegler:

He accepted in a spirit of mingled curiosity and ribaldry. The mood survived until the Queen appeared and her guests were presented. 'Suddenly I felt physically ill,' he said. 'My legs felt weak, my head swam and my mind went totally blank. "So you're writing about such-and-such, Mr—" said the Queen. I had no idea what I was writing about, or even if I was writing a book at all. All I could think of to say was, "What a pretty brooch you're wearing, ma'am." So far as I can recall she was not wearing a brooch at all. Presumably she was used to such imbecility; anyway, she paid no attention to my babbling and in a minute or two I found that I was talking sense again.' Looking back, he says that he feels not so much shame as surprise. 'I have never felt like that before. I hope that I never do again. I would not have believed that I could have reacted in such a way.' Would this man have reacted in the same way if confronted by Marlene Dietrich, Jacqueline Kennedy, Dame Rebecca West? No, because he had met all three of them and though he had found the first and third in their separate ways impressive he was in no way overawed. Royalty touched some atavistic chord of whose existence he had previously been unaware.

The Queen does not smoke. Neither does the Duke, though he used to do so quite heavily. Nor incidentally does Prince Charles who can be uncharacteristically testy with those who do in his presence. But cigars and cigarettes are offered at these luncheons. Afterwards coffee is served, and the conversation continues, next door.

Guests at State Banquets are expected to wear full evening dress with decorations; but the rules are no longer strictly applied. On the occasion of the Romanian State Visit in 1978, it was agreed in advance that the Romanian men at the banquet should wear lounge suits. And when Pietro Nenni, the Italian Socialist leader, was invited to a State Banquet at Windsor he asked if he really must wear a tailcoat and white tie. He was told, of course, he need not, though the other men would. He wore a black tie but, choosing not to make himself conspicuous, he apparently withdrew to another room when the photographs were taken.

The wearing of ordinary suits or a black tie at a State banquet would, of course, have horrified King Edward VII in whose time neither ladies nor foreign diplomats were immune from his censure and his Household and Ministers came in for particularly sharp abuse for negligence. Before his continental tour in 1903 his entire suite were paraded on the deck of the royal yacht. 'The sea was rough, and it was somewhat painful staggering about the deck in full uniform, but it seemed to amuse the King to see us,' wrote Charles Hardinge. 'Our clothes were criticized without exception.' As for Lord Rosebery, the King considered him quite outrageous. Once he had the temerity to appear aboard the royal yacht for dinner wearing a white tie with a Yacht Squadron mess-jacket. The King eyed him angrily all through dinner. And when Rosebery came to an evening reception at Buckingham Palace in trousers instead of the prescribed court dress of black velvet breeches that buckled below the knee, black silk stockings and pumps, the King growled at him: 'I presume you have come in the suite of the American Ambassador.'

In those days American diplomats were not as punctilious as others in wearing court dress; but they did not reject it entirely. Walter Hines Page, the American Ambassador at the Court of St James's before the First World War, sometimes wore knee-breeches at Buckingham Palace and assured a friend how 'nice and comfortable' they were, though 'a devil of a lot of trouble to put on'. In 1929, however, when President Hoover despatched as Ambassador to London the blunt, outspoken Chicago banker, Charles G. Dawes, the wearing of knee-breeches by Americans at the English Court almost caused a crisis in Anglo-American relations. On being asked at a press conference before his departure whether or not he would wear the attire so demeaning to a republican, Mr Dawes replied that he would not. When this reply was reported in England, the Court was profoundly disturbed. King

George v, convalescing at Windsor Castle after a serious illness, was informed, and, in the words of the Lord Chamberlain, Lord Cromer, was 'extremely upset', not only because of the intended flouting of court etiquette but also because the Ambassador's incorrect attire might be taken as an affront to the Queen who, because of her husband's weakness, would be obliged to hold Court alone. The Foreign Office were called in to help; pressure was put upon the staff of the American Embassy; the Marshal of the Diplomatic Corps was urgently consulted. The Lord Chamberlain, having failed to persuade Mr Dawes to change his mind, at length approached the Prince of Wales.

The Prince who knew and liked Dawes and confessed to being 'much amused by the furore', made the ingenious suggestion that he should leave the Embassy wearing trousers to conceal the knee-breeches which he had on underneath; the trousers could be removed in a room at the palace, and replaced when it was time to go home. 'It's a little devious,' the Prince conceded, 'and I imagine Mr Dawes may take persuading. But of this much I am sure: he'll never leave his own Embassy in knee-breeches.'

Lord Cromer asked the Prince if he himself would approach the Ambassador with this suggestion. But the Prince declined, maintaining that 'good Anglo-American relations' meant far more to him than a breach of court etiquette, and that he did not 'want to spoil any good will' he might have built for himself in America 'by offending so important a citizen'.

'In that case,' said Lord Cromer, gloomily, 'I suppose I am still left with the hot potato.'

The next evening the Court was held; and the royal family and Household awaited Mr Dawes's arrival with trepidation. 'My mother must have looked glacial, while I hid a mildly disapproving glance behind the bearskin cap I was cradling in my right arm,' the Prince recalled. 'Did I detect a certain self-consciousness in Mr Dawes's demeanour, as he advanced to make his bow? If I did, it was only a flash, for he walked with the same deliberation and self-assurance with which he might have taken the chair in the United States senate. When it was all over, my mother murmured: "Papa will not be pleased; what a pity that such a distinguished man should be so difficult."'

Eventually the Ambassador's bluff charm and friendliness overcame the prejudice that his unconventional attire aroused; and it was accepted at Court that Americans must be regarded in a special light. Yet when Dawes resigned his appointment in 1932 his successor did not feel obliged to follow his example: in 1935 at the principal Jubilee Banquet at Buckingham Palace the new American Ambassador, Robert Bingham, was seen in knee-breeches. By the time of Joseph

Kennedy's resignation, however, a new tradition for American Ambassadors had been firmly established. 'I don't like to be out of the picture,' Kennedy had told Lady Airlie. 'But if I were to take to wearing English knee-breeches I'd offend folks in America. Bingham loved England so much that he ended up half an Englishman – and lost America. I'm not going to do that.'

It was not only with American diplomats that the Household of King George V experienced problems over court dress. For the new King was almost as punctilious in this regard as his father. Lord Stamfordham recalled an occasion when His Majesty firmly refused to allow one of his Ministers into his carriage because he was wearing a bowler hat instead of the top hat which the occasion demanded. And Sir Samuel Hoare, a former Secretary of State for India, wrote of the King's horror at having to receive Mahatma Gandhi, the 'rebel Fakir', who arrived at the palace 'with no proper clothes on and bare knees'. The interview got off to an extremely sticky start until Gandhi's 'beautiful manners' and the King's 'simple sincerity' combined to 'smooth the course of the conversation'. But, even so, Hoare 'more than once became nervous when the King looked resentfully at Gandhi's knees'.

Problems over dress assumed a new and disturbing importance when Ramsay MacDonald's Labour Government came into office in 1924. Ramsay MacDonald himself was not at all averse to pomp and ceremonial. Besides he liked and respected the King whom he did not want to offend both for political and personal reasons. He wrote:

If royalty had given the Labour Government the cold shoulder, we should have returned the call. It has not. It has been considerate, cordially correct, human and friendly. The King has never seen me as a Minister without making me feel that he was also seeing me as a friend. I record a remark I made to one of the Left incorruptibles who asked why I had been to the Palace: 'Because its allurements are so great that I cannot trust you to go.' ... These braids and uniforms are but part of an official pageantry and as my conscience is not on my back, a gold coat means nothing to me but a form of dress to be worn or rejected as a hat would be in relation to the rest of one's clothes. Nor do I care a fig for the argument that it is part of a pageantry of class, or royalty or flunkeyism ... If the poor spirits that are disturbed by pageantry only felt the spirit of ceremony, how much richer they would be and how much more powerful as the pioneers of a new world.

Many of MacDonald's colleagues did not agree with him. J. R. Clynes, who was appointed Lord Privy Seal and later became Home Secretary, much disliked the idea of having to wear court dress, and resented 'the waste of time caused by dressing and undressing' from 'morning dress for one function, afternoon dress with plumes and swords to consort with some arriving prince, and evening dress for a State banquet'. But,

196

as he wrote, MacDonald 'was our leader, and our first days of office were hardly a suitable time in which to open a disagreement among ourselves. We drifted into acquiescence because none of us realized at the time that strong feeling would arise in the Party concerning our ceremonial attire.'

For his own part the King, while attaching supreme importance to the proper observance of all forms of court etiquette, was quite prepared to compromise with his Labour Ministers and certainly did not want them to have to pay more for court dress than they could afford, particularly for the full Levee dress for which the Court Tailor charged £73 25s 6d. To allay their fears as to cost Lord Stamfordham wrote to the Chief Whip, B. C. Spoor: 'I have ascertained from Messrs Moss Bros, 20 King Street, W.C.2. ... which is I believe a well known and dependable Firm, that they have in stock a few suits of Household, Second Class, Levee Dress from £30 complete. This comprises trousers, coat, cock-hat and sword and is the regulation dress.'

The high cost of the dress, however, as Stamfordham was told, was only one of the Ministers' objections to it. Having to wear the uniform was objectionable enough; for former working men to have to wear a sword in 1924 they deemed absurd.

Eventually it was decided in Cabinet that the Prime Minister would try to arrange with Stamfordham that Ministers attending Levees should be allowed to do so in plain evening dress and knee-breeches; that a panel of Ministers, who had procured or were willing to procure the necessary uniform, should be drawn up; and that when Ministers were required to attend the King at Court they should be drawn from this panel, those Ministers not possessing uniforms being excused from attending functions at which they were obligatory.

'This question of uniform is becoming very intricate and confused,' the King noted in a minute when some such proposals were put to him. 'Whatever decision the Cabinet Ministers come to, I will agree to, but they must all do the same. It would look very odd if some were in uniform and some in evening clothes at a Levee ... In no case do I expect anyone to get more than the Levee coat; full dress is not necessary on account of the expense.'

At a Levee at St James's Palace on 11 March 1924 the incongruity of his Ministers' dress was quite as pronounced as the King had foreseen and feared. A photograph published in newspapers the next day showed a group of Ministers arriving at the palace. They included MacDonald himself who was accompanied by Thomas Griffiths, the Member for Pontypool and Treasurer of the King's Household. MacDonald, hatless, was wearing a long cloak which failed to conceal the broad stripe in his levee trousers and the tip of his sword; Griffiths was also in levee dress but his was complete with a plumed hat. Two other Ministers, the very small President of the Board of Trade, Sidney Webb, and the extremely tall Minister of Agriculture, Noel Buxton, 'the dwarf and the stork', were both in knee-breeches and opera hats.

Copies of this photograph, labelled 'Was this what you voted for?', were circulated by the Independent Labour Party. And after that Sidney Webb – who most reluctantly became Lord Passfield in 1929 – declined to wear knee-breeches at Court. This much distressed the King, as did Lady Passfield's determination to go on calling herself Mrs Beatrice Webb. He consulted his friend, J. H. Thomas, about it. 'Well,' Thomas explained to the King with the customary twinkle in his eye, 'poor Sidney can't put the breeches on because 'is wife wears 'em.' The King, delighted by this remark, repeated it to everyone, so that it eventually came to the ears of Lord Passfield himself who decided to abandon his protest and wear knee-breeches at Court after all.

When Attlee's Labour Government came into power in 1945 the wearing of knee-breeches at Court and of frock coats at Privy Council meetings was no longer required. Attlee himself deserved credit for this, wrote his Chancellor of the Exchequer, Hugh Dalton, 'and it was accepted on his suggestion, almost as a matter of course, by the Palace'. Nowadays, since court dress is no longer worn, such problems do not arise.

12 *The Fount of Honour*

In the earlier years of the nineteenth century, when the bestowal of titles and orders had largely replaced the payment of money as a reward for political services, the honours system had become unwieldy and corrupt. For a time Sir Robert Peel managed to bring it under control by insisting that it be limited and highly select and that honours should be bestowed on the meritorious rather than the rich or influential. But by the time the Marquess of Salisbury became Prime Minister honours were far more freely bestowed and easily available. The new rich demanded and obtained higher social rank; the growth of the Empire led to the creation of new and the extension of old knightly orders; political instability and the frequent dissolutions of Parliament and changes of government led to an immense increase in the hereditary awards and knighthoods which politicians and others had learned to expect upon such occasions. In the year of the Queen's Golden Jubilee, 1887, Lord Salisbury was inundated with requests for honours from men who would never have considered themselves candidates in earlier years. He endeavoured to keep the list as short as possible, as he did in the year of the Diamond Jubilee, 1897; but he found it impossible to strike as many names off the lists as he would have liked. Yet, indiscriminate as the honours·lists had become in Queen Victoria's reign, they became far more so in the next century.

Lloyd George's attitude towards the system was notorious – no less than twenty-five thousand Orders of the British Empire were bestowed during the years of his War and Coalition Cabinets between 1917 and 1922 – and the sale of honours which was carried on so profitably in his time caused King George v the greatest concern, particularly as those who bought the honours were frequently quite unworthy of them, while he was often kept in the dark about them until the deals were made. In 1916, for instance, Lloyd George asked for the King's consent to the granting of a peerage to a Conservative Member of Parliament so as to provide a safe seat for another man the Prime Minister wanted in his Government. The King replied that he could not approve of the honour as the public services of the Member in question did not call 'for such special recognition'. He had to give way, however, when it appeared that the man had already been told of his forthcoming elevation and the Conservative Association in his constituency had been warned that an immediate by-election would be necessary. Again, a few years later, in 1922, the King was asked to confer peerages on two men both of whom had been suspected of dishonest dealings. He wrote a letter of angry protest to Lloyd George, complaining that this 'brought things rather to a climax', though 'for some time,' he added, 'there have been evident signs of growing public dissatisfaction on the excessive number of honours conferred; and the questionable circumstances under which the honours in certain instances have been granted ... I do appeal most strongly for the establishment of some efficient and trustworthy procedure in order to protect the Crown and the Government from the possibility of similar painful if not humiliating incidents.'

Lloyd George's Conservative successors were more discriminating in their use of the honours system. But when MacDonald came into office in 1924, the King thought it as well to send him a memorandum on the subject of 'Honours and Appointments':

It is hoped that a firm hand will be kept on the distribution of Honours. With the exception of the last Government [Baldwin's first], the bestowal has been extravagant. Especial care should be taken with regard to appointments to the Privy Council. Mr Gladstone said that a Privy Councillorship used to be regarded as a greater honour than a Peerage.

Before any person is offered an Appointment under the Crown, or an Honour, the King's approval should be obtained, until which time the individual in question should not be approached on the subject ...

Except in very special cases, Submissions for Honours are only made twice a year, i.e., New Year's Day and the King's Birthday.

The number of names submitted on each occasion for Baronetcies and Knighthoods, other than those for the Dominions, should not respectively exceed 8 and 24.

The King deprecates the bestowal of Honours on Ministers while in office.

The King's strong feelings on the subject eventually led to the appointment of a Royal Commission under the chairmanship of Lord Dunedin which was itself followed by the Honours (Prevention of Abuses) Act of 1925. Thereafter the names put forward for the King's consideration were less open to censure; yet there were still to be found amongst them those of men of whom the King could not really approve. He often protested, but usually in vain, though he was successful in preventing the award of the Order of Merit to John Singer Sargent whom he admired neither as a painter nor as a man. He himself was never anxious to press names upon his Prime Minister, though his father had not been so forbearing. Indeed, King Edward VII as Prince of Wales was often importunate; and in 1881 worried Gladstone by a strong recommendation for baronetcies for four men, not one of whom was considered worthy of the honour. 'It is perhaps hardly fair to say so,' Gladstone's secretary, Edward Hamilton, noted in his journal, 'but these recommendations have rather an ugly look about them. A respectable clergyman [the Rev. H. W. Bellairs] wrote not long since to say that he was in possession of information to which he could swear, that there were certain persons scheming for hereditary honours, and bribes to people in very high life ... that a gentleman told him that he had been offered a baronetcy by the Prince of Wales ... on condition that he would pay £70,000 to the Prince's agent on receiving the title.' Only one of the four men recommended by the Prince was 'known to ordinary fame', Hamilton added. This was a rich building contractor, C. J. Freake, and for him a knighthood would have been quite sufficient. Yet the Prince 'persistently and somewhat questionably (if not fishily)' pressed Freake's name upon Gladstone.

King George v, on the contrary, only once asked for a title to be conferred on someone whom he knew. This was an inventor of flying boats whom the King considered worthy of a knighthood. The Prime Minister's reply, however, was not helpful: there were other inventors who had prior claims. Besides 10 Downing Street was 'snowed under' with applications.

Nowadays applications from the royal family are uncommon; and all recommendations for political honours have to be accompanied by a declaration signed either by the leader of the party concerned or by an accredited representative, usually the Chief Whip, to the effect that 'no payment or expectation of payment to any party or political fund is directly or indirectly associated with the recommendations' made. The recommendations are then carefully vetted by the Political Honours Scrutiny Committee and by the Ceremonial Officer of the Civil Service Department, R. L. Sharp, a scrupulous Scotsman who gained a first in classics at Cambridge.

The Prime Minister can, however, insist on an honour to which the Political Honours Scrutiny Committee has taken exception, as Sir Harold Wilson was alleged in the Press to have done when in his final Honours List he put forward the names of various people who were, it was claimed, unlikely either to make any significant contribution to public affairs or, in the case of certain peers, to the business of the House. Nor can the Queen herself overrule this insistence, though she can protest as her grandfather did. On his resignation in 1963 Mr Harold Macmillan – while declining for himself the Order of the Garter and the earldom which had traditionally been offered to retiring Prime Ministers for generations – asked for and obtained an unprecedented number of honours for his staff and loyal supporters. Sir Harold

Wilson, who has accepted the Order of the Garter but would not accept an earldom, decided on coming to power to reduce the number of honours which had in the past been conferred each year as a matter of course. And, although his later lists led to much criticism and some ridicule, he did ensure that his first Honours List was, as he put it himself, 'welcomed by the press as less stuffy, more original and more representative of the kind of people who made Britain tick'.

'There were no hereditary peerages, nor baronetcies,' Sir Harold continued. 'Life Peerages then, and subsequently, were based not only on the test of distinction but on that of having something of importance to say, in the national forum which the House of Lords provides ... Sports, entertainment and the arts had more representatives ... and many leading industrialists, surprisingly the forgotten men of Conservative lists, were included. It was at this time I instituted a new citation in my recommendations to the Queen for "services to export".'

The Queen's Awards for Export and Technology, as they are now known, are presented to about a hundred firms a year on Her Majesty's birthday, 21 April; and the formal letter confirming them is couched in splendidly grandiose terms:

Greeting! We being cognisant of the outstanding achievement of the said body as manifested in the furtherance and increase of Export Trade ... and being desirous of showing Our Royal Favour do hereby confer upon it
THE QUEEN'S AWARD FOR EXPORT ACHIEVEMENT
for a period of five years ... and do hereby give permission for the authorised flag of the said Award to be flown during that time by the said body and for the device thereof to be displayed in the manner authorised by Our Warrant ...

And we do further hereby authorise the said body during the five years of the currency of this Our Award further to use and display in like manner the flags and devices of any current former Awards by it received. ... Given at our Court of St. James's under Our Royal Sign Manual

Sir Harold Wilson was created a Knight of the Most Noble Order of the Garter in 1976 as his predecessor as Labour Prime Minister, Earl Attlee, had been twenty years before. It was Attlee who, as Prime Minister in 1946, agreed to the suggestion of King George VI that the Garter should be a non-political honour in the sovereign's gift. It was the oldest order of knighthood anywhere existing, having been established by King Edward III in the fourteenth century. Yet it was no longer that illustrious and exclusive Christian fellowship which once it had been. Charles II had bestowed it freely upon his illegitimate children; in the next century it had become a political honour; George III had increased its original number of twenty-five knights so as to make room for as many of his sons or of his successors' sons as he might choose to elect. By the nineteenth century it was so little coveted that

Lord Melbourne was able to say he liked the Garter well enough because there was no 'damned merit in it'.

King George VI was determined to rescue the Garter from further deterioration in public esteem. Rejecting Winston Churchill's romantic suggestion that he should revert to the principles of Edward III and knight 'young paladins', he decided to appoint to the seven vacancies that existed in 1946 only such distinguished men as had performed some great service for their country. Winston Churchill was naturally one of them, but he declined the honour for the moment. So did the Prime Minister. The Labour and Opposition Leaders of the House of Lords were, therefore, invested together with five war leaders, the soldiers, Alexander, Alanbrooke and Montgomery, the sailor, Mountbatten, and the airman, Portal. This early example set by the King in making the Order a reward of merit and service to the State was unfortunately not always followed, even by himself. And several knights since elected to the Order, of which the Queen is Sovereign, have not had careers which have distinguished them as national figures, though those unknown to common fame – like Lord Middleton, a Yorkshire landowner, who confessed himself 'dumbfounded' when selected for the honour – have certainly devoted much of their time to the unpaid duties of public life.

Like the Garter, the next most illustrious Order of Chivalry, the Most Ancient and Most Noble Order of the Thistle, which is limited to sixteen knights of Scottish descent, is also in the sovereign's gift. So is the Royal Victorian Order, which was founded in 1896 by Queen Victoria who thought that too much patronage was left in the hands of politicians. So, too, is the Order of Merit, founded in 1902 as an order of special distinction limited to twenty-four members on whom no title is conferred. The Royal Family Order, which consists of a miniature portrait of the Queen, surrounded by diamonds on a bow of yellow watered silk, is entirely at her disposal and is awarded to female members of the royal family only.

Both the Royal Victorian Order – which is awarded for personal service to the sovereign and, with a quite lavish generosity, to foreign officials with whom the sovereign comes into contact on State visits – and the Order of Merit are open to women, although there were only two female members of the Order of Merit in 1978 and if Edward VII, in whose reign it was founded, had had his way there would have been none at all: being 'reluctant to give it to women', he 'hung fire', so Francis Knollys told Balfour's secretary, when it was proposed to award it to the aged Florence Nightingale who did eventually become the first woman to have the Order bestowed upon her in 1907.

The other principal orders of chivalry, which are not in the sovereign's gift, are the Most Honourable Order of St Michael and St George, the Most Excellent Order of the British Empire, and the Order of the Companions of Honour. The last of these is limited to sixty-five members and is open to women. But, like the Order of Merit, it has relatively few female members: of the fifty-six members in 1978, only four were women.

About fourteen times a year various of these honours are bestowed by the Queen at investitures at Buckingham Palace. Each investiture lasts for about an hour and a quarter of a weekday morning and requires skilful organization and great concentration. The men and women who are to be honoured, for the most part accompanied by the two members of their families they are permitted to take with them into the palace, drive through the arch at the far end of the forecourt of Buckingham Palace, park their cars in the courtyard, walk through the great doors and across the red carpet of the Grand Hall, past the Carrara marble columns with their gilt bronze capitals and up the impressive Grand Staircase between troopers of the Household Cavalry. They then enter the Ballroom, a vast cream and gold apartment almost a hundred and twenty-five feet long with a ceiling forty-five feet high from which hang six pink lustre chandeliers. At the far end, raised on a dais under a canopied recess, enclosed by Corinthian columns, are two thrones which were made in Paris in 1902 under the direction of the art dealer, Lord Duveen. While, in the musicians' gallery, an orchestra of one of the regiments of the Household Division plays those bland and familiar tunes, mostly from popular musical comedies and usually by American composers, which are considered appropriate to such occasions, those recipients who are to receive medals have hooks fitted to their lapels or dresses. They are told to walk towards the Queen when their turn comes, to bow or curtsy, not to say anything while she is putting on the medal unless she speaks to them, to take three steps backwards, to bow or curtsy once more before turning and walking away. Men receiving knighthoods are required to kneel on a red stool placed in front of the throne; the Queen will tap them on each shoulder with a sword handed to her by an equerry; they will stand up (without being commanded 'Arise, Sir —') and shake the Queen's offered hand lightly before backing away.

The imminent arrival of the Queen is indicated by the appearance just before eleven o'clock of five Yeomen of the Guard who march down the Ballroom to take their places behind the throne. The Queen herself then comes into the room with a few members of the Household. Those who have been sitting on the chairs arranged in rows on the parquet floor beneath the Gobelin tapestries stand up. The orchestra plays the national anthem. Each person to be honoured awaits his turn standing by a Gentleman Usher and moves forward to the Queen as his name is read out by the Lord Chamberlain. The Secretary of the Central Chancery of the Orders of Knighthood places the appropriate medal on to a cushion held by a member of the Household. The Queen takes up the medal to place on the hook provided, saying a few words or smiling in a friendly, sometimes charmingly conspiratorial way. When the last medal has been accepted the Lord Chamberlain steps forward to face the Queen; the national anthem is played again; and the ceremony is over.

To some it is a rather tiresome ordeal but to most a moving and memorable occasion. A Fire Brigade officer, who was presented with the British Empire Medal, spoke for many when he said: 'I thought it would be just another ceremony. But now that I've been, it's something I'll remember for the rest of my days.'

13 Royal Finances

In November 1969, during the course of an interview on television in America, the Duke of Edinburgh was asked how the royal family was managing with inflation. After a pause he replied, quite casually, that they were not coping very well. He explained that the money allowed by the Government to the Queen, known as the Civil List, had been 'based on costs of eighteen years ago', and that they would be going 'into the red next year'. He added, in a comment which the Prime Minister described as 'clearly jocular', that they would probably have 'to move into smaller premises'.

At the beginning of her reign the Queen's Privy Purse, sometimes described as her 'salary', was fixed at £60,000 a year under the Civil List Act of 1952. She was granted in addition an annual allowance of £306,800 for the salaries and expenses of her Household, a Royal Bounty of £13,200 which was to be given back to the people each year in the form of 'alms and services', and a Supplementary Provision of £95,000 a year to allow for inflation and to make allowances for certain members of the royal family who have no fixed annuity granted to them by Parliament but are nevertheless presumed to be precluded by their position from taking up paid employment. These sums, totalling £475,000 a year, were granted to her in return for the income (£6,500,000 in 1977–8) derived from the lands and property which used to belong to the monarch personally – much of it taken from the Church at the time of the Reformation – and which, theoretically still in royal hands, have, since the time of George III, been surrendered to the Government at the beginning of each new reign. These Crown Lands, which include much valuable property in the West End of London and the Home Counties, are managed on the Government's behalf by the Crown Estate Commissioners.

As well as the interest on her large private fortune – the exact amount of which is the subject of constant and often, in the words of Lord Cobbold, 'wildly exaggerated guesswork' – the Queen also has an income from the Duchy of Lancaster, a collection of estates, extending to about 52,000 acres, spread all over England from Yorkshire to Buckinghamshire, and Shropshire to Lincoln, most of which were acquired by the Crown in the Middle Ages and which are a private property, not part of the Crown Estate. The Duchy – which transferred £485,000 to the Privy Purse for the year mid-1977 to mid-1978 – also owns properties in various towns in England, including Bedford, Bristol, Leeds, Leicester and Northampton, and in London, both in the Strand, where it is still the landlord of the Manor of Savoy, and in the City.

The Duchy of Cornwall is also a private estate. It is vested in the eldest son of the sovereign or, if there is no son, it lies dormant in the Crown. It covers an area of nearly 130,000 acres, for the most part agricultural land in the West Country, principally in Cornwall, Devon and Somerset, though it also has property in London, including a residential estate in Kennington and the Oval cricket ground. Its net income, which amounts to about £230,000 a year, is now at the disposal of the Prince of Wales, who is also Duke of Cornwall.

The Prince of Wales is not liable to pay tax on this income, an 'incredible amount' of which he gives away, in the words of Anthony Gray, Secretary and Keeper of the Duchy's Records, being 'hideously generous with his money' and 'hardly ever' ignoring a request for help from an organization within the Duchy. But it was announced in 1969 that, until he marries or there is some other change in his circumstances, the Prince of Wales would voluntarily surrender half the annual sum to the Government, the late Duke of Windsor, as Prince of Wales, having surrendered about thirty per cent of the Duchy income in lieu of taxation. It was also announced that Prince Charles would contribute his naval officer's pay, after tax, to the King George VI's Fund for Sailors.

The Queen is exempt from income tax and surtax as well as capital gains tax, capital transfer tax and death duties,* whilst other members of the royal family, apart from the Prince of Wales, are liable for tax on any income left after paying their official expenses. They have to complete tax returns as ordinary members of the public; and, after their expenses have been agreed with the Inland Revenue, the balance of income is taxed in the normal way. As the official expenses of these

---

* As well as being exempt from income tax and death duties, the Queen has many other privileges, most of them unique to herself. She cannot be sued in a court of law or made to give evidence; she is not required to pass a driving test; her four principal cars carry no number plates; she does not need licences for the dogs (which, as has often been related, she feeds herself, at Buckingham Palace on white plastic sheets spread upon the carpet, placing the meat in the bowls with a silver fork and spoon brought to her by a footman). She cannot, however, vote in a parliamentary election. Nor can the royal dukes as peers of the realm, though they may speak in the House of Lords. The Queen Mother, Princess Margaret and other female members of the royal family do have a right to vote; but they do not take advantage of the privilege since they must, like the Queen herself, be above party.

other members of the royal family are high, only a modest balance of taxable income is left.

The Queen's Civil List and her untaxed income from the estates of the Duchy of Lancaster are supplemented by what has been termed the 'hidden subsidy' of public funds, that is to say the Department Votes which are contributed each year by various ministries and government departments.

The royal yacht *Britannia* – which, costing about £2,150,000 to build, was designed for alternative use as a hospital ship in times of emergency – is maintained, with a crew of 276 on long sea voyages and 189 in harbour, by the Ministry of Defence at an estimated cost in 1977–8 of £3,250,000. It serves the Queen and other members of the royal family as a mobile official residence, an administrative headquarters in both home and foreign waters and, less often, usually for no more than about one week a year, as a pleasure craft – the Queen is not such a bad sailor as popular mythology suggests. It also takes part in naval exercises from time to time and is occasionally employed on hydrographic duties.

The Queen's Flight, which transports Ministers and senior members of the armed forces as well as the royal family, is also maintained by the Ministry of Defence at a cost of about £1,800,000 a year. The Post Office provides free postal and telecommunications services valued at £1,000 a week; British Rail paid £228,500 in 1976–7 for royal train journeys and the maintenance of the royal train. The salaries of equerries do not come out of the royal purse; nor does the cost of stationery and office machinery, while the Department of the Environment pays at present some £4,545,000 a year for the upkeep of the royal palaces and residences in which it employs about 350 people.* The total of these so-called 'hidden subsidies' now runs at about £10,000,000 a year.

Like the crown jewels, various other pieces of personal jewellery and the royal art collections, Windsor Castle and Buckingham Palace are considered by both the Queen and the Treasury solicitor as 'inalienable by the occupant of the throne' and not 'at her free personal disposal'. Also considered as the property of the State are Kew Palace; the Palace at Holyroodhouse; Kensington Palace which provides London houses for various members of the royal family, including Princess Margaret, Princess Alice Duchess of Gloucester, the Duke and Duchess of Gloucester, Princess Alice, Countess of Athlone and Prince Michael of Kent; St James's Palace where the Queen Mother lives in Clarence House and the Duke and Duchess of Kent have apartments at York

---

* The Department of the Environment is also responsible for maintaining Hampton Court Palace, Queen Charlotte's Cottage and Kensington State Apartments at an estimated cost in 1977–8 of £1,374,000. These costs are included in the expenditure for Ancient Monuments.

House; and Hampton Court, a part of which consists of Grace and Favour residences, houses and apartments at the Queen's disposal, whose occupants (mostly elderly and of limited means) pay rates but no rent.*

Balmoral and Sandringham are held to be privately owned by the sovereign who pays rates on them but no tax on the farm profits. As critics of the monarchy have often maintained, however, they were both bought with money saved from income either provided by the State or derived from the Duchy of Cornwall. This is true of Sandringham which was purchased together with some 7,000 acres, in 1862 for £220,000 – a further 4,000 acres were acquired later – and on which £60,000 was spent on improvements and additions. Both sums of money came from the accumulated revenues of the Duchy of Cornwall. Most of the money for Balmoral, however, came not from savings which the astuteness of Prince Albert had been able to make from Queen Victoria's Civil List but from the fortune of about £250,000 bequeathed to her by John Camden Nield, an eccentric miser. The estate at that time had 17,400 acres. In 1978 the nearby estate of Delnadamph of 6,700 acres, mainly grouse moor, was purchased by the present Queen for a price of about £700,000. She also paid about £300,000 for a country estate with some 500 acres for Princess Anne in Gloucestershire where another 500 acres were later acquired from a neighbouring farmer.†

For the first few years of the Queen's reign the Civil List proved adequate to meet the expenses for which it had been allocated without her having to call upon the Supplementary Provision of £95,000. Most of this Provision could, therefore, be saved and invested until the rising tide of inflation made it necessary to spend it. In 1962, however, the expenditure exceeded the allowances by a considerable sum, and thereafter by sums increasingly large, until in 1969 the amount left in reserve could not be expected to meet the deficit for the following year.

When the Duke of Edinburgh's remarks revealing this state of affairs on American television were broadcast in England they caused uproar

---

* There used to be about 140 of these Grace and Favour residences in all, but the numbers have been greatly reduced in recent years as most of them are uncomfortable and inconvenient and so expensive to modernize that they are not being reallocated when the occupants die. At Hampton Court there are now only about twenty still in use.

† The Prince of Wales's country home, Chevening House in Kent, was left to the nation by Lord Stanhope. Under the terms of the Chevening Estate Act the resident may be either the Prime Minister, another Cabinet Minister, the widow or a lineal descendant of King George VI or the spouse, widow or widower of such a descendant. After the Act was passed Lord Stanhope expressed the hope that the house would one day be occupied by the Prince of Wales who accepted nomination as the resident in 1974. Originally a Tudor mansion, the existing exterior was designed by Inigo Jones. The estate of about 3,000 acres is managed by a body of trustees and no public funds are involved. Lord Stanhope endowed the property with enough money for the trustees to pay for the renovation of what had become a rather dilapidated house.

in the Press. Sympathizers with the monarchy, horrified by what they took to be the Government's neglect, demanded an emergency debate in the House of Commons and the immediate establishment of a Select Committee to review the whole position of the Civil List. Lord Shinwell was quoted as having said, 'If we want a monarchy we have to pay them properly. We can't have them going around in rags.' At the same time others professed themselves to be outraged by the Duke of Edinburgh's comments which, they maintained, should have been raised at home, if in public at all, and which made no reference either to the support given to the royal finances by grants from various government departments or to the discussions which had been going on for several months between the Queen's advisers and Treasury officials in an effort to help the Crown meet the growing cost of its obligations. In an article in the *New Statesman*, Richard Crossman, for example, wrote of the Prince's 'truly regal cheek'.* He and various other members of the Cabinet met to consider the implications of what the Prime Minister, Harold Wilson, termed 'a crisis' in its affairs. Crossman recorded in his diary:

We discussed it at length. Suddenly Barbara [Castle, Secretary of State for Employment] blew up and said what I had been feeling: 'I must say this is absolutely outrageous ... I think we should make some political capital out of this. Now that Prince Philip has put all this before the public, complaining about the Government as though we are being unfair to them, at least let's have a Select Committee to look into the private fortune of the Queen.' This is something I've thought about for many years. The Queen pays no estate or death duties, the monarchy hasn't paid any since these taxes were invented and it has made her by far the richest person in the country. Not only has the family accumulated pictures and riches, but their estates and actual investments must have accumulated and they are inordinately wealthy.

Roy Jenkins, the Chancellor of the Exchequer, Crossman added, was, like Barbara Castle and himself, a republican, which was 'striking': 'We don't like going to Court or feel comfortable there, and we know the Queen isn't comfortable with us.' But it was only these three and Michael Stewart, the Foreign Secretary, who disliked Court ceremonial and public dinners. Fred Peart, the Lord President of the Council, was apparently appalled by Barbara Castle's outburst:

Not only did he think it was politically unwise to have any radical taint to what we do but he naturally adores being Lord President of the Council and gets on with the Queen just like George Brown and Callaghan do. Callaghan said, 'I am a loyalist. I wouldn't like to see the royal family hurt and I think Prince

* Nothing detracts so much from the general popularity of the monarchy in Britain as discussion of royal finances. Public opinion polls indicate that only about 10% of the population would prefer a republic, but the figure tends to rise sharply at times when an increase in royal expenditure is proposed or authorized. The figure rose to about 16% in 1969 and almost 20% in 1971.

Philip is a very fine fellow.' My God, Jim made a speech of such banality and appalling conventionalism, attacking the sentiments of middle-class intellectuals. He really is putting himself forward as the spokesman of the conservative working man, and his new role is growing on him . . . And roughly speaking, it is true that it is the professional classes who in this sense are radical and the working-class socialists who are by and large staunchly monarchist. The nearer the Queen they get the more working-class members of the Cabinet love her and she loves them.

As for Harold Wilson, the Prime Minister, he did, according to Crossman, say something to this effect: 'Most rich men feel that part of the job of a rich man is spending a good part of his wealth for charitable and public purposes. It takes royalty to assume that all their private income is to be kept to themselves and accumulated and that they are not obliged to spend any of it on seeing them through their private life.' But Wilson 'had apparently no sense of indignation with Edinburgh, no anxiety to take the opportunity to get death duties applied to royalty or all the other things we naturally wanted to do. He is a steady loyalist.'

On 11 November the Prime Minister made a statement in the House of Commons which, in his own phrase, was intended to 'defuse' the crisis. He revealed that in recent years there had been 'a progressive transfer of expenditure, previously borne by the Royal Household, to provide funds by Departmental Votes', citing, as examples, the remuneration of staff engaged on maintenance of the royal palaces, and the reimbursement to the Crown of costs incurred on royal tours overseas, rail travel to royal functions in this country, and expenses relating to State entertainments. He pointed out that 'in the previous six years there had been two efficiency investigations of the Royal Household, one by the Organization and Methods Division of the Treasury, the other by an industrialist commissioned by the Queen's advisers, which had led to a number of cost-saving improvements'. And he further informed the House that over a period of months there had been 'detailed discussions between the Queen's advisers and Treasury officials, as a result of which the Government authorized a communication to the effect that a new Select Committee would be appointed at the beginning of the succeeding Parliament. Earlier action was not required.' Wilson concluded: 'I hope that the House will accept that in this important – and, I do not need to stress, delicate – matter, the Government have proceeded in full discussion with the Queen's advisers, on a basis capable of dealing with the problem which is developing, and of dealing with it in time, having regard both to increasing costs and to a proper regard for restraint in public expenditure.' The House of Commons Select Committee which the Prime Minister promised in his speech was duly appointed and met in June and July 1971.

211

Having considered all the evidence which they were able to gather, the Committee came to the conclusion that the Civil List was, indeed, wholly inadequate and that, while there was 'no question in any ordinary sense of a "pay increase" for the Queen', the allowances made to her and to her family would have to be greatly increased to enable them to meet their mounting expenses and the salaries of their staffs. Accordingly, an Act was passed which raised the Civil List to £980,000 a year, more than double its previous figure. The annuities payable to members of the royal family, other than the Queen, were also increased considerably: the Queen Mother's to £95,000, the Duke of Edinburgh's to £65,000, the late Duke of Gloucester's to £45,000, Princess Margaret's to £35,000 and Princess Anne's to £15,000 which was to be raised to £35,000 after her marriage. An additional £60,000 a year was allowed for those members of the royal family – the present Duke of Gloucester, the Duke of Kent, Princess Alexandra and Princess Alice, Countess of Athlone – who were not otherwise provided for, yet who carried out a variety of public duties. Provision was also made for contingent future payments of £20,000 a year to the younger sons of the Queen, Prince Andrew and Prince Edward, at the age of eighteen and before marriage and £50,000 after marriage; of £60,000 to any widow of the Prince of Wales; of £20,000 to any widow of a younger son; and £20,000 to the widowed Princess Alice, Duchess of Gloucester. The Queen undertook to forego the element of £60,000 in the Civil List which had previously been described as her salary and which had, in any event in the past, been confused with other expenditure.

Despite the large rises provided for by the Civil List Act of 1972, by the beginning of 1975 they had once again been overtaken by inflation and the Prime Minister felt obliged to ask the Commons for another increase. He stressed that, 'thanks to continuing economies in the administration of the Royal Household', royal expenses had not risen nearly as fast as the Retail Price Index, and that the increase was necessitated principally by the need to meet the rises in salaries and wages of the palace staff which, gradually reduced in numbers over the years, had formerly been paid considerably less than people engaged in similar work elsewhere. Household wages and salaries, it was explained, had risen from £580,000 in 1972 to £985,000 in 1975; other Household expenses had risen from £291,000 to £385,000. Food bills now ran at £73,061; laundry at £12,878; the maintenance of the royal gardens cost £23,736; garden parties, £39,477. £11,244 was spent on flowers; £9,357 on official presents; and £24,253 on ceremonial horses, as opposed to the Queen's race-horses which, of course, are her private property and paid for personally. The Queen herself, it was made known, had had to contribute £150,000 towards the Civil List in 1975.

While this was seen as generosity in some quarters, in others it was maintained that she could well afford such sums which were relatively paltry when compared with the enormous income she enjoyed. And the matter of her immunity from taxes was raised once more. Michael Stewart declared:

We are now living in a community where we are always exhorting each other to show respect for the law, to have some sense of national unity and to have a fair sharing of burdens. The example of a Head of State who is immune from that part of the law that requires us to pay taxes is unfortunate ... I am not talking about the size of the bill. I am saying that immunity from tax exposes the Monarchy to unnecessary criticism. I am saying that this way of paying for the Monarchy by granting an inadequate Civil List, because the Queen does not have to pay income tax, is slovenly and an undignified way of going about the matter.

Ninety Members of Parliament voted against the increase; but the Civil List Act 1975 passed into law, raising the royal allowances to £1,820,000 a year. There will be no other similar Acts, for increases in the Civil List are now simply included in the public expenditure Estimates and no longer require a parliamentary order. Under this new procedure there have been further increases every year since 1975. In 1977 the annuities payable to certain members of the royal family were also raised after discussions between the three royal trustees, that is to say the Prime Minister, the Chancellor of the Exchequer and the Keeper of the Privy Purse. The Queen Mother's annuity was increased to £155,000, Princess Anne's to £50,000 and Princess Margaret's to £55,000. The Duke of Edinburgh's annuity, which had been raised from £65,000 to £85,000 in 1976, remained the same; so did Princess Alice of Gloucester's which had been raised from £20,000 to £25,000. Allowances, which were paid for personally by the Queen, were made in 1977 to the Duke of Gloucester (£26,000); the Duke of Kent (£48,000); Princess Alexandra (£50,000) and Princess Alice, Countess of Athlone (£6,000).

In 1978 it was announced that an increase in the Civil List from £2,620,000 in the current year to £2,860,000 for the following year had been proposed. This was an increase of less than ten per cent; and, since royal expenditure had increased by eighteen per cent in 1977 due to the Jubilee celebrations, it was considered by the Government to be reasonable. But William Hamilton, the Labour Member for Fife Central and a persistent critic of the royal family, strongly opposed it. The request for an increase in 1969 had been condemned by Hamilton as 'the most insensitive and brazen pay claim made in the last two hundred years'. He now deplored the fact that the royal family should be given yet another increase without Members of Parliament having an opportunity to find out whether it was justified or not, and declared that there would be 'a nationwide sense of outrage' if it was proposed to increase the payment made to Princess Margaret whom he condemned for not carrying out her proper share of public duties. Finally he demanded 'a return to the practice pertaining up to 1972, namely, that of subjecting the financing of the institution of the Monarchy to critical examinations by a Select Committee; that such examinations be held at not less than five-yearly intervals; and that the royal annuitants themselves be invited to submit both oral and written evidence'.

When the allocations from the Civil List to the various members of the Royal Family were later announced, Hamilton renewed his attack for not only was Princess Margaret's annuity increased by £4,000 to £59,000, but all the other allowances were raised as well – the Queen Mother's by £20,000 a year to £175,000, the Duke of Edinburgh's by £8,500 to £93,500, Princess Anne's from £50,000 to £60,000, Princess Alice of Gloucester's by £5,000 to £30,000, the Duke of Gloucester's by £13,000 to £39,000, the Duke of Kent's by £12,000 to £60,000, Princess Alexandra's by £10,000 to £60,000, and Princess Alice's by £500 to £6,500. In addition Prince Andrew who reached the age of eighteen on 19 February 1978, became eligible for £20,000; but as he was still at school and not undertaking any royal duties the amount was initially limited to £518 a year, the balance being accumulated by the Royal Trustees.

Hamilton's demands for the reconvening of a Select Committee on the Civil List found little support on either side of the House. Ministers were anxious not to be concerned with any moves that might suggest a tendency to republicanism, while the Labour left wing, sympathize though they might with Hamilton's feelings, considered that public opinion was so strongly in favour of the monarchy that any concerted effort to bring it under close parliamentary scrutiny would be electorally damaging in the months before a general election.

The Conservatives for their part were perfectly content with the proposed increase. 'Supply for the monarchy should never be skimped,' Lord Home maintained. 'It would be a totally false economy.' He emphasized, as others have, the enormous benefit the country derives from the Queen's overseas tours alone for which the Government pays, though it leaves her responsible for providing the many presents she is expected to give away. Lord Home knew of no royal tour which had not made 'a deep and favourable impact on the people and Government of the country visited'. The Queen's appearances abroad 'do more in days to gain goodwill for Britain', he added, 'than all the politicians and diplomats lumped together could achieve in years'. Many diplomats are inclined to agree with him. Lord Caccia, once British Ambassador in America, told Harold Macmillan that the Queen's visit to the United States 'made a tremendous effect' there and 'buried George III for good and all'. Even Aneurin Bevan, by no means a convinced monarchist, admitted that the Queen's visit to America had been a great success, though he could not resist replying, when asked by a journalist in New York what he thought as an Englishman of her enthusiastic reception there, 'I'm not an Englishman. I'm a Welshman. But I'm naturally delighted at the success here of anyone descended, however remotely, from our House of Tudor.'

Including the amount spent on these foreign tours, the Civil List and Department Votes, the office of the Head of State now costs the nation some £14,000,000 a year. Large as this sum is, it is relatively paltry when compared with what is spent elsewhere: well over five times as much is expended upon the promotion of cigarettes; well over half as much again is spent by the National Health Service on anti-depressant drugs; over £61,000,000 is spent on the Arts Council; £215,000,000 on football pools; and a total of almost £5,000,000,000 on Bingo and gambling machines. In the United States the budget for the White House offices alone, in the fiscal year 1977, was $17,236,000.*

---

* Since this chapter was written rising costs have led to further increases in the annuities payable to the royal family. The full allocation, which stood at £2,560,462 in 1978, has been increased to £2,821,200. Of this sum, the Queen's Civil List accounts for £2,134,200. The other annuities now stand at £200,000 for the Queen Mother, £98,000 for the Duke of Edinburgh, £63,000 for Princess Anne, £64,000 for Princess Margaret, £30,000 for Princess Alice, Duchess of Gloucester, £57,000 for the Duke of Gloucester, £75,000 for the Duke of Kent, £72,000 for Princess Alexandra and £8,000 for Princess Alice, Countess of Athlone. Prince Andrew's allowance has been increased to £20,000 but the amount paid to him will be limited to £1,000, the balance accumulated by the Royal Trustees as it was last year.

14 The Royal Family

Preferring as her father and grandfather did, the regular to the unexpected, and not sharing her great-grandfather's passion for foreign travel, the Queen is content to leave untouched the pattern of her yearly moves from one royal home to another. Provided that overseas tours allow, she spends Christmas at Windsor, then moves to Sandringham for the New Year and January. Easter and Ascot Week are spent at Windsor; a week or so, usually in July, at Holyroodhouse; and a summer holiday at Balmoral, her presence in each residence being indicated by the royal standard flying from a flagpole.

In Queen Victoria's time included among the guests there was always a Minister in Attendance. So there usually was in Edward VII's and occasionally in the earlier years of the reign of George V. But the practice was abandoned after the First World War when communications were considered sufficiently advanced to render it unnecessary. In 1919 the King, while at Balmoral, was informed of the railway strike by telephone; and two years later a letter to him was dropped over the grounds from an aeroplane. The Prime Minister of the day and his wife, however, are normally asked every year for a week-end to Balmoral where they are likely to occupy, as the Macmillans did, 'a suite of rooms on the ground floor of the Castle with the well-known maple furniture, Stuart tartan curtains, brass ink-stands and Winterhalter prints which must have been used by many Prime Ministers for more than a century'. These visits 'in an entirely informal atmosphere', Sir Harold Wilson thinks, are 'one of the highlights of the prime ministerial year'.

A Minister is also usually included amongst the 'dine and sleep' guests who are invited to join the Queen at Windsor at Easter. In 1978 the Chancellor of the Exchequer and Mrs Denis Healey were asked, together with the Marquess of Anglesey; the Polish Ambassador; the High Commissioner for New Zealand; Professor Sir George Porter, Director of the Royal Institution of Great Britain and Fullerian Professor of Chemistry; and the Reverend Kenneth Slack, the Presbyterian Director of the Christian Aid Division of the British Council of Churches, all of whom were accompanied by their wives. The following Thursday evening the dinner guests who stayed the night in the Castle with their wives were the Prime Minister; the Secretary General of the United Nations; the Turkish Ambassador; the High Commissioner for Australia; Sir Arthur Armitage, Vice Chancellor and Professor of Common Law, Victoria University of Manchester; and Dr Roy Strong, Director of the Victoria and Albert Museum.

These 'dine and sleep' guests, who are asked to arrive between six and seven and told that 'dinner jackets will be worn', assemble in the Green Drawing-Room of the Castle before dinner, and follow the Queen into the white-and-gold panelled dining-room at half past eight. After the meal, they are usually taken round parts of the Castle by the Queen who shows them some of its treasures, including those in the Royal Library, about which she talks with enthusiasm and knowledge. After this tour of inspection they return to the drawing-room where drinks are laid out and where Prince. Philip, alert, watchful and astringent, moves about, drawing people into conversation. He and the Queen generally retire to bed before midnight, saying goodbye to their guests as they will not see them again in the morning. The guests are served breakfast in their rooms to which the visitors' book is also brought up for them to sign.

'The Queen is a pleasant, easy hostess,' one of these guests has commented, 'far easier to talk to than one had imagined.' A patient, interested listener, she is quickly responsive to a neatly turned phrase, readily amused by a good story and a gifted raconteuse herself, animated, spontaneous and sometimes quite witty. She does not pretend to any deep love or understanding of music or the visual arts. She prefers watching television to reading books. She is not, in fact, in any sense intellectual. Yet she is as astute as she is conscientious and honest, as perspicacious as she is painstaking and sensible, far more prone to self-mockery than to self-satisfaction, and disarmingly aware of her own weaknesses and foibles: she is superstitious, disliking the idea of thirteen places at table, straightening crossed forks, and throwing spilled salt over her shoulder; she also betrays her nerviness when ill at ease by twisting her rings round her fingers. As a child, though generally happy, she was prone to worriment and anxiety; and, as is frequently the case with such children, she was excessively neat and careful not to waste anything. Before her governess and her far less orderly sister teased her out of the habit, she would get out of bed more than once to make sure her clothes were properly arranged and her shoes set quite straight; meticulously rolled ribbons and bits of smoothed coloured paper were stored in chocolate boxes. Her father used to refer to her 'fretwork'. This increased after she realized that she would one day take over the responsibilities of a monarch, of which he spoke to her often; and her grandmother on her mother's side told Lady

Airlie that she ardently prayed for a baby brother so that she would not have to be Queen.

In public, even after the repeated successes of her appearances during the Jubilee year of 1977, she is still sometimes rather shy and can appear to be both haughty and censorious when she is merely unsure of herself or of her effect on others. 'Under the limelight of public occasions, her sense of responsibility overlays her innate sense of fun,' wrote Godfrey Talbot, the broadcaster, who was the official BBC observer accredited to Buckingham Palace between 1948 and 1969 and had many opportunities of watching the Queen both at work and in her leisure hours. 'And there are times when, intent on the job in hand, her face seems expressionless ... Trained like a trooper to resist displays of emotion ... she brings down an inscrutable curtain of stiffness when many people would be clapping their hands ... She loves children – and her own family life is a sustainer of her existence – and yet I have seen her "freeze" extraordinarily during a young people's rally or a walk round boys' and girls' hospital wards. These severe moments are not frequent ... but [they] are noted.' As Sir Godfrey Agnew told Richard Crossman, her attempts to control her emotions are rarely successful; and Crossman noticed this himself: 'When she is deeply moved and tries to control it she looks like an angry thunder-cloud. So, very often when she's been deeply touched by the plaudits of the crowd she merely looks terribly bad-tempered.'

She has a proper sense of her own dignity and can – as her grandmother, Queen Mary, so often appeared – be intimidating: an unfortunate remark may well be greeted in grim silence with a baleful stare. She can also be demanding; for, setting extremely high standards for her own conduct, she expects the same from those whose work brings them into contact with her. Like her father and her grandfather, George v, she is occasionally capable of sudden outbursts of anger. But, as with the far louder, less controlled and more alarming explosions of Edward vii's temper, these outbursts and the irritation that follows them are soon overcome. In any case, they are rare. As a member of her Household has been quoted as saying: 'She is patient and cheerful. When you think of all the demands made upon her, it makes you appreciate all the more how she conducts herself so cheerfully. Of course, being human, she does sigh occasionally about some particularly irritating detail, but fundamentally she does not complain about the things she has to do.'

What she would really like to do, she once confessed as a girl to her riding-master, would be to live like an ordinary 'lady in the country with lots of horses and dogs'. And it is in the country with her family, close friends and animals that she still feels most contented and at home. For many of those who see her there – a small figure with deep blue eyes, walking about in an old tweed skirt, head scarf and gum boots, occasionally emitting a piercing and most unqueenly whistle at her dogs, or, in the evening, in helpless laughter as she plays charades, delighting in those simple, earthy jokes and absurd antics to which she is as ready happily to abandon herself as her mother and her eldest son – it is difficult to believe that this is the same woman who plays her dignified part in great occasions of State as 'Her Most Excellent Majesty Elizabeth the Second, by the Grace of God, of the United Kingdom of Great Britain and Northern Ireland and of Her other Realms and Territories Queen, Head of the Commonwealth, Defender of the Faith, Sovereign of the British Orders of Knighthood'. She is the fortieth monarch of her country since the Norman Conquest, descended from kings who reigned in Britain long before the Normans came, as well as from Charlemagne, Rodrigo the Cid, Saint Louis, King of France, Mary Queen of Scots, Llewellyn-ap-Gruffyd, Prince of all Wales, and the Emperor Barbarossa. She is also a sixth cousin twice removed from George Washington – to whom few people, says Garter King of Arms, can, therefore, be related more closely – and when the poet, Robert Graves, came to receive from her the Queen's Medal for Poetry he informed her that they were both descended from the Prophet Mohammed, information which she received without apparent surprise.

Shortly before the Queen's accession, 'Chips' Channon was invited to a ball at Windsor Castle during Ascot week. He arrived at the Castle about ten o'clock and found fifty or sixty other guests in the Green Drawing-Room waiting for the beginning of the dancing which was to go on until dawn. 'The rooms were banked with flowers and the lit vitrines full of china,' Channon wrote. 'The Edinburghs made a somewhat late appearance ... and they looked divine. She wore a very high tiara and the Garter.' The Duke was wearing the Windsor uniform of dark blue coat with gold buttons and red collar and turned-back cuffs which had been worn on such occasions at Windsor by the royal family and certain members of the Household since the time of George III. Channon thought they both 'looked like characters out of a fairy tale, and quite eclipsed Princess Margaret, who was simply dressed. But already she is a public character, and I wonder what will happen to her? There is already a Marie Antoinette aroma about her.'

Princess Margaret was nineteen then and deeply attached to one of her father's equerries, Group Captain Peter Townsend, who, as a brave survivor of the Battle of Britain, had joined the Royal Household in February 1944 when she was fourteen and he twenty-nine. At his first interview with the King in the green-carpeted Regency Room at Buckingham Palace, His Majesty, so Townsend wrote, 'did not try, or even need, to put me at my ease ... Despite his easy manner I felt impressed and so kept well within myself. But sometimes he hesitated in his speech, and then I felt drawn towards him, to help keep up the flow of words. I knew myself the agonies of a stammerer.'

Townsend found his duties, which consisted largely of introducing visitors to the King, extremely tedious; and the hours spent waiting for His Majesty's bell to ring were rendered all the more wearisome by the gloom of the Equerries' Room, a dark, high-ceilinged apartment whose windows faced north and whose drab walls were at that time lined with shelves of religious and outdated historical books. He got on well, however, with most of his fellow-courtiers; and, though alarmed by the frightening glare in the blue eyes of his sometimes inordinately angry master, he grew very fond of the King. The Queen he adored; and, like many others, had cause to be grateful to her for calming her husband down when he started 'to rant noisily'. 'Once she held his pulse,' he wrote, 'and, with a wistful smile, began to count – tick, tick, tick – which made him laugh and the storm subsided. In those moments he was like a small boy, very lovable. "The most marvellous person in the world", the King called his wife ... I came, within my limits to think so, too.'

As time went on, however, and Townsend's term of duty, intended initially to last for a few months only, extended into years, it was the King and Queen's younger daughter who came to mean more to him than either of her parents and to preoccupy his thoughts. This is how he described her, contrasting her with her elder sister:

Princess Elizabeth was the King's pride; she was his heir, his understudy, his affectionate admirer, and played her role, as he did his, dutifully, punctiliously, and charmingly.

Princess Margaret was the King's joy. She amused ... delighted ... enchanted him ... She was a girl of unusual, intense beauty ... She was capable, in her face and in her whole being, of an astonishing power of expression. It could change in an instant from saintly, almost melancholic, composure to hilarious, uncontrollable joy. She was, by nature, generous, volatile ... If her extravagant vivacity sometimes outraged the elder members of the household and of London society, it was contagious to those who still felt young – whether they were or not ... She was a *comédienne* at heart, playing the piano with ease and verve, singing in her rich, supple voice the latest hits, imitating the favourite stars. She was coquettish, sophisticated. But what ultimately made Princess Margaret so attractive and lovable was that behind the dazzling façade, the apparent self-assurance, you could find, if you looked for it, a rare softness and sincerity. She could make you bend double with laughing; she could also touch you deeply.

Although Townsend was far from alone in finding her disconcertingly attractive and endearing, there were those who quietly lamented – or have since outspokenly complained of – the 'ill-educated and ill-informed' Princess Margaret's quite unjustified self-regard, her tactlessness, her insistence on unnecessarily expensive arrangements being made for her accommodation and transportation, her tendency to petulance and moods of sullen obstinacy, her tiresome habit of encouraging people to feel completely at home with her, then haughtily checking them, as her uncle, Edward VIII, used to do, for some supposed *lèse-royauté*. It has been suggested, too, that her 'all too voluntary vocal sessions at any piano within reach' were neither gifted nor as welcome as her less critical admirers averred. Yet these harsh and often unjust judgements have not gone uncontested. Lord Fisher of Lambeth, the former Archbishop of Canterbury, who grew to know her well and may be supposed to have been less susceptible to her physical allure than Group Captain Townsend, described her as 'always friendly, always intelligent, always entertaining all through [his] experience of her'. 'I used to meet her fairly often,' Lord Fisher once said, 'and always enjoyed it immensely . . . I became especially devoted to her.'

Peter Townsend's devotion to her, and her devotion to him, eventually became a problem to which both the Government and the Church had to address themselves. It was not so much that Townsend, the Haileybury-educated son of an official in the Burmese Civil Service, was a middle-class commoner, nor that he was almost sixteen years older than Princess Margaret, but that his marriage, hastily contracted during the war and productive of two children, had ended in divorce. And in 1953, when Princess Margaret told her sister and mother of her feelings for him, such a husband for the new Queen's sister was scarcely to be contemplated, particularly, as Winston Churchill pointed out, in coronation year. The young Queen liked Townsend; so did her mother who appointed him Comptroller of her Household after her husband's death. But both of them appreciated the constitutional difficulties placed in the way of his marriage to Princess Margaret by the Royal Marriage Act of 1772. This Act, instigated by King George III, provided that no member of the royal family could marry without the sovereign's consent, though, if that consent were refused to someone over twenty-five, a year's notice could be given to the Privy Council and then the marriage could take place despite the sovereign's refusal. The Act was – and is – still in force; and the Queen was, therefore, bound to consult the Prime Minister about her sister's proposed marriage and to act in accordance with his advice.

If Mr Churchill was firmly opposed to the necessary consent being given, the Queen's Private Secretary, Sir Alan Lascelles, was even more so. In his memoirs Peter Townsend writes of the 'mutual affection' that existed between himself and Lascelles, of his admiration for the Secretary's 'dry, pungent wit', though he admitted to admiring it 'less when it turned into pitiless sarcasm'. But there was little sympathy between them when Townsend went to see Lascelles 'to broach the news'.

Townsend entered his 'sombre but spacious office'. Lascelles remained seated, regarding him darkly through his steel-rimmed spectacles.

I stood before him [Townsend recalled], and told him, very quietly, the facts: Princess Margaret and I were in love. Visibly shaken, all that Tommy could say was: 'You must be either mad or bad.' I confess that I had hoped for a more helpful reaction. Though not entitled, perhaps, to any sympathy from him, it would, all the same, have helped ... There was great kindness in him, but in purely human affairs, affairs of the heart to be more precise, he had an archaic, uncomfortable outlook which irked me ... Profoundly perspicacious in political and constitutional matters, he was, I felt, on the human side, cold, rigid and inhibited.'

Lascelles may well have been tempted to observe that not only was the Royal Marriage Act still in force, so was the Statute of Treasons of 1352 under which 'encompassing the virtue of the King's daughter' is High Treason and, accordingly, an offence punishable by death. Certainly he felt that the Queen's interests, which it was his duty to protect, could best be served by Townsend leaving the Queen Mother's Household, as Townsend himself had offered to do, and by being banished abroad, as Townsend naturally had no wish to be. Neither the Queen nor her mother considered such steps necessary for the moment; but soon the crisis deepened. On the morning of Coronation Day newspaper reporters were closely watching both Princess Margaret and Group Captain Townsend. They saw her approach him after the service, looking exhilarated and, in his words, 'superb, sparkling, ravishing'. She talked to him excitedly for a few moments, then affectionately brushed a bit of fluff off his uniform. The next day this intimate gesture and its implications were the subject of a front-page story in the New York *Journal-American*. Other American newspapers soon printed further stories; and on 14 June the English Sunday newspaper the *People* informed its readers: 'It is high time for the British public to be made aware of the fact that newspapers in Europe and America are openly asserting that the Princess is in love with a divorced man and that she wishes to marry him ... Every newspaper names the man as Group Captain Townsend ... The story is of course utterly untrue. It is quite unthinkable that a royal princess, third in line of succession to the throne, should even contemplate a marriage with a man who has been through the Divorce Courts.'

Agreeing that the idea was, indeed, unthinkable, but knowing it to be far from untrue, Lascelles went to see the Prime Minister the following day having already consulted the Queen's stonewalling Press Secretary, Commander Richard Colville. Churchill now agreed that Townsend must go abroad for a year, and proposed to say so to the Queen at his audience on the Tuesday. The Queen considerately delayed Townsend's departure, softening the blow by inviting him to accompany her to Northern Ireland as Equerry-in-Waiting on 30 June. Soon after their return, however, Townsend left for Brussels where he had been found an appointment in the British Embassy as Air Attaché.

For a year he and Princess Margaret did not meet, though they wrote to each other almost every day; and when they did meet again they assured one another that their feelings had not changed. But there was still another year to wait before Princess Margaret was twenty-five, the age at which the Royal Marriage Act allowed her to give notice to the Privy Council of her decision to marry him. And in the end she decided not to give that notice.

Sir Anthony Eden, now Prime Minister, had been obliged to advise – though divorced himself – that in the event of her marriage, Princess Margaret would have to relinquish not only her royal rights and functions but also her income. If she did nevertheless insist on marrying Townsend it was probable that Lord Salisbury, a strong High Anglican and one of the most influential members of his Government and leader of the House of Lords, would choose to resign rather than introduce the enabling Bill into the House. Apart from this, there were the theological considerations of which Princess Margaret, a sincere upholder of the Church of England and much attached to its rituals, was only too well aware. Also, there was the widespread feeling, as expressed in a leader in *The Times*, that since the royal family was a symbol of united family life for the Queen's subjects throughout the Commonwealth, the marriage of Princess Margaret to Group Captain Townsend could not but damage its prestige.

On the afternoon of the day that this leading article appeared Peter Townsend made up his mind that Princess Margaret must no longer delay in informing the world that she had decided not to marry him. He wrote a few phrases on a piece of paper which he took to Clarence House. Having read the words, Princess Margaret told him: 'That's exactly how I feel.' A few days later she went to see the Archbishop of Canterbury at Lambeth Palace to tell him of her decision. Fisher was waiting for her in his study; and, believing that she was coming to consult him upon the theological points involved, he had laid out various reference works upon his desk. 'Archbishop,' she said as she walked into the room. 'You may put your books away. I have made up my mind already.'

The following Monday, 31 October 1955, the Princess's statement was broadcast:

I would like it to be known that I have decided not to marry Group Captain Townsend. I have been aware that subject to my renouncing my rights of succession, it might have been possible for me to contract a civil marriage. But mindful of the Church's teaching that Christian marriage is indissoluble, and conscious of my duty to the Commonwealth, I have resolved to put these considerations before others. I have reached this decision entirely alone, and in doing so I have been strengthened by the unfailing support and devotion of Group Captain Townsend. I am deeply grateful for the concern of all those who have constantly prayed for my happiness.

It seemed that the prayers of these people were answered when, less than five years later, Princess Margaret announced her engagement to Antony Armstrong-Jones, soon to be created Earl of Snowdon. A Court Ball was held before the marriage at Buckingham Palace; and Noël Coward, one of the guests, described the Princess as looking 'radiant'. She 'arrived late,' he added, 'and we wandered about and bobbed and bowed and had a lovely time. Her dress split and an Adonis footman produced a pin and we screened her while she fixed it up more or less satisfactorily ... The bridegroom is a charmer and I took a great shine to him, easy and unflurried and a sweet smile.'

It could not have been expected that the bride's grandfather, King George V, would have approved of Antony Armstrong-Jones or of his father, a Welsh barrister whose third wife had once been an airline hostess. But to less prejudiced observers Princess Margaret's choice seemed a happy one. Armstrong-Jones was kind, amusing, attractive and talented. He had coxed the eight at Eton and if his subsequent career at Cambridge had not been distinguished and he had failed to qualify as an architect, he had since established a reputation as a highly distinguished photographer and capable, versatile designer. The friends he had made were far removed from the circles in which husbands for English princesses were usually found: as *The Times* pointed out, there was 'no recent precedent for the marriage of one so near to the Throne outside the ranks of international royalty and the British peerage'. But Armstrong-Jones was highly adaptable. The Queen and her mother both liked him. He was quite prepared to accept an earldom and, while continuing to work hard for his living, to adjust himself both to the duties and to the conventional outdoor pursuits of royalty.

In March 1976, however, it was announced that the Snowdons' marriage, which had long been foundering, had at last broken up. It had been known for some time that Lord Snowdon was finding his wife unreasonably possessive, that she, in turn, obviously unhappy and overweight, was finding him selfishly neglectful and had had to consult a psychiatrist, that the different milieux from which they came – despite their own once apparent compatability and shared interest in the arts – were felt to be irreconcilable after all. The public were officially informed that the couple, who had been leading different social lives for a long time, were to separate: Lord Snowdon was to have enough money to buy a house in Launceston Place, Kensington; Princess Margaret was to have custody of the children. Both were to remain on the best of terms with the Queen who was as fond as ever of her sister and whose affection for her brother-in-law was undiminished. When Princess Margaret, 'against her personal wishes but on the strict advice of her doctors', was prevented by gastro-enteritis from attending her daughter's confirmation at Windsor Castle in April 1978, Lord Snowdon was there, joined in the royal celebrations afterwards and was invited to take photographs of the Queen with her first grandchild, Princess Anne's son.

During the two years' separation Princess Margaret was the butt of much ill-natured criticism, particularly when it became known that she had been on a fifth indiscreet holiday at Les Jolies Eaux – a villa on the Caribbean island of Mustique – with Roderick Llewellyn, a *soi-disant* landscape gardener seventeen years younger than herself who, once a member of a farming commune in Wiltshire, harboured inopportune hopes of becoming a pop star. Accusations were also made that the Princess was neglecting those public duties for which she was recompensed out of public funds to perform, though these accusations were, incidentally, strongly denied by various representatives of organizations and charities who were grateful for what one of them called 'her unstinted support'.

To the annoyance of the Archbishop of Canterbury, who disapproves of this kind of public discussion, some church leaders, too, voiced their protests at Princess Margaret's conduct. The Bishop of Truro, for example, in answer to questions put to him as Chairman of the Church of England Board for Social Responsibility, declared that she should consider withdrawing from public life, a declaration roundly condemned by the Princess's friend, the Bishop of Southwark, who said: 'Princess Margaret has been President of the Friends of Southwark Cathedral for many years. She has always gone out of her way to help and support many good causes in the diocese ... What she has done for Southwark is only the tip of the iceberg of the good she has done in

Great Britain and elsewhere. Public recognition of these achievements is far more important than the censoring of her private life, whatever that may be.'

This view was one which most reasonable and compassionate people shared. As *The Times* observed:

Princess Margaret's present association with Mr Roddy Llewellyn ought not [to have] and does not have [any] disabling effect on her public position. The high standing and efficient work of the monarchy does not require that every member of the extended royal family should be a paragon of virtue or a model of decorum, and that all who fail that test should be withdrawn out of range of royal duties and rewards. There is very common sympathy for Princess Margaret arising from the observation that the duties of her royal station and the dictates of her heart have crossed to make personal life one of unusual difficulty.

The *Daily Telegraph*, in expressing similar views, suggested that it was part of the price of a hereditary system 'that the good must be accepted with the less good', and that to expect not only the occupant of the throne but the entire royal family to provide a perpetual exemplar of moral and aesthetic perfection was 'to ask too much, and would be to ask too much even in a society which was far clearer than ours is about what constitutes these ideals'.

By the time of the announcement that Princess Margaret and Lord Snowdon were to seek a divorce, criticism of her had become less strident. It was accepted that, being by then no more than sixth in the line of succession to the throne, she could be seen in a different light from her sister, and that the divorce, which the Church of England had not opposed, in no way disabled her from carrying out those public duties which it was her obvious intention to continue to perform as she had done in the past.

Indeed, the public attitudes towards divorce and the monarchy had changed radically since the Princess's announcement of her decision not to marry Group Captain Townsend, as the personal histories of some other members of the royal family have demonstrated.

Prince Charles, as heir to the throne the second most important member of this Family, says that the realization that he would one day have to succeed his mother dawned upon him 'with the most ghastly inexorable sense'. There was a time when this realization filled others, too, with apprehension. For, it was rumoured, he was rather a backward boy. Pleasant looking, though with a slightly undershot chin, near-set eyes and prominent ears, he did better at his preparatory school than is generally supposed, being 'good at all arts subjects', so one of his masters there has said, and 'only let down' by mathematics, playing in the school's first Rugby football team and captaining the first Soccer eleven. But it was not until he had left school that he began to develop that sensitive charm and amiability that have made him so popular. His time at Cheam was followed by five years at his father's old public school in Scotland, Gordonstoun, as well as by six months at Geelong Grammar School in Australia; and finally by three years at Cambridge where, living in college, he gained a respectable honours degree, was awarded a half blue for polo, played the cello in the orchestra and took a lively part in the baroque antics of Trinity College revues. He began, in fact, to display that versatility which has characterized his later career and to develop those wide-ranging interests, from opera, anthropology and reading to field-sports and the company of lively and attractive women that still give him stimulus and pleasure.

Before being invested as Prince of Wales at Caernarvon, he was sent to the University College of Wales where, it was announced, he would 'study the history, language and current problems of Wales, as well as continue the subjects he [was] studying at Cambridge. He joined the Royal Air Force, learned to fly a supersonic jet, then entered the Royal Navy in 1971 and took command of a mine hunter in 1975. In 1978, as Colonel-in-Chief of the Parachute Regiment he was presented with his parachute wings badge after successfully, but evidently not fearlessly, completing the course. Cheerful, kind-hearted, articulate, disciplined, if very occasionally prone to the family failing of quick flashes of temper in moments of stress, adventurous yet unabashedly conservative, Prince Charles has been described without undue hyperbole as the most promising Prince of Wales since the time of the Black Prince.

He often gets behindhand with his paperwork for which he has little natural inclination; and it is not at all uncommon for him to fall asleep when bored. But, helped by a young staff of two private secretaries, a press secretary, an equerry and two valets, he fulfils his public duties conscientiously and with disarming verve; and takes an active and helpfully positive interest in the numerous organizations and institutions with which he is closely connected. Far more demands are made upon him than he can possibly satisfy – at a recent meeting, held to discuss his programme for the ensuing six months, over a thousand proposed engagements had to be considered – yet he still confesses himself unsure of what exactly an heir to the throne in his position ought to do and be. 'My great problem,' he said to some Cambridge undergraduates in November 1978, 'is that I do not really know what my role in life is. At the moment I do not have one, but somehow I must find one for myself.' He has also recently said that the Queen will never abdicate and that he expects to be her heir for another thirty years. In the meantime, since appointments such as the Governor-Generalship of

Australia are unlikely to be considered for political reasons, he has resolved to devote himself to learning as much as he can about aspects of the country's life with which he is unfamiliar, to travelling abroad as a kind of roving ambassador, and to choosing a suitable wife – an undertaking which, at the moment that this is written, assumes increasing importance.

Romantic and impressionable – he admits to having fallen in love 'countless times' and has been seen in tears when listening to Berlioz – he is also, on occasions, ingenuous, giving the impression of being far younger than a man in his early thirties and of having a decidedly immature sense of humour. Encouraged by a sensible and affectionate mother, indulged by a loving grandmother, chivvied, guided and profoundly influenced by an admired father, and more gently advised by his father's uncle, Lord Mountbatten, whose wisdom is not marred by his vanity, Prince Charles has overcome the extreme sensitivity and shyness of his childhood, though he is still both introspective and sometimes unsure of himself. It is not a disadvantage that he should be so. Unlike his great uncle, Edward VIII, he is prepared patiently to listen to advice as well as determined to do well. It seems most unlikely that he will not succeed.

After his two younger brothers, Prince Andrew and Prince Edward – whose schooldays have been less probed by journalists than those of Prince Charles – next in order of succession to the throne is Princess Anne. She has not received so good a press as her eldest brother and is consequently less well liked. A determined, competitive, resolute young woman, she has overcome her natural impatience and impetuosity, and recovered resiliently from several injuries and disappointments, to become what her trainer has described as 'a tough horsewoman ... capable of competing on equal terms with Olympic champions'. Educated at Benenden, the girls' public school in Kent – where her academic work, though not of a standard likely to have recommended her for a place at university had she wished to attend one, was not discreditable – she has since displayed a quick intelligence less marred by that overweening confidence in her opinions which was noticed in her earlier years. Since her marriage to Captain Mark Phillips, a pleasant, cheerful, inarticulate former officer in the 1st the Queen's Dragoon Guards, she has also trained herself to become more capable of carrying out her public duties, and to appear before an exasperatingly inquisitive public without revealing the boredom and irritation which a young woman of her naturally imperious nature is bound to feel. Their son, Peter, now fifth in order of succession to the throne, was born in 1977. His father has no title, so he has none, and has not been granted one. In accordance with what a left-wing Labour Member of

Parliament has termed 'a misguided, spurious egalitarian notion', his mother is referred to as Princess Anne, Mrs Mark Phillips, whereas she should properly be styled, as the daughter of a duke, Princess Anne, Lady Anne Phillips, just as Princess Alexandra is really Lady Alexandra Ogilvy, not as she chooses to call herself the Honourable Mrs Angus Ogilvy.

Next in order of succession after Peter Phillips, are Princess Margaret and her two children, Viscount Linley and Lady Sarah Armstrong-Jones, both of whom are at Bedales, the co-educational public school in Hampshire. Then comes the Duke of Gloucester, whose elder brother, a gifted and high-spirited professional diplomat, was killed while piloting an aeroplane in 1972. The Duke, whose wife is the daughter of a Danish lawyer, is a Cambridge-trained architect and author of books on the architecture and statues of London. He is still in practice, though his official duties and a large family estate in Northamptonshire, allow him little time to give to this work. His son, the Earl of Ulster, was born in 1974 and their second child, Lady Davina Windsor in 1977.

His cousin, the Duke of Kent, who went to Eton and Sandhurst, was commissioned into the Royal Scots Greys; and, belying a rather droopily Hanoverian appearance and a reputation as an effete man-about-town with a habit of smashing cars, he proved himself an efficient and talented officer. Had he not, as an obvious target for the IRA, been withdrawn from his regiment after it had been posted to Northern Ireland, he would have commanded it, thus fulfilling a long-held ambition. Disappointed by this set-back, he left the Army to work for the British Overseas Trade Board, of which he is now the conscientious and astute vice-chairman. He is married to the attractive and popular daughter of a Yorkshire landowner, and they have three children, the Earl of St Andrews, a clever boy who won a scholarship to Eton, Lady Helen Windsor and Lord Nicholas Windsor.

Their uncle, Prince Michael of Kent, is a major in the Royal Hussars and a former winner of the British bobsleigh championships. In 1978 he obtained the Queen's permission to marry Baroness Marie-Christine von Reibnitz, an Austrian interior decorator, whose first marriage to Thomas Troubridge, a merchant banker, was dissolved by mutual consent. As Princess Michael is a Roman Catholic, the Prince, who was sixteenth in line of succession to the throne, was excluded from the line under the terms of the Act of Succession of 1700, though any children of the marriage will not be excluded provided they are baptized into the Church of England.

His sister, Princess Alexandra, is universally admired for her good looks, spontaneous charm and gaiety. She lives at Thatched House

Lodge, Richmond, Surrey, with her husband, the Honourable Angus Ogilvy, brother of the Earl of Airlie. A highly successful businessman, he once held over fifty directorships, but his conduct of one of them having been harshly criticized in a government report, he has since become far less active in the City, though he is still closely connected with several charitable organizations. They have two children, a son, James, and a daughter, Marina, who is named after her grandmother who was a daughter of Prince Nicholas of Greece.

These two children are respectively nineteenth and twentieth in order of succession. The twenty-first in the order is the seventh Earl of Harewood, the elder son of the Queen's aunt, the Princess Royal. Managing Director of the English National Opera, as well as, amongst many other appointments, Chancellor of the University of York, President of the English Football Association and a member of the Arts Council, he has little time or inclination for royal duties, for which there is, in any case, no call for him to perform. Sued for adultery by his first wife, he had a child by his second, formerly his secretary, before his marriage to her. In order to remarry he had to obtain the Queen's consent under the provisions of the Royal Marriage Act.

Reminding her audience of a bishop's attitude towards sin – he was against it – the Queen once said that this was just like her own attitude to family life: she was for it. So is Prince Philip. And it was his determination to protect his family from what he took to be an interfering and damaging intrusion into their privacy which led to so many of the misunderstandings he once had with the Press.

Even more than the Queen, so it seemed to his then Private Secretary, Michael Parker, he had been shocked and dismayed by King George VI's death. Appalled by the thought of how radically their lives would have to change, 'he looked as if you'd dropped half the world on him'. 'Within the house and whatever we did, it was together,' the Prince said later, referring to the earlier years of his marriage. 'I suppose I naturally filled the principal position. People used to come to me and ask me what to do. In 1952 the whole thing changed.' He had hoped that at least they might not have to leave St James's where they had settled happily into Clarence House. But Winston Churchill, backed by King George's Household, was implacably insistent that they must move to Buckingham Palace where, much as he wanted to help the Queen and lighten the load of her work, he knew that it would be difficult to do so without appearing officious. It was a long time, in fact, before he could persuade various members of the Household not to bother the Queen with questions which he could easily answer and problems which he could perfectly well settle himself, and before they understood that he had no wish to interfere in matters which were not his concern.

It was recognized immediately, however, that the work he did outside the Palace could be of inestimable benefit to the Queen. Being free to go to places where she cannot go, and to talk to innumerable people, he can act as a kind of Chief of Staff who, to quote Michael Parker again, is able to give her 'the lowdown on absolutely anything'. In this capacity he travels some 75,000 miles a year, fulfilling about three hundred engagements, making between eighty and ninety speeches, all of which he writes himself – sometimes working on them until one o'clock in the morning – well aware that if he strays far beyond the usual clichés he will be 'setting out across thin ice'; but refreshingly determined to do so all the same. In March 1978, to take one random month as an example, his official duties required him to attend, amongst other functions, five receptions, four dinners and four luncheons; he opened a conference; he performed various duties as Captain-General of the Royal Marines, Colonel-in-Chief of the Queen's Own Highlanders and the Intelligence Corps, Chancellor of Cambridge University and President of the Central Council of Physical Recreation, of the School Natural Science Society and the City and Guilds of London Institute. He visited a hospital, a broadcasting station and the headquarters of a professional body; he went to a service in Westminster Abbey, a rugby match at Twickenham and the Royal Film Performance in Leicester Square; he presented awards to the British Sub-Aqua Club. He paid official visits to Glasgow, Kent, Staffordshire, Warwickshire, Devon, Reading, Northamptonshire and Carlisle.

With a mind fully responsive to new experiences and always open to new knowledge, he receives as many varied and authoritative accounts of what is going on in the country as any other man in public life. But, trying to fit as much as is conceivably possible into a day's work, there are, not surprisingly, occasions when he makes an inadequate speech; and naturally, too, there are times when a quick rejoinder turns out to be an unfortunate gaffe. There are those, of course, who are ill at ease in his company, who point to the way in which he used to play polo, or his impatience when he is driving a car, as characteristic of a nature which is excessively competitive. Certainly, he is often impatient, as restless, energetic, impulsive men are bound to be. He does not suffer fools or sycophants gladly, and has little sympathy, it must be said, with those whose views differ essentially from his own, while an example of careless thinking or an illogical argument may well be greeted by a dry, rather contemptuous laugh or a sharp, sarcastic retort. But those who know him well all agree that he is fundamentally kind as well as highly intelligent and able.

THE COURT OF ST JAMES'S

The members of his staff, so Basil Boothroyd wrote in a biography published some eight years ago, 'learn to live briskly, eat fast and have the answers ready'.

His foibles sometimes madden, more often amuse, seldom alienate affection, never reduce respect [Boothroyd continued]. He is always Sir to his face, and to third parties Prince Philip or 'P.P.' at a pinch. He has no nickname among his staff, or familiar reference, but is the pervading topic, and their whole preoccupation is to smooth his path. If they mess up the arrangements, and say so before the event, he's likely to laugh first, and then see how things can be put right. To leave it until it happens doesn't go so well. If he's sharp for no reason, he'll find a way of saying something at the next encounter that has the flavour of an apology if not the form. Among their few complaints is his general taking for granted, the calm assumption that the cars will be there, the airways cleared for take-off, the bags packed, the uniforms laid out. They usually are, but he isn't pleased if they aren't. He knows perfectly well what goes into all this. 'The trouble is that I'm spoilt – everything's nearly always right, so the odd occasion when they go wrong is more noticeable.'

These complaints – so Lord Rupert Nevill, his Private Secretary since 1976 and friend of many years, has observed – are not heard now. 'He is never unreasonably demanding,' Lord Rupert says. 'He works so hard we all have to work hard, too. But he takes mishaps quite philosophically when things go wrong through nobody's fault. He inspires great respect here, and also great affection.' Like the Queen he sets high standards for himself, and expects them in others. But he is never unduly exacting. And of his effectiveness there can be no doubt. He has become adept at dealing with crowds and is particularly good with children. He can talk to almost anyone about almost anything, and as he is the repository of countless bits and pieces of miscellaneous information he is able to give the useful impression that he knows more about a subject than he does or, indeed – since he is expected to show interest in subjects so disparate – than he can possibly be expected to do. In fact, the interest is rarely assumed. There are few aspects of life that do not intrigue him, from etymology and cooking to the conservation of nature and the construction of boats. He has 'an obvious enthusiasm for all that is energetic, progressive and masculine in the nation's life and work,' Dermot Morrah has written, 'especially in industry, technology and sport'. A man of high and varied talents and of formidable vigour, he is at once a stimulus and a provocation.

In the past Britain has been no more fortunate with her sovereigns and consorts than any other nation. The fifteenth century produced its adventurers, the sixteenth its parvenus, tyrants and zealots, the seventeenth its dogmatists, the eighteenth its dullards and diehards. And by the beginning of the nineteenth century, when the mind of King George III was deranged by porphyria, it was said, with what Walter Bagehot called, 'a possible approximation to truth', that not only he but every other hereditary monarch in Europe was insane. Since then over thirty royal dynasties have tumbled into oblivion. It seemed at times that the Court of St James's might tumble, too, tarnished as its reputation was by George III's extravagant and vexatious sons – 'the damnedest millstone around the neck of any government that can be imagined', in the opinion of the Duke of Wellington – and forceful as republicanism grew in the middle years of the reign of his granddaughter, Queen Victoria. But in her later years the tide of republicanism turned; it was kept at bay by her son, that popular *bon vivant*, King Edward VII; and was finally overcome by her grandson, the dutiful, unaffected and understanding King George V. Following his example, and that of her father, Queen Elizabeth II has ensured that the British monarchy, and the Court of St James's which embodies so many of its atavistic traditions, remain institutions which her people still hold dear.

Principal Sources

AGA KHAN, *The Memoirs of the Aga Khan* (Cassell, London 1954).

AIRLIE, MABELL, Countess of, *Thatched with Gold: Memoirs*, ed. Jennifer Ellis (Hutchinson, London 1962).

ALEXANDRA OF YUGOSLAVIA, Queen, *Prince Philip: A Family Portrait* (Hodder & Stoughton, London 1960; Bobbs-Merrill, New York 1960).

ASQUITH, MARGOT, COUNTESS OF, *The Autobiography of Margot Asquith*, ed. Mark Bonham-Carter (Eyre & Spottiswoode, London 1962; Houghton Mifflin, Boston 1963).

AVON, THE EARL OF, *Eden Memoirs: Full Circle* (Cassell, London 1960; Houghton Mifflin, Boston 1960).
Eden Memoirs: Facing the Dictators (Cassell, London 1962; Houghton Mifflin, Boston 1962).
Eden Memoirs: The Reckoning (Cassell, London 1965; Houghton Mifflin, Boston 1965).

BAHLMAN, DUDLEY R. (ed.), *The Diary of Sir Edward Walter Hamilton: 1880–1885* (Clarendon Press, Oxford 1972; Oxford University Press, New York 1972) 2 vols.

BATTISCOMBE, GEORGINA, *Queen Alexandra* (Constable, London 1969; Houghton Mifflin, Boston 1969).

BEATON, CECIL, *Photobiography* (Odhams, London 1951; Doubleday, New York 1951).
The Wandering Years: Diaries, 1922–39 (Weidenfeld & Nicolson, London 1961; Little, Brown, Boston 1962).
The Strenuous Years: Diaries, 1948–55 (Weidenfeld & Nicolson, London 1973).
The Parting Years: Diaries, 1963–74 (Weidenfeld & Nicolson, London 1978).

BEAVERBROOK, LORD, *The Abdication of King Edward VIII*, ed. A. J. P. Taylor (Hamish Hamilton, London 1966; Atheneum, New York 1966).

BENNETT, DAPHNE, *King Without a Crown: Albert, Prince Consort of England, 1819–1861* (Heinemann, London 1977; Lippincott, Philadelphia 1977).

BIRKENHEAD, THE EARL OF, *The Life of Lord Halifax* (Hamish Hamilton, London 1965; Houghton Mifflin, Boston 1966).
Walter Monckton: The Life of Viscount Monckton of Brenchley (Weidenfeld & Nicolson, London 1969).

BLAKE, ROBERT, *Disraeli* (Eyre & Spottiswoode, London 1966; St Martin's Press, New York 1967).
The Unknown Prime Minister: The Life and Times of Andrew Bonar Law, 1858–1923 (Eyre & Spottiswoode, London 1955); published as *Unrepentant*

Tory: The Life and Times of Andrew Bonar Law, 1838–1923, Prime Minister of the United Kingdom (St Martin's Press, New York 1956).

BOLITHO, HECTOR, *My Restless Years* (Max Parrish, London 1962).

BOOTHROYD, J. BASIL, *Philip: An Informal Biography* (Longmans, London 1971); published as *Prince Philip: An Informal Biography* (McCall, New York 1971).

BRUCE LOCKHART, SIR ROBERT, *The Diaries of Sir Robert Bruce Lockhart, 1915–1938*, ed. Kenneth Young (Macmillan, London 1973).

BRYANT, SIR ARTHUR, *King George V* (Peter Davies, London 1936).

BUTLER, R. A., *The Art of the Possible: The Memoirs of Lord Butler* (Hamish Hamilton, London 1971).

CHANDOS, VISCOUNT, *Memoirs: An Unexpected View from the Summit* (Bodley Head, London 1962; New American Library, New York 1962).

CHANNON, SIR HENRY, *Chips: His Diaries*, ed. R. Rhodes James (Weidenfeld & Nicolson, London 1967).

CHURCHILL, RANDOLPH S., *They Serve the Queen* (Hutchinson, London 1953).

CHURCHILL, WINSTON S., *The Second World War* (Cassell, London 1948–54; Houghton Mifflin, Boston 1948–54).

CLARK, ALAN (ed.), *A Good Innings: The Private Papers of Viscount Lee of Fareham* (John Murray, London 1974).

CLARK, SIR KENNETH, *The Other Half: A Self-Portrait* (John Murray, London 1977; Harper & Row, New York 1978).

CLARK, STANLEY F., *Palace Diary: Authentic Account of the Crowded Days of Queen Elizabeth's Life from the Time of her 21st Birthday* (Harrap, London 1958; Dutton, New York 1958).

CLYNES, J. R., *Memoirs, 1924–1937* (Hutchinson, London 1937).

COLVILLE, LADY CYNTHIA, *Crowded Life: Autobiography* (Evans, London 1963).

COLVILLE, JOHN, *The New Elizabethans, 1952–1977* (Collins, London 1977).

COOLICAN, DON, AND LEMOINE, SERGE, *Charles, Royal Adventurer* (Pelham Books, London 1977).

COOPER, LADY DIANA, *The Light of Common Day* (Hart-Davis, London 1959; Houghton Mifflin, Boston 1959).

COOPER, SIR A. DUFF, *Old Men Forget* (Hart-Davis, London 1953; Dutton, New York 1954).

CORBITT, F. J., *Fit for a King: A Book of Intimate Memories* (Odhams, London 1956).

CROMER, RUBY, *Such Were These Years* (Hodder & Stoughton, London 1939).

CROSS, COLIN, *Philip Snowden* (Barrie & Rockliff, London 1966).

CROSSMAN, RICHARD, *The Diaries of a Cabinet Minister*, vols 1–3 (Hamish Hamilton, London 1975–7; Holt, Rinehart & Winston, New York 1978).

DALTON, HUGH, *Call Back Yesterday: Memoirs, 1887–1931* (Muller, London 1953).

DAVID, EDWARD (ed.), *Inside Asquith's Cabinet: From the Diaries of Charles Hobhouse* (John Murray, London 1977; St Martin's Press, New York 1978).

DAVIDSON, J. C. C., 1ST VISCOUNT, *Memoirs of a Conservative: Memoirs and*

Papers, 1910–1937, ed. R. Rhodes James (Weidenfeld & Nicolson, London 1969; Macmillan, New York 1970).

DEAN, JOHN, *H.R.H. Prince Philip, Duke of Edinburgh: A Portrait by his Valet* (Robert Hale, London 1954); published as *Prince Philip* (Holt, New York 1955).

DIMBLEBY, JONATHAN, *Richard Dimbleby* (Hodder & Stoughton, London 1975).

DONALDSON, FRANCES, *Edward VIII* (Weidenfeld & Nicolson, London 1974; Lippincott, Philadelphia 1975).

DRIBERG, TOM, *Ruling Passions* (Jonathan Cape, London 1977; Stein & Day, New York 1978).

DUNCAN, ANDREW, *The Reality of Monarchy* (Heinemann, London 1970).

ECKARDSTEIN, BARON VON, *Ten Years at the Court of St James's, 1895–1905* (Thornton Butterworth, London 1921).

EMDEN, PAUL H., *Behind the Throne* (Hodder & Stoughton, London 1934).

ERSKINE, MRS STEUART (ed.), *Twenty Years at Court: From the Correspondence of the Hon Eleanor Stanley* (J. Nisbet, London 1916).

ESHER, REGINALD, 2ND VISCOUNT, *Cloud Capp'd Towers* (John Murray, London 1927).
Journals and Letters (1870–1930) ed. M. V. Brett, 4 vols, Nicholson & Watson, London 1934–8); published as *The Captains and the Kings Depart: Journals and Letters (1910–1930*, 2 vols (Scribners, New York 1938).

FEILING, KEITH, *The Life of Neville Chamberlain* (Macmillan, London 1946).

FISHER, NIGEL, *Iain Macleod* (Deutsch, London 1973).

FITZROY, SIR ALMERIC, *Memoirs* (Hutchinson, London 1925), 2 vols.

FOOT, MICHAEL, *Aneurin Bevan: A Biography, II, 1945–1960* (Davis-Poynter, London 1973).

FRERE, J. A., *The British Monarchy at Home* (Gibbs & Phillips, London 1963).

FULFORD, ROGER, *The Prince Consort* (Macmillan, London 1949).
Hanover to Windsor (Batsford, London 1960; Macmillan, New York 1960).

GASH, NORMAN, *Peel* (Longman, London 1975; Longman, New York 1976).

GORE, JOHN, *King George V: A Personal Memoir* (John Murray, London 1941; Scribners, New York 1941).

GREVILLE, CHARLES, *Memoirs, 1814–1860*, eds Lytton Strachey and Roger Fulford, 8 vols (Macmillan, London 1938).

GUEDALLA, PHILIP, *The Queen and Mr Gladstone* (Hodder & Stoughton, London 1933; Doubleday, New York 1934).

HAMILTON, WILLIE, *My Queen and I* (Quartet Books, London 1975).

HARDINGE OF PENSHURST, BARONESS HELEN, *The Path of Kings* (Blandford, London 1952).
Loyal to Three Kings (William Kimber, London 1967).

HASSALL, CHRISTOPHER, *Edward Marsh: Patron of the Arts* (Longmans, London 1959); published as *Biography of Edward Marsh* (Harcourt Brace, New York 1959).
(ed.) *Ambrosia and Small Beer* (Longmans, London 1964).

HEILPERN, JOHN, 'A King in the Making' and 'Prince Charles: the Dangerous Years' (*Observer*, London, 12 and 19 November 1978).

HIBBERT, CHRISTOPHER, *The Court at Windsor: A Domestic History* (Longmans, London 1964; Harper & Row, New York 1964).
Edward VII: A Portrait (Allen Lane, London 1976); published as *The Royal Victorians: Edward VII, His Family and Friends* (Lippincott, Philadelphia 1976).

HOBHOUSE, CHARLES, *see* DAVID, EDWARD (ed.)

HOLDEN, ANTHONY, 'The Monarch in Waiting' (*Sunday Times*, London, 12 November 1978).

HOLROYD, MICHAEL, *Augustus John: A Biography*, II *The Years of Experience* (Heinemann, London 1975; Holt, Rinehart & Winston, New York 1975).

HOME, LORD, *The Way the Wind Blows* (Collins, London 1976; Times Books, New York 1977).

Honours and Titles in Britain (Central Office of Information, London 1976).

HOUGH, R. A., *Louis and Victoria: The First Mountbattens* (Hutchinson, London 1974).

HOWARD, PHILIP, *The British Monarchy* (Hamish Hamilton, London 1977; Mayflower Books, New York 1978).
'Prince Charles at 30' (*The Times*, 13 November 1978).

HYDE, H. MONTGOMERY, *Baldwin: The Unexpected Prime Minister* (Hart-Davis, MacGibbon, London 1973).

INGLIS, BRIAN, *Abdication* (Hodder & Stoughton, London 1966; Macmillan, New York 1967).

JENKINS, ROY, *Asquith: Portrait of a Man and an Era* (Collins, London 1964; Chilmark Press, New York 1964).

JONES, THOMAS, *Diary with Letters, 1931–1950* (Oxford University Press, London 1954).

KAVANAGH, DENNIS, *see* ROSE, RICHARD

KILMUIR, 1ST EARL OF, *Political Adventure: Memoirs* (Weidenfeld & Nicolson, London 1962).

KING, CECIL, *The Cecil King Diary, 1965–1970* (Jonathan Cape, London 1972).
The Cecil King Diary, 1970–1974 (Jonathan Cape, London 1975).

LACEY, ROBERT, *Majesty: Elizabeth II and the House of Windsor* (Hutchinson, London 1977; Harcourt Brace, New York 1977).

LAIRD, DOROTHY, *How the Queen Reigns: An Authentic Study of the Queen's Personality and Life Work* (Hodder & Stoughton, London 1959; World Publishing, New York 1959).
Queen Elizabeth, the Queen Mother, and her Support to the Throne during Four Reigns (Hodder & Stoughton, London 1966).

LEE, SIR SIDNEY, *King Edward VII: A Biography*, 2 vols (Macmillan, London 1925–7).

LEE, VISCOUNT, *see* CLARK, ALAN (ed.)

LEVIN, ANGELA, 'The Men who Paint the Queen' (*Observer Magazine*, London, 15 January 1978).

LONGFORD, ELIZABETH, COUNTESS OF, *The Royal House of Windsor* (Weidenfeld & Nicolson, London 1974; Knopf, New York 1974).

Victoria R.I. (Weidenfeld & Nicolson, London 1964); published as *Queen Victoria: Born to Succeed* (Harper & Row, New York 1964).

LOWNDES, MARIE BELLOC, *Diaries and Letters* (Chatto & Windus, London 1971).

LUTYENS, MARY (ed.), *Lady Lytton's Court Diary, 1895–1899* (Hart-Davis, London 1961).

LYTTELTON, THE HON MRS HUGH WYNDHAM (ed.), *The Correspondence of Sarah Spencer, Lady Lyttelton* (John Murray, London 1912).

McCLINTOCK, MARY HOWARD, *The Queen Thanks Sir Howard* (John Murray, London 1945).

MACMILLAN, SIR HAROLD, *Winds of Change, 1914–1939* (Macmillan, London 1966; Harper & Row, New York 1966).
Tides of Fortune, 1945–55 (Macmillan, London 1969; Harper & Row, New York 1969).
Riding the Storm, 1956–1959 (Macmillan, London 1971; Harper & Row, New York 1971).
Pointing the Way, 1959–1961 (Macmillan, London 1972; Harper & Row, New York 1972).
At the End of the Day, 1961–1963 (Macmillan, London 1973; Harper & Row, New York 1973).

MAGNUS, PHILIP, *King Edward the Seventh* (John Murray, London 1964; Dutton, New York 1964).

MARIE-LOUISE, PRINCESS, *My Memories of Six Reigns* (Evans, London 1956; Dutton, New York 1957).

MARQUAND, DAVID M., *Ramsay MacDonald* (Jonathan Cape, London 1977; Rowman & Littlefield, Totowa, NJ 1977).

MARTIN, KINGSLEY, *The Crown and the Establishment* (Hutchinson, London 1962).

MIDDLEMAS, KEITH, AND BARNES, JOHN, *Stanley Baldwin* (Weidenfeld & Nicolson, London 1969; Macmillan, New York 1970).

Monarchy in Britain, The (HMSO, London 1977).

MONYPENNY, WILLIAM FLAVELLE, AND BUCKLE, GEORGE EARLE, *The Life of Benjamin Disraeli*, revised edn, 2 vols (John Murray, London 1929; Macmillan, New York 1929).

MORAN, CHARLES McM. W., 1ST BARON, *Winston Churchill: The Struggle for Survival, 1940–1945* (Constable, London 1966); published as *Churchill: The Struggle for Survival, Taken from the Diaries of Lord Moran* (Houghton Mifflin, Boston 1966).

MORLEY, JOHN, *The Life of William Ewart Gladstone*, 2 vols (Macmillan, London 1906).

MORRAH, DERMOT, *The Work of the Queen* (William Kimber, London 1958).

MOSLEY, DIANA, *A Life of Contrasts* (Hamish Hamilton, London 1977; Times Books, New York 1978).

MURRAY-BROWN, JEREMY (ed.), *The Monarchy and its Future* (Allen & Unwin, London 1969).

NICOLSON, HAROLD, *King George V: His Life and Reign* (Constable, London 1952; Doubleday, New York 1952).

ed. Nigel Nicolson, *Diaries and Letters, 1930–1939* (Collins, London 1966; Atheneum, New York 1966).

ed. Nigel Nicolson, *Diaries and Letters, 1945–1962* (Collins, London 1968; Atheneum, New York 1968).

ORMATHWAITE, LORD, A. H. J. WALSH, BARON, *When I was at Court* (Hutchinson, London 1937).

PELLING, HENRY, *Winston Churchill* (Macmillan, London 1974; Dutton, New York 1974).

PETRIE, SIR CHARLES, *The Modern British Monarchy* (Eyre & Spottiswoode, London 1961; International Publications, New York 1961).

PONSONBY, ARTHUR, *Henry Ponsonby: His Life from his Letters* (Macmillan, London 1942).

PONSONBY, SIR FREDERICK, *Recollections of Three Reigns*, ed. Colin Welch (Eyre & Spottiswoode, London 1957).

Sidelights on Queen Victoria (Macmillan, London 1930; Sears Publishing, New York 1930).

POPE-HENNESSY, JAMES, *Queen Mary, 1867–1953* (Allen & Unwin, London 1959; Knopf, New York 1960).

Private Life of the Queen [Victoria], *The*, By one of Her Majesty's Servants (Pearson, London 1901).

PURCELL, WILLIAM, *Fisher of Lambeth* (Hodder & Stoughton, London 1969).

Queen, The (Penguin Books, Harmondsworth 1977).

RHODES JAMES, ROBERT, *Rosebery: A Biography of Archibald Philip, 5th Earl of Rosebery* (Weidenfeld & Nicolson, London 1963; Macmillan, New York 1964).

Victor Cazalet: A Portrait (Hamish Hamilton, London 1976).

See also CHANNON and DAVIDSON.

ROOSEVELT, ELEANOR, *On My Own* (Harper & Row, New York 1958; Hutchinson, London 1959).

ROSE, KENNETH, *The Later Cecils* (Weidenfeld & Nicolson, London 1975; Harper & Row, New York 1975).

ROSE, RICHARD AND KAVANAGH, DENNIS, 'The Monarchy in Contemporary British Culture', *Comparative Politics*, July 1976, 8, 4.

ROSKILL, STEPHEN, *Hankey: Man of Secrets*, II *1919–1931* (Collins, London 1972; St Martin's Press, New York 1972).

ST AUBYN, GILES, *Edward VII: Prince and King* (Collins, London 1979).

SAMPSON, ANTHONY, *The New Anatomy of Britain* (Hodder & Stoughton, London 1971; Stein & Day, New York 1973).

Select Committee on the Civil List: Report with Minutes of Evidence (HMSO, London 1971).

SYKES, CHRISTOPHER, *Nancy: The Life of Lady Astor* (Collins, London 1972).

TALBOT, GODFREY W., *Ten Seconds from Now: A Broadcaster's Story* (Hutchinson, London 1973).

TAYLOR, A. J. P., *English History, 1914–1945* (Oxford University Press, London and New York, 1965).

Beaverbrook (Hamish Hamilton, London 1972; Simon & Schuster, New York 1972).

TEMPLEWOOD, LORD, *Nine Troubled Years* (Collins, London 1954).

TOWNSEND, PETER, *The Last Emperor: Decline and Fall of the British Empire* (Weidenfeld & Nicolson, London 1975; Simon & Schuster, New York 1976).

Time and Chance: An Autobiography (Collins, London 1978; Methuen Inc., New York 1978).

TURNER, E. S., *The Court of St James's* (Michael Joseph, London 1959; St Martin's Press, New York 1960).

WELDON, MAJOR F. W. C., 'The King's Troop, Royal Horse Artillery' (*RA Journal*, LXXVIII, 1951).

WHEELER-BENNETT, JOHN W., *King George VI: His Life and Reign* (Macmillan, London 1958; St Martin's Press, New York 1958).

WILLIAMS, FRANCIS, *A Prime Minister Remembers: The War and Post-War Memoirs of the Rt Hon Earl Attlee* (Heinemann, London 1962); published as *Twilight of Empire: Memoirs of Prime Minister Clement Attlee* (Barnes & Noble, New York 1962).

Nothing So Strange: An Autobiography (Cassell, London 1970).

WILSON, SIR HAROLD, *The Labour Government, 1964–1970: A Personal Record* (Weidenfeld & Nicolson/Michael Joseph, London 1971).

The Governance of Britain (Weidenfeld & Nicolson/Michael Joseph, London 1976; Harper & Row, New York 1977).

WINANT, JOHN G., *A Letter from Grosvenor Square* (Hodder & Stoughton, London 1947; Houghton Mifflin, Boston 1947).

WINDSOR, DUCHESS OF, *The Heart has its Reasons* (Michael Joseph, London 1956; McKay, New York 1956).

WINDSOR, HRH THE DUKE OF, *A King's Story* (Cassell, London 1951; Putnam, New York 1951).

A Family Album (Cassell, London 1960).

WOODHAM-SMITH, CECIL, *Queen Victoria: Her Life and Times*, I *1819–1861* (Hamish Hamilton, London 1972; published as *Queen Victoria from her Birth to the Death of the Prince Consort* (Knopf, New York 1972).

WOOLTON, THE 1ST EARL OF, *Memoirs* (Cassell, London 1959).

YOUNG, KENNETH, *Arthur James Balfour: The Happy Life of the Politician, Prime Minister, Statesman and Philosopher, 1848–1930* (Bell, London 1963).

Sir Alec Douglas-Home (Dent, London 1970; Fairleigh Dickinson University Press, NJ 1972).

See also BRUCE LOCKHART

ZIEGLER, PHILIP, *Crown and People* (Collins, London 1978; Knopf, New York 1978).

Index

Queen Elizabeth II is referred to in this index as
Elizabeth II, and the Queen Mother as Queen Elizabeth.